THE WORLD OF
CHARLES
DICKENS

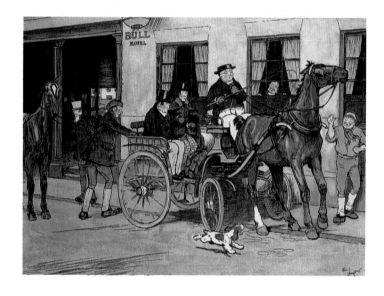

THIS IS A CARLTON BOOK

Design copyright © 1997 Carlton Books Limited

Text copyright © 1997 Martin Fido

This edition published by Carlton Books Limited 1997
20 St Anne's Court
Wardour Street
London
W1V 3AW

A CIP catalogue for this book is available from the British Library

ISBN 1 85868 342 4

PROJECT EDITOR: Sarah Larter
SENIOR ART EDITOR: Zoë Maggs
DESIGNER: Tony Truscott
PICTURE RESEARCH: Rachel Leach
PRODUCTION: Sarah Schuman

Printed and bound in Italy

THE WORLD OF
CHARLES
DICKENS

The Life, Times and Work
of the Great Victorian Novelist

MARTIN FIDO

CARLTON

CONTENTS

Introduction

THE PRINCE REGENT'S ELEGANT DEPORTMENT, CONTEMPTUOUSLY CARICATURED IN MR TURVEYDROP ("BLEAK HOUSE").

THE GREAT VICTORIANS. Gladstone and Disraeli. Tennyson and Browning. The Queen herself and Albert the Good. Dickens and Thackeray. The inevitable Charles Dickens. The Inimitable Boz. Creator of a powerful image of Victoria's age: overstuffed furniture and overfed aldermen; canting public piety and private improprieties; overt squeamish prudery averting its eyes from salacious pornography and satire, extensive street prostitution, and and the covert sale of flesh in the upper class matrimonial stakes. All set in glacial Great Houses, sooty slums, chilly churches, rattling coaches, and snorting trains. Few writers have left so permanent an impression of their age. Few have been accepted so enthusiastically at home and abroad as the national self-portrait painters more than a century after the conditions they described have passed away.

Yet much that we think of as typically "Dickensian" describes the era before Victoria. When Dickens was born in 1812, George III was still on the throne, though his porphyria – "The Madness of King George" – had finally condemned him to permanent dementia the year before, and his fat profligate son had entered upon the Regency that gave its name to an age of elegance. Regent's Park and its beautiful adjoining terraces were born at the same time as Dickens: Regent's Street came into being during his first three years. And the world of jolly stage coachmen downing hearty meals before blazing inn fires, their passengers exhilarated by fresh frosty air on the "outside", or steaming in the fug of the "inside", was a memory as nostalgic for Dickens the

writer as it is Christmas-card sentimental for us. Dickens was twenty-five by the time the Queen whose era he represents came to the throne, and all his life he inclined to set his fiction back in the reign of her predecessor, William IV, even though the foppish aristocrats and dandies of that era ceased to be prominent among his characters, and the new social questions of the mid-century were more important to him than the victories gained over the slave trade or the rotten parliamentary boroughs during his youth.

Indeed, during his childhood Dickens was actively opposed to the great reforms, insofar as a child could understand them. He heard, he later said:

> in confidence, from one whose father was greatly connected, being under Government, of the existence of a terrible banditti, called 'The Radicals', whose principles were, that the Prince Regent wore stays, and that nobody had a right to any salary, and that the army and navy ought to be put down – horrors at which I trembled in my bed, after supplicating that the Radicals might be speedily taken and hanged.

Yet this was the writer who would mercilessly mock the Prince Regent's memory – corsetted indeed! – whose name would become a byword for progressive reform; and whose ultimate declaration of radical democracy would be, "My faith in The People governing, is, on the whole, infinitesimal; my faith in The People governed, is, on the whole, illimitable."

It was The Great Reformer and The People's Friend who was mourned when he died, and whose scathing satires on the rich ruling classes and warm populist sympathy for the poor and powerless made him the Soviet Union's favourite illustrator of capitalist Britain in its heyday. But it is the creator of a vivid gallery of characters, incidents and places who lives on for us today: his creations reproduced in pub names and designs, plays and films, and vignettes on plates and tobyjugs.

And our strong sense of what Dickens' world looked like points to another crucial element in his popularity. Striking and vital as his own descriptions were, they were brought still more fully to life by the brilliant illustrators of all but his latest novels. Like Lewis Carroll's Wonderland characters, Dickens' stand before us because we have always known what Mr Pickwick and Bill Sikes and Mr Pecksniff and and Ebenezer Scrooge look like. Cruikshank and Phiz and Cattermole and Leech created caricatures to grip our imagination long before we could read the stories. There must have been disappointment for many a child in the discovery that spindly, bald-pated Tom Pinch offers little comic entertainment in the text, and some surprise that he bears no relationship to the faintly similar skull-capped Old Martin Chuzzlewit. It is a mark of Dickens' own imaginative creativity that we all have a visual image of Miss Havisham, frail and ghostlike among her spider-ridden feast, even though no artist brought her instantly to life. Conversely we have no common notion of what Mr Pumblechook or Mr Wopsle – let alone Mr Hubble the wheelwright! – looked like. *Our Mutual Friend* would be immensely more popular than it is had Phiz's untidy visualization, rather than young illustrator Marcus Stone's realistic propriety, realized Silas Wegg and Mr Venus. Mr Podsnap is one of Dickens' finest creations, but he is a character most people have heard praised by critics and commentators while knowing terribly little about him; not one who is recognized with the immediacy of the far inferior but highly illustratable and illustrated Barnaby Rudge.

This book is not a life of Dickens, though it includes a biographical outline. This is biased to consciously stressing aspects of Dickens' life which help to illumi-

nate his writing. Thus his childhood, whose memory informed his observation all his life, is given very full treatment. His marital breakdown and relationship with Ellen Ternan, which had far less impact on his fiction than some early twentieth century critics imagined, is given less space. Both learned and popular books attempting a general picture of Dickens the man abound – I have written one myself. This is a study of Dickens the writer in his world and ours. This will explore the wonderful mixture of optimism and despair, energy and squalor on "the roaring streets" around the author, where, as he said, "the noisy and the eager, and the arrogant and the froward and the vain, fretted and chafed, and made their usual uproar." It will look at the ways in which an observer with no obvious advantages of birth or education made himself the foremost lamp illuminating those streets. And it will see how he and his streets have lived on for us, making the World of Dickens a real presence in our world.

DICKENS IN 1859: PORTRAIT BY W.P. FRITH WHICH LANDOR THOUGHT MADE HIM LOOK TOO BUSY AND DICKENS THOUGHT LOOKED AS IF HE'D JUST HEARD HIS HATED NEIGHBOUR'S HOUSE WAS BURNING DOWN.

Chronology

1809	Gladstone, Tennyson and Darwin born	John Dickens, naval pay clerk, marries Elizabeth Barrow. Family lives at Portsea, Hampshire.
1810	Chopin and Schumann born	Elizabeth's father absconds. Fanny Dickens born
1811	George III mad; Regency established	
1812	Browning born; Byron awakes famous	**Charles Dickens born**
1813	*Pride and Prejudice* published	
1814	Scott's first novel (*Waverley*)	Family moves to London
1815	Battle of Waterloo	
1816	Coleridge writes *Kubla Khan*	Family moves to Chatham. Letitia Dickens born
1817	Jane Austen dies	Happiest period of Dickens' childhood, with sister Fanny, little sweetheart Lucy Stroughill and her brother George as playmates; Mary Weller as family nursemaid; mother as elementary teacher; father as friendly companion promising him possibility of owning Gad's Hill Place
1818	*Frankenstein* published	
1819	George Eliot and Walt Whitman born	
1820	George III dies. Cato St conspiracy	Fred Dickens born
1821	Napoleon and Keats die. George IV crowned	
1822	Shelley dies	Alfred Lamert Dickens born
1823	Rugby football first played	Dickens family moves to London
1824	Beethoven's IXth symphony performed	John Dickens in the Marshalsea; Charles at blacking factory. Unhappiest period of childhood.
1825	First organized baseball club	Wellington House Academy
1826	Cooper's *Last of the Mohicans* published	
1827	Turks lose Battle of Navarino	Clerk at Ellis and Blackmore's
1828	Duke of Wellington Prime Minister	Augustus ("Boses/Boz") Dickens born
1829	Locomotive "The Rocket" wins prize	Doctors' Commons' reporter
1830	William IV succeeds George IV. Tennyson publishes poems	In love with Maria Beadnell
1831	New London Bridge opened	Parliamentary Reporter
1832	Reform Act democratizes Parliament	
1833	Slavery abolished in British Empire	
1834	Coleridge dies	
1835	Phineas T. Barnum exhibits "160-year-old"	*A Dinner at Poplar Walk* (first fiction)
1836	Davy Crockett dies at the Alamo	*Sketches by Boz*; marries Catherine Hogarth; *Pickwick Papers*
1837	Queen Victoria succeeds William IV	Charles jr. born. Move to Doughty Street. Mary Hogarth dies
1838	Railway Post Office, Birmingham-Liverpool	Mary Dickens born. *Nicholas Nickleby*
1839	Fox-Talbot and Daguerre invent photography	Kate Dickens born. 1 Devonshire Terrace leased

1840	Victoria marries. Nelson's column erected	*The Old Curiosity Shop*
1841	E.A.Poe writes first detective story	Walter Landor Dickens born. *Barnaby Rudge*
1842	Grace Darling saves nine shipwrecked people	Dickens' first visit to America
1843	Wordsworth appointed poet laureate	*Martin Chuzzlewit; A Christmas Carol*
1844	Marx meets Engels	Francis Dickens born; move to Italy; The Chimes
1845	Newman converts to Roman Catholicism	Alfred Dickens born
1846	First Christmas card designed	*Daily News;* move to Switzerland; *Dombey and Son*
1847	*Jane Eyre* and *Wuthering Heights* published	Sydney Dickens born
1848	Revolutions all over Europe, but not UK	
1849	Disraeli leads Conservative party	Henry Dickens born; *David Copperfield*
1850	Wordsworth dies; Tennyson poet laureate	Dora Dickens born; *Household Words*
1851	Great Exhibition in Hyde Park	Dora died; move to Tavistock House
1852	Wellington dies; Asquith born	Edward ("Plorn") Dickens born; *Bleak House*
1853	Queen Victoria has chloroform in seventh labour	
1854	Crimean War breaks out	*Hard Times*
1855	Florence Nightingale nurses in Crimea	Re-encounter with Maria Beadnell. *Little Dorrit*
1856	Oscar Wilde and George Bernard Shaw born	Gad's Hill Place purchased
1857	Indian Mutiny	
1858	Burton and Speke find source[s] of the Nile	Public readings; marital break-up; Garrick Club row
1859	Samuel Smiles' *Self Help* published	*All the Year Round; A Tale of Two Cities*
1860	Abraham Lincoln elected US president	*Great Expectations*
1861	American Civil War breaks out	
1862	Bismarck Prime Minister of Prussia	Second series of public readings
1863	Lincoln emancipates slaves	Walter Dickens dies in India
1864	Tolstoy's *War and Peace* starts appearing	*Our Mutual Friend*
1865	Civil War ends; Lincoln assassinated	
1866	Dr Barnado opens homeless boys' refuge	Third series of readings
1867	Garibaldi's failed "March on Rome"	Second visit to America
1868	Disraeli and Gladstone successively PMs	Last series of readings
1869	Suez Canal opened	
1870	Papal infallibility propounded	*Edwin Drood.* **Dickens' death at Gad's Hill Place**

THE AGE OF DICKENS

It was the best of times, it was the worst of times, it was the age of wisdom, it was the age of foolishness, it was the epoch of belief, it was the epoch of incredulity, it was the season of Light, it was the season of Darkness, it was the spring of hope, it was the winter of despair, we had everything before us, we had nothing before us, we were all going direct to Heaven, we were all going direct the other way – in short, the period was so far like the present period, that some of its noisiest authorities insisted on its being received, for good or for evil, in the superlative degree of comparison only.

Thus Dickens' great bravura opening to *A Tale of Two Cities*. Thus he recognizes our universal tendency to judge ourselves and our universe and our history ego-centrically, as though our own perspective in itself gave us some great hold on the essential truth. But thus, too, with dubious self-awareness, Dickens describes a willingness to rush to extremes, and claims that he stands above such shallow judgment.

Yet his readers, be they admiring or critical, must surely feel that he of all men loved judging in black and white; felt most at ease when he could declare a Little Nell to be supremely virtuous; a Daniel Quilp to be a monster of malignity. It was Dickens whose mistrust of the past led him to hold up the Rack and the Block as exemplary features of the great Age of Faith; whose doubts about the present never led him to look back to a Golden Age; whose hopes for the future were expressed with unbounded confidence in his youth, and with unreserved excoriation of the Old Institutions –

"Physician, Bar and Bishop" – that still stood in their way as he aged prematurely.

And what amazing wisdom and foolishness, light and darkness, hope and despair Dickens' lifespan really did cover. The wisdom of Charles Darwin, patiently following nature and reason to truth without losing toleration; the foolishness of an intelligent man like Disraeli, who could diminish Darwin's thinking to "Is man an ape or an angel?" and unblushingly declare, "I am on the side of the angels." The belief that swallowed phrenology and human spontaneous combustion and a world created in six days with woman fashioned from a man's rib; the incredulity that thought men would die at speeds above forty miles an hour. The light of the great movements which struggled for the abolition of chattel slavery in the western hemisphere; the darkness that perverted Darwin's perception of the unity of all life into a discriminatory hierarchical order with – what a surprise! – northern European man the last and finest creation of God. The hope that led the muddled little bands of Christian Socialists and Young England Tories and Men of Good Will to try and ameliorate sad social conditions; the despair that led to nihilism on the one hand and ruthless authoritarianism on the other; to anarchists practising terrorist assassination and imperialists carrying out punitive expeditions.

This Dickens lived through and saw. Much of it he described. And in this, as his contemporaries recognized, he was normally and remarkably, an influence for good. In a better sense than Disraeli's, Dickens was on the side of the angels.

DICKENS' DREAM:
R.W. BUSS'S FAMOUS
POSTHUMOUS TRIBUTE.

Politics
AND Society

THE POLITICS OF DICKENS' forma-
tive years were dominated by memories
of the French Revolution. Napoleon,
the last hungover belch of Revolutionary
intoxication, retreated from Moscow the year Charles
was born, and was exiled to St Helena three years later.
Yet when the Emperor surrendered to the British, the
government dared not let him set foot in England. He
was too popular with the masses. His presence might
have incited revolution, and, to middle class
Englishmen, that meant mob rule; the Terror of Paris in
1793 recalling only too vividly London's anti-Catholic

Gordon riots of 1780. Charles Dickens, the People's
Friend, would memorably recreate both these occasions
when The People were The Enemy.

Dickens' parents were patriotic Tories. His paternal
grandparents were butler and housekeeper to Lord Crewe,
and "Upstairs-Downstairs" conservatism came naturally to
the family. Lord Crewe's patronage brought his housekeeper's son John a clerk's post in the Navy Pay Office.
John's son Charles recalled his mother – "God forgive her,"
he remarked facetiously – lifting him as a small child onto
a low wall in Chatham to cheer the Prince Regent. The
adult Dickens furiously rejected aristocratic pretensions.

THE STORMING
OF THE BASTILLE,
1789, BY J.P.HOUET.

The war had expanded the navy, bringing Elizabeth Dickens' father Charles Barrow, a music teacher from Lambeth, into the Pay Office in 1801, whence he fled to the Isle of Man nine years later before it could come out that he had embezzled nearly £6000. A year before his disgrace, his nineteen year-old daughter married twenty-three-year-old John Dickens who had been in the Pay Office for four years.

For twelve years after the birth of his first son, John Dickens worked loyally for King and Country, serving that long succession of Tory governments whose reactionary mediocrity was relieved only by the short-lived rise of the brilliant progressive Tory, George Canning. Extremist opposition dwindled to the dotty efforts of spy-controlled subversives. The infant Trade Unions looked silly and dangerous when they used secret oaths and ceremonies. As late as 1841 Dickens satirized these absurdities through Sim Tappertit's antics in *Barnaby Rudge*. The Tolpuddle martyrs had not got through to him.

The long Tory hegemony was broken by the Reform Act of 1832. At last the growing industrial cities were enfranchised at the expense of those underpopulated "Rotten Boroughs" which handed control of the Commons to great landowners. But reform did little for the workers. They fretted under the industrial revolution which had covered the country, covering it with mills, smoke and dirt. Industrial city slums were a dreadful blemish on civilization. The country labourer suffered continuing semi-feudal domination because England's tradition of land-renting prohibited an independent peasantry. So the workers seethed. Luddite rioters burned new machines which threatened jobs. The middle classes easily confused these malcontents with the intelligent Chartists, who demanded universal suffrage with paid annual parliaments.

Dickens was not politically astute about all this. He reported the reform agitation as a journalist, and despised the rhetoric inseparable from the democratic process. He was far less alive to the claims of Chartism than the Tory Disraeli, let alone the Christian Socialist Charles Kingsley or the north-country Unitarian Mrs Gaskell. He threw his sympathies in with the alternative middle-class agitation against the Corn Laws, demanding removal of the protective tariff on wheat which safeguarded Tory landowners' profits at the expense of cheap bread for all. Nor did he fully appreciate the revolutionary change from Old High Toryism to New Modern Conservatism that Robert Peel initiated when he split his party by repealing the Corn Laws. Dickens despised the essential concomitant for this longterm change: a Whig leader, Palmerston, whose essentially conservative and administrative bent did not frighten the right into reactionary extremism.

Dickens, like William Blake before him, pinned his faith on "revolutionary" America – until he visited it, and was appalled by slavery and its continuing racist underprops. He was, in fact, a broad humanitarian with Little England instincts; a populist who never shook off middle class attitudes. He demanded the reform of scattered social evils, and his heated demands were heartfelt. He came to feel there was something intangibly wrong with the whole of society, but he never really contemplated the "root and branch" social change that true Radicalism implied.

By the end of his life, he was totally disgusted with politicians' claptrap and so felt himself to be growing more Radical by the minute. Yet Disraelian Romantic Conservatism and Gladstonian, Peelite, Liberalism, by replacing the Whigs and Tories of his youth, had transformed most of the electorate and governing classes into much the sort of moderate piecemeal reformers he represented. And as economic growth extended the personal prosperity he desired for as many people as possible, and since he celebrated the kind of jollification that appealed to proponents of Merry England as well as the well-wishers of the poor, Charles Dickens became an overwhelmingly acceptable voice for his nation and his time.

ORANGE STREET: A LONDON SLUM OF 1870, DRAWN BY GUSTAVE DORÉ.

BENJAMIN DISRAELI.

Literature
AND THE Arts

ONE YEAR BEFORE DICKENS was born Jane Austen published her first novel *Sense and Sensibility*. One year after his birth, her popular favourite *Pride and Prejudice* came out. Three years and two novels later she died. A more perfect artist than Dickens, she is the one English novelist who seriously challenges his claim to be "the greatest". But she appears to have had no influence whatsoever on him.

SIR WALTER SCOTT
IN 1822, BY
HENRY RAEBURN.

Sir Walter Scott contributed mightily to winning respect for prose fiction by the time Dickens entered the field. Still an "editor" of folk ballads who had graduated to writing long – often very long – narrative poems in indifferent but highly esteemed verse by 1812, Scott was sufficiently aware of intellectual contempt for fiction that he presented all his novels as "By the Author of *Waverley*" just as Miss Austen's work appeared as "By a Lady" or "By the Author of *Pride and Prejudice*".

Scott's achievement was to take serious historical subjects and reinterpret them. His originality lay in careful thought about historical personages and movements. His vision proved so enticing that his interpretations often represent clichés

historians are now anxious to dispel: Richard the Lionheart as noble and chivalrous warrior, for example, or Bonny Prince Charlie as dashing hero. Yet Scott was not repeating hackneyed opinion. In 1815 everyone recalled Prince Charles Edward at the end of his life: a fat drunken sponger drifting around Europe. Scott reasoned that he must have had charisma in 1745 to have rallied the clans.

Scott also showed historical events affecting all classes in society, from the warring aristocracy to the humblest peasants and outlaws, with middle-class tradesfolk and clerics putting in their pennyworth for good measure. This breadth of vision compensated for some poor characterization: for wooden heroes and heroines, stilted love interest, turgid descriptions and empty assertions that he was creating some immensely funny characters without actually doing so. His novels were long, and published in three expensive volumes apiece. They were "a good read" and they bred imitators.

Dickens grew up in a period of poor English fiction. Jane Austen had no worthy successors. Scott spent the last ten years of his life, 1822–32, writing far too much far too quickly in the desperate – if honourable and successful – need to pay his creditors after bankrupting himself by building a palace at Abbotsford. Thomas Love Peacock's was the only voice of real individuality and interest among the English novelists of the 1820s, and his deft conversaziones satirizing the foibles of the intellectual classes could never command a large popular audience. Nor could the finest British novelist of the period, James Hogg "the Ettrick Shepherd", whose reputation as a sort of carefree lesser Burns completely eclipsed his dark masterpiece study of diabolic hypocritical corruption, *Confessions of a Justified Sinner*.

Trailing along behind Scott, Captain Marryatt's bluff narratives of naval adventure passed the reader's time without deeply engaging his imagination. The young dandies Bulwer Lytton and Benjamin Disraeli wrote "silver fork" novels of fashionable life, offering models of supposedly aristocratic taste for middle-class social-climbers. Mrs Catherine Gore turned the form to really insipid romances, parodied by both Dickens and Thackeray. Bulwer – who would try anything – also produced some dull sub-Scott historical fictions, and a couple of novels following the fortunes of the imaginary highwayman Paul Clifford and the historical murderer Eugene Aram. Harrison Ainsworth followed Bulwer's lead, fixing a misleadingly romantic image of Dick Turpin in the British mind with his first great success, *Rookwood*. Dickens himself raised the novel to a higher plane, his example encouraging Thackeray who, in turn, was revered by the Brontës. And the mature Dickens' editorial eye encouraged Mrs Gaskell and recognized George Eliot.

If fiction was poor, drama was worse. Even Jane Austen seems unaware how sheerly rubbishy is the translated *Sturm und Drang* melodrama her characters act in *Mansfield Park's* private theatricals. The stage was dominated by "frantic German tragedies" – the complaint is Wordsworth's – and vapid farces and operettas. Between Sheridan and Wilde – more than Dickens' lifetime – not one lasting English play appeared.

Poetry was England's early nineteenth century literary glory. Yet it was only gradually winning recognition. The great Romantics, Wordsworth and Coleridge, Byron, Shelley and Keats, had to create the taste by which they were approved. And this took time. Byron, the most conservative of them, achieved overnight fame by imitating, reducing and popularizing Wordsworth's vision of an elevating force in natural grandeur. Privately, Byron rather despised both Wordsworth and Keats, and ultimately found his own *métier* in hearty, upper-class-

confident comic satirical verse. Wordsworth soldiered on till the middle of the century, writing poetry that became increasingly dry and sententious so that he met ponderous Victorian taste, even while the best judges were truly valuing the magnificence of his best early work. Keats and Shelley had a huge influence on poetic technique. The Victorian poets, with Tennyson (three years older than Dickens) and Swinburne (twenty-five years younger) in the lead, mastered a remarkable lyrical beauty, which Browning (Dickens' exact contemporary) would challenge through his bold use of gritty colloquial language and demanding condensed syntax.

English music of the period, if not as bad as the drama, was still inescapably minor. Painting was, unusually, the art in which we excelled. Constable's use of colour and freshness in his landscapes; Turner's perception of light and willingness to distort form in the interest of impression and expression: these were great pointers to an international future, and recognized as great in Europe.

Alas, outside literature, Charles Dickens was unremittingly Philistine. He liked colour. But he wanted every picture to tell a story or evoke a sentimental sigh. In his preference for minor sententious or sentimental verse; his appreciation of little music rising above the level of operetta; his acceptance of the most improbable cat-tearing melodrama on stage, he was again a perfect representative of his nation and his audience.

TURNER, "RISE OF THE CARTHAGINIAN EMPIRE". DICKENS WAS THREE WHEN THIS APPEARED. TURNER WOULD GO ON TO BECOME THE GREATEST OF HIS CREATIVE ENGLISH CONTEMPORARIES.

LITERATURE AND THE ARTS

Early Childhood

ICKENS WAS BLESSED with remarkably acute memories of his earliest days: his mother and his nurse sending him toddling from one to the other across the kitchen floor as he learned to walk, for example, or the exact view of the garden from the window when he was two. This gift may be associated with a creative imagination: Scott, Tolstoy and Compton Mackenzie also enjoyed it. And in Dickens' case it was peculiarly important, for it led to memorable creations of childhood in *David Copperfield* and *Great Expectations*, and some persistent attitudes that coloured his work all his life.

His birthplace in Hampshire can cause confusion: some books call it Portsmouth; others Portsea or Portsea Island; others again, Landport, or even, erroneously, Southsea. Portsea Island, bridged into peninsularity, lies twenty miles southeast of Southampton facing the Isle of Wight where Southampton Water joins the Solent. Portsmouth, a town in the southeast of the island, was the oldest settlement. However, the largest in 1812 was Portsea lying just to its north and based around the Royal Naval Dockyard. Landport, north again and just a mile from the main entry to Portsmouth, was a new residential area on the road leading off the island. Here John and Elizabeth came in 1809 after a short honeymoon. They were married on June 13 at St Mary-le-Strand

DICKENS' BIRTHPLACE, PRESERVED AS A MUSEUM BY PORTSMOUTH CITY COUNCIL.

in London, and John was posted to Portsmouth to help pay off ships on their arrival in dock. The young couple took the end house of a new terrace of four: solid early nineteenth-century lower middle-class accommodation, with two parlours on the ground floor, two bedrooms on the first floor; kitchens in the basement and servants' rooms in the attic. Fanny Dickens was born here in the autumn of 1810, and Charles on February 7, 1812.

The house has been beautifully preserved and fitted out with simple Regency furniture. To stand in the small, plain bedroom where Charles was born is to realize how loyal he was to his roots. Wealth and success made his own homes larger and more comfortable than his parents' yet, without hesitation, Dickens placed his moral centres in the simple clerical station to which he was born rather than the upper middle class aristocracy of intellect to which he ascended. This is the sort of rented house where Rumty Wilfer of *Our Mutual Friend* would have felt comfortable: to which the Cratchits of *A Christmas Carol* could have aspired. John Dickens' home was markedly smaller than that supposedly cramped parsonage where the Perpetual Curate of Haworth, Patrick Brontë, brought up his brilliant children. Charles Dickens was unashamed of being an entertainer and, like many good entertainers, he worked for support from the great audience of the decently educated and modestly self-supporting, rather than the select audience of the very well-educated and modestly affluent, or the mass audience of the relatively ignorant and deprived. He appreciated lower-middle-class lower-middlebrows because he was born among them.

He was two years old when the war effort wound down and John Dickens was recalled to the Navy's head office in Somerset House. The family lodged in Cleveland Street, where Elizabeth taught Charles to read. When the boy was four, John was transferred out of London again: this time to the naval dockyard in Chatham. The next five years were among the most important in Dickens' life. He looked back on his boyhood in the Medway towns as idyllic. He apparently regarded himself as a man of Kent: he honeymooned in Chalk; vacationed in Broadstairs; patronized "The Leather Bottle" in Cobham; finally settled in the house near Rochester he had admired when walking as a small boy with his father. He called the eight mile walk between Rochester and Maidstone one of the finest in the land. Mr Pickwick's first travel notes describe the Medway towns: "The principal production of these towns … appear to be soldiers, sailors, Jews, chalk, shrimps, officers, and dockyard men." His creator's unfinished last novel is set in Rochester. David Copperfield is rescued by Aunt Betsey in Dover and sent to a good school in Canterbury. No part of *Martin Chuzzlewit* takes place in Kent, yet both the eponymous hero and his more admirable servant-companion Mark Tapley are casually described as coming from the county.

The little Chatham boy was small for his age and sickly; subject to "spasms", which prevented him from being a cricketer. He compensated by reading avidly: *Robinson Crusoe*, *Tom Jones* and *Peregrine Pickle* from his father's small library and *The Arabian Nights* and oriental *Tales of the Genii*, which would always spring to his mind when he imagined something peculiarly beautiful, romantic or exotic.

He played with his protective older sister Fanny and retained a deep affection for the sisterly relation. Good sisters recur in his characterizations. He was in love with curly-haired blonde blue-eyed Lucy Stroughill, the little girl from almost next door. He recalled this childhood emotion with great clarity, re-creating it perfectly and unsentimentally in David Copperfield's early devotion to Little Em'ly. Lucy's brother George was his companion in games of pirates and robbers. Local girl Mary Weller was the Dickens children's happily loved nursemaid. Chatham

St MARY LE STRAND

Baptist minister William Giles gave Charles his earliest and best formal education at his little private school.

But this Eden of childhood was under threat. Even in Portsea, John Dickens had moved house twice as over-expenditure forced him into cheaper accommodation. The decent house in Ordnance Terrace, Chatham, still standing as no.11, had to be abandoned, too, for a not too dissimilar but cheaper house next to Mr Giles' chapel in St Mary's Place, now demolished. And when Charles was ten, the family made a fateful move, as John was recalled to London again. With dismal hindsight, Dickens recalled this move as leaving "everything that had given his ailing little life its picturesqueness or sunshine."

ST MARY-LE-STRAND WHERE DICKENS PARENTS WERE MARRIED AND WHOSE SQUALID BURIAL YARD IS FEATURED IN "BLEAK HOUSE".

EARLY CHILDHOOD

Warren's Blacking

BAYHAM STREET, Camden Town is flat and enclosed. Ordnance Terrace, Chatham is high and airy. The Bayham Street houses which John Dickens rented were comparatively cramped. Despite the proximity of the country in 1822, Charles retained no happy memories of Camden Town.

His father became increasingly pressed by debt, and less and less able to play the proper parent. In the following years the Dickens children saw their paterfamilias hide from angry tradesmen who shouted through the letterbox.

Another bad experience was the neglect of Charles' education. His sister Fanny, was sent as a boarder to the newly opened Royal Academy of Music. Somehow the thirty-eight guineas a year fees were found and kept up. But Charles education was effectively abandoned. Elizabeth Dickens taught him the rudiments of Latin. But the boy was principally used for household errands, and felt that nobody cared what became of him.

Camden Town itself was a decent neighbourhood. But it abutted on Brill, where areas of criminal slums abounded. It is to one of these that "Good Mrs Brown"

abducts little Florence Dombey to steal her clothes and turn her out in rags, an actual form of crime at the time, perpetrated against a jeweller's five-year-old son by the evil Whitechapel bodysnatcher Eliza Ross. The odious Noah Claypole evokes Fagin's silent contempt in *Oliver Twist* by his cowardly preference for stealing money from little children out on errands. Bearing in mind that Charles was small for his age and aware of it, unfitted for mildly rough games like "Prisoners' Base", there can be little doubt that he was frightened when sent to buy bread or milk in a district where big bullies preyed on small children.

By 1823 the wolf was at the door in the form of furious creditors. Elizabeth made a heroic but hopeless attempt to rescue their fortunes. Renting a larger house in Gower Street, she had a brass plate made and fly-sheets printed, and tried to open a genteel private school. The project failed completely. Though Charles pushed leaflets through all the neighbouring letterboxes, nobody came. There was no money, and John Dickens was hauled off to debtors' prison.

At this point, Elizabeth's cousin by marriage, James Lamert, came up with an idea. He was associated with a project to manufacture boot blacking. The market-leading brand of the time was (Jonathan) Warren's Blacking of 30 The Strand. Lamert's cousin George and Jonathan Warren's cousin Robert had secured a decaying warehouse over the Thames at Hungerford Stairs and used a label deceptively mimicking the greater firm. Lamert offered work at the blacking factory for Charles. So the twelve-year-old trudged daily from Bloomsbury to the river, and mastered the art of pasting labels round the pots.

James Lamert's intentions were excellent. He had lodged with the Dickenses and made Charles a toy theatre in Camden. He gave him lessons in the lunch hours for his first few weeks at the factory. When Elizabeth and the younger children moved to lodge in the Marshalsea Prison with John, and Charles felt lonely, boarding in Camden Town with the taciturn old family friend Mrs Roylance (Mrs Pipchin of *Dombey and Son*), Lamert found him lodgings in Lant Street, close to the prison. But Charles felt deserted and ruined. "And so I became a little labour-

ing hind," muses David Copperfield over his fictional parallel experience in Murdstone and Grinby's. Charles felt relegated to the working class. The older boys in the warehouse usually treated him kindly, calling him "the little gentleman". One of them, Bob Fagin, even tried to see him home from work when he was taken ill. Dickens didn't really appreciate the other boys' generosity in hardly resenting his superior accent and special lunchtime lessons. Filled with boyish ambitions for a great future, he felt that all his hopes had been dashed. The experience was so terrible that he told no one about it in adult life until he drafted some memoirs which he passed to his friend John Forster, who was to be his official biographer, and then felt he should at last tell his wife. His works contain furtive references to Warren's Blacking, and its famous advertising doggerel. Those working days and the journeys home with meals bought in pie-shops burned into his mind the feeling of being a brave and frightened small boy alone in London, recaptured so brilliantly in *David Copperfield*. But all his life he felt that this episode, for which no blame could attach to him, was the most humiliating experience he had ever undergone. Release should have come when a small

legacy freed his father from prison. But the weekly six shilling wage was too valuable to be relinquished. He went on labelling blacking-pots until his father quarrelled with the Lamert, removed him, and sent him to school.

Elizabeth Dickens tried to repair the quarrel. She visited Lamert and arranged that Charles should return to work. John rejected the proposal, and Dickens stayed at school. But he never forgave his mother. He ridiculed her brave attempts to save the family finances. He caricatured her savagely as Nicholas Nickleby's vain, silly and dangerous mother. And he would never thereafter believe that a flirtatious feminine woman could possess sound sense.

MR MICAWBER ESCORTS HIS "FRIEND COPPERFIELD", DICKENS' MEMORY OF HIS EXPANSIVE BUT FECKLESS FATHER.

WARREN'S BLACKING

Education AND Apprenticeship

WELLINGTON HOUSE ACADEMY, just south of Mornington Crescent, was not much of a school. The silhouette of schoolboy Dickens in a stiff, top-heavy mortar-board, displayed at the birthplace suggests a petty snobbish outfit covering a petty smatterer's approach to learning. In any case, he was not to remain there for long. John Dickens' finances were soon complicated again, and, by the time he was fifteen, Charles had to return to the world of work.

CHARLES DICKENS IN 1830. THIS MINIATURE IS PROBABLY BY HIS AUNT JANE BARROW WHO MAY HAVE MODELLED FOR MISS LA CREVY.

Elizabeth Dickens took the initiative, and obtained for her son a clerk's position, first with a solicitor of Lincoln's Inn, and from May 1827 to November 1828 with Ellis and Blackmore, attorneys of Gray's Inn. He was not especially grateful. The distinction between legality and justice seemed to him humbug. It would prove fruitful in his later work: from Buzfuz to Jaggers his lawyers are memorable creations, and *Bleak House* remains England's greatest satire on the law's incompetence and delays. Charles Dickens lasted just one year as a law clerk.

He was never dull, however. He enjoyed the cut-price man-about-town's life of a junior clerk. He made friends with Thomas Potter and got drunk with him and went to theatres, including one which allowed them and other patrons to act for a small fee. A glance at the life of Dick Swiveller, or David Copperfield carousing with Steerforth, shows how keenly Dickens remembered the experience of getting drunk when immature, and how callow he felt himself to have been. There may also be significance in "The Finches" of *Great Expectations* locating themselves in "The Grove": "The Grove of the Evangelist" was common slang for St John's Wood, centre of kept women and up-market prostitution. And the young fashionable carousers meet in Covent Garden, the major downmarket red light district of eighteenth- and nineteenth-century London. When Pip uses the Covent Garden Hummums as a place where he can get a bed at any hour of the night, he reveals his familiarity with a notorious assignation house, although Dickens discreetly declines to mention this.

The new career for which Charles abandoned the law was instigated by his father. John Dickens was not unenterprising. Unemployable in the Navy Pay Office as a former debtor, he learned shorthand and became a parliamentary reporter. Charles followed his example, using the British Museum library to broaden his reading and master the difficult "brachygraphy" of the day. He began his reportorial career by transcribing the proceedings in Doctors' Commons. This specialized branch of the law handled the business of the pre-Reformation Ecclesiastical Courts, and became the Court of Admiralty, Divorce and Probate by the time of Dickens' death. But during his youth it met in the Court of Arches under St Mary-le-Bow church in Cheapside, and its specialist attorneys, the proctors, had offices adjacent to St Paul's Cathedral. A "lazy old nook," Steerforth calls it, where they "play all kinds of tricks with obsolete old monsters of acts of Parliament, which three-fourths of the world know nothing about, and the other fourth supposes to have been dug up, in a fossil state, in the days of the Edwards." Dickens shared this low opinion of the institution when he had the young David Copperfield contemplate becoming a proctor and marry a proctor's daughter.

Typically, his brilliant recall of subjective emotion carried him back to his profoundest feelings of the time he worked among the proctors when he fell more intensely in love than he ever would again. Maria Beadnell was a senior bank clerk's daughter, living in Lombard Street. She was a pretty, flirtatious tease who collected admirers. It seems unlikely that Dickens was ever as important to her as she was to him, and their passage of love was further confused by her giggly, girly gossiping about him with her friend Mary Anne Leigh. Miss Leigh, the original of the wonderful *poseuse* Julia Mills in *David Copperfield*, enjoyed being a go-between, and provoked lovers' quarrels between Charles and Maria, once even leading Charles to expostulate furiously with his sister Fanny for not having revealed her silly goings-on. As he remembered it later, the Beadnells disapproved of his poor prospects, and sent Maria to finishing school in Paris to forget about him. However, Michael Slater has shown that his memory was at fault; Maria went to Paris before her association with Dickens ended, and it clearly petered out because he was only one of the many strings to her bow.

By the time he was twenty, Dickens had graduated to reporting Parliamentary proceedings. His speed and accuracy made him hugely in demand. The offer of a permanent position on the *Morning Chronicle* led him to set aside the ambition of going on the stage which had actually reached the point that the manager of Covent Garden theatre offered him an audition. He travelled the country reporting the great Reform agitation and the subsequent election. He wrote on his knees

in coaches, meeting deadlines and establishing fine professional journalistic habits. But he despised the politics he described, and hoped for a career more satisfying to his artistic nature. He wrote a short humorous piece "A Dinner at Poplar Walk," and glowed with the pride of authorship when the *Monthly Magazine* accepted it in December 1833. By 1835 he was contributing regular comic and descriptive "Sketches of London Life" to the *Morning* and *Evening Chronicles*, and signing them "Boz": his youngest brother Augustus' family nickname.

When the publisher John Macrone brought out the *Sketches* in book form, the young man was set fair to becoming an author. But nobody could have guessed that he would leap to the position of his country's most popular novelist, and hold it for the rest of his life.

MARIA BEADNELL POSED AS A MILK-MAID. WATER-COLOUR BY SIR HENRY AUSTIN

Early Triumph AND Tragedy

LEFT TO RIGHT:
GEORGINA HOGARTH,
CATHERINE AND
CHARLES DICKENS
IN 1843. SKETCH
BY DANIEL MACLISE.

E ARLY IN 1836, publisher William Chapman visited the bachelor chambers in Furnival's Inn, Holborn, where Dickens had been living for two years. He had a proposal for young Boz. The recently formed firm of Chapman and Hall had just brought out *The Squib Annual*, including comic plates of sporting incidents by popular artist Robert Seymour. They now wanted to publish four new Seymour plates every month. They contemplated the adventures of a "Nimrod Club" of Londoners, distinguished by their incompetence at the sports they tried to practice. They would pay a jobbing writer £14 per part to supply text to accompany the prints and the author of the *Sketches* was recommended as a useful creator of short comic cockney pieces.

The fee was irresistible though the commission was not flattering. Monthly part-issue of caricaturists' work had proved successful in the 1820s, with Cruikshank's drawings of the sporting swells Jerry Hawthorn and "Corinthian Tom" especially popular, and Rowlandson's *Tour of Doctor Syntax* appearing in Ackermann's *Poetical Magazine*. It was the illustrators' artwork that commanded popularity. Pierce Egan, who wrote the story of Tom and Jerry's nightlife, was a sporting journalist rather than a novelist; William Combe's verses on Dr Syntax were the highlight of an undistinguished career of pamphleteering and casual writing. Dickens was accepting hackwork.

But young and almost unknown though he was, he set his stamp on it immediately. Objecting that he knew nothing about sport, he insisted on a club boasting Mr Pickwick's antiquarian interests and Mr Tracy Tupman's sexless romantic ardour, as well as Mr Winkle's sporting incompetence. Economical with his own work, he had chance-met characters tell stories which used up unsold sketch-like material he had on the stocks. Robert Seymour found himself illustrating such sentimental melodrama as "The Dying Clown" instead of the concurrent series of sporting incidents he had anticipated. In the wake of *Pickwick's* success, the original narrative proposal would be far better executed in Robert Surtees' *Jorrocks* novels.

The awkward facetiousness of the opening chapters gave little impression of the characters' appearance. Seymour imagined a thin Pickwick; Edward Chapman objected that fatness and good humour went together, and described his friend John Foster of Richmond, "a fat old beau who would wear, in spite of ladies' protests, drab tights and black gaiters". And so the memorable character of Pickwick was visualized by someone else.

Before he had completed more than three illustrations for the second part, Seymour shot himself in a fit of depression. The venture might have stopped then and there, but Dickens could not afford to lose the income. Robert Buss illustrated the third number. His style was like Seymour's, but his engraving technique proved inadequate. Dickens energetically interviewed other would-be artists, including the young Thackeray and prentice John Leech, before settling on Hablot Knight Browne who adopted the *nom-de-plume* "Phiz" to match Dickens's "Boz", and deservedly became famous with the writer to whose success he contributed.

Still the *Pickwick Papers* might have terminated. Sales were poor: the laidback villainy of Mr Jingle; the jollity of Mr Wardle at Dingley Dell; the flesh-creeping spying of the Fat Boy failed to attract readers. It was the introduction of Sam Weller – a stock comic cockney manservant copied from the comic actor Sam Vale – that saved the day. Dickens's linguistic invention flowered in giving Sam his extended similes, and "as the soldier said …" tags. The public rushed to buy it. And "Boz's fun" swept society from top to bottom. Judges read the new numbers on the bench when cases lagged. Consultants read them in their carriages between patients and, at the bottom of the market, a host of imitative pirates copied the characters and reduced their adventures to crude knockabout, often with Sam Weller as clear hero and Mr Pickwick a silly butt. What had started by earning Dickens £29 for the first two numbers brought him a clear £500 bonus with the twelfth, and when it ended earned him £3000 more than the stipulated £280. Chapman and Hall made a profit of £14,000.

Had Dickens only been able to command the profits of spin-off merchandise, he would have been financially secure at once. Pickwick cloths and chintzes, cabs and canes, hats and coats were marketed. Boz clubs sprang up. At twenty-four Dickens had suddenly become the object of a popular mania, which was useful. On receiving the original commission he had pressed forward with his plans to marry Catherine Hogarth, the daughter of his colleague George, the *Morning Chronicle*'s music critic. It was three or four years since his passion for Maria Beadnell had made him miserable, and Catherine's character was gentler and more tractable. They married quietly and returned to Furnival's Inn, where their first son, Charles Culliford Boz Dickens was born. When the success of the part-issued novel became clear, they moved to a comfortable house in the newly-built private road, Doughty Street. Catherine's younger sister Mary came to stay with them, giving Kate support and help with the baby, and Charles the backing he found most conducive to household harmony. Here Mary died, suddenly aged eighteen, after a visit to the theatre with her sister and brother-in-law. Charles sat up through the night with her when

the spasm of a probable heart attack keeled her over on the landing. She died in his arms, leaving an intense and essentially unfortunate impression on him. He was so distressed that he delayed for a month before producing the next numbers of *Pickwick* and *Oliver Twist*, which he had already started. The rumour flew round that Boz was dead, or had gone insane from overwork. In fact he was alive and energetic as ever. But he felt he had experienced true tragedy. Henceforth he would tend to expect the good to die young, and his theatrical tendency to morbid melodrama would find expression in some elaborately overwritten childhood deaths.

MR PICKWICK, ON DICKENS' DOUGHTY STREET DOORSTEP.

Fame AND Friendship

THE SUCCESS of *Pickwick* brought offers of new work. The young publisher Richard Bentley invited Dickens to edit a magazine and contribute a serial to it. So *Oliver Twist* appeared in *Bentley's Miscellany*. Fanny Dickens had married a fellow singer, and their interest in the newly opened St James' Theatre encouraged Charles to collaborate with another ex-pupil from the Academy in contributing an operetta, *The Village Coquettes*, to its repertoire. Charles signed an incautious contract promising Bentley two more novels on terms reflecting his beginner's status rather than his massive commercial success. For the next few years he would worry over *Gabriel Vardon, the Locksmith of London* until his friend John Forster negotiated away his commitment to Bentley, and the work could appear as *Barnaby Rudge*.

Forster was the most important friend Dickens made in his early twenties. He, too, was a journalist, but though he had once seen Dickens representing reporters in a dispute with management, Charles was rather a reserved and shy figure in the press gallery. Thomas Beard, best man at his wedding, was the only lasting friend of his reporting days. Forster was friendly with another young writer in Bentley's stable, the "Newgate novelist" Harrison Ainsworth. With Dickens' blessing, Ainsworth would take over the *Miscellany* when he gave it up.

Since his second novel featured Fagin's criminal gang, Dickens too was briefly seen as one of the "Newgate school"; and he shared, further, a taste for the dandiacal dress and colourful waistcoats Ainsworth affected. But the more robustly sober figure of Forster appealed to him immensely when the two met at Ainsworth's table, and both made energetic efforts to improve the acquaintance. Soon they were going for long afternoon rides together whenever possible – Dickens was a keen horseman, and enjoyed going to the races without actually racing himself. They took long walks across Hampstead Heath or the southern environs of London. Forster helped his friend regain control over his own copyrights, even though Macrone demanded an exorbitant £2000 to relinquish the right to reissue the *Sketches*. Forster's birthday coincided with the Dickenses' wedding anniversary, and the three made a practice of celebrating every year with a private dinner at one of their favourite inns, like the Star and Garter at Richmond. Forster was invariably present at the congratulatory dinner parties Dickens enjoyed with his men friends, and ultimately wrote the great standard biography which rested heavily and convincingly on their voluminous lifelong correspondence, and lies behind every serious subsequent description of Dickens.

PAINTERS, POETS AND PERFORMERS

"Mr Vice-President" at dinners congratulating Dickens on the completion of each new book was frequently Serjeant Thomas Noon Talfourd, a barrister and MP nearly twenty years older than the author. Talfourd had

JOHN FORSTER.

worked as a reporter for *The Times* early in his career. He contributed literary criticism to literary journals and had a *succès d'estime* with his classical tragedy *Ion*. By 1856 he was a judge with a knighthood, and one must wonder whether even this good-natured radical heartily welcomed Dickens's presenting him as David Copperfield's best friend in the heavily patronized guise of Tommy Traddles.

Daniel Maclise the painter was closer to Dickens in friendship, as he was in age. He was producing a series of portraits of all the leading men and women of letters for *Fraser's Magazine* at the time when Dickens came to prominence and his painting of the young Dickens, now in the National Portrait Gallery in London, was acclaimed by all his friends as the most perfect likeness, and so exhibits for us the astonishing brightness, life and energy written across his face, just as Forster and others describe it. "Mac" became a dear friend, whose inadequacy as a correspondent Dickens would lament when awaiting letters from England during his first American tour.

When Forster, Dickens and Maclise went on holiday to Cornwall in 1841, their fourth companion was another painter, Clarkson Stanfield. Older than his three companions, Stanfield had been a scene painter at Drury Lane and was to help Dickens materially in his later theatrical ventures, painting drop-scenes for his melodramas which Dickens used to decorate the offices of his journal *All the Year Round* in 1859. Another older friend, who was nonetheless close, was William Macready, greatest tragic actor of the day. His Macbeth and Lear were unrivalled; his temper, especially with fellow-actors, was uncertain. But he was proud to know Dickens as Dickens was to know him. And Macready and his wife kindly and reliably took care of the Dickens children when Charles and Kate visited America in 1840.

The roll-call of Dickens' friends among the established radical writers and journalists of the time is almost the index from a literary history. From the older generation: Samuel Rogers, the banker poet; Leigh Hunt, who suffered imprisonment for libelling the Prince Regent; B.W. Procter ("Barry Cornwall"); Thomas Carlyle, the dyspeptic sage of Ecclefechan; Albany

Fonblanque the *Examiner's* proprietor; poet Walter Savage Landor; Lady Blessington whose scandalous liaison with the ten-year-younger dandy Count Alfred D'Orsay was disreputably sealed by D'Orsay's token marriage to her young daughter. Dickens' friendship with this last pair marks the extent to which his domestic morality tolerated pre-Victorian attitudes in his early days. Forster's lists of younger writers and great contemporaries give his biography rather a name-dropping quality. Dickens probably preferred association with those whose distinction did not challenge his own: Tennyson, whose poetry he greatly admired, pre-eminent in a different field; or R.H. Horne the "spasmodic" poet, clearly his inferior. But from engineer Brunel to painter Landseer, and excepting only the politicians, Dickens' circle of friends is a remarkable listing of the great and less-great early Victorians.

MACREADY AS MACBETH, HIS MOST FAMOUS AND VIOLENT ROLE.

MR MACREADY AS MACBETH.
Pub.d by M & B SKELT, 11 Swan St Minories London.

Family AND Travels

THEATRICALS, MONTREAL, 1842. THE PROGRAMME DICKENS SENT FORSTER WITH SCREAMERS HIGHLIGHTING KATE'S PERFORMANCE.

KATEY, WALTER, CHARLIE AND MAMIE DICKENS IN 1842. THIS PORTRAIT BY MACLISE, WENT WITH CHARLES AND KATE TO AMERICA.

ORSTER'S LIFE OF DICKENS respects Victorian proprieties and handles the Dickenses' publicly broken marriage as discreetly as possible. So we may have too strong an impression of Dickens the intellectual man's man, throwing himself into social activities with fellow-writers and artists.

He was equally centred in his family life and strongly attached to his wife Kate at first. They both missed their children deeply when visiting America in 1842 – Charles junior had been followed by two girls, Mary and Katey, and a second baby boy, Walter. Kate would bear Charles another six children, one of whom, Dora, died in infancy. Charles' tact, love and sympathy with his wife in this tragedy were profound and genuine.

He was an ebullient and rather domineering father. He gave the children extravagant nicknames: Alfred, the youngest, would always be known as "Plorn", short for "Plornishmaroontigoonter". He kept an array of pets for their and his delight – dogs, two ravens, a donkey. Their children's parties were the envy of their contemporaries, as Charles whirled the fun along and dazzled the company with conjuring displays. Yet he was never their friend and companion as Thackeray was for his daughters. His passion for a neat and perfectly run household was too exacting. His contempt for traditional academic education left them inadequately prepared for the society ordered by competitive examinations which succeeded the age of patronage into which he had been born. His need to be the centre of attention left little room for childish self-assertion. Only one of his sons, Henry, would be a real success in life and he achieved this by resisting his father's prejudices against old institutions, and reading law at Cambridge.

MAN OF THE WORLD

The zest for life – it seems too tame a phrase – that Dickens evinced in entertaining his children showed in his holidaymaking as well. Until he took to summers in France in the 1850s, and then moved to Gad's hill Place in 1860, he summered out of town in rented cottages at Putney, Finchley and Petersham – rural spots in the 1840s. There he organized visitors in energetic country sports: high-jumping, bowling, quoits and the like. He was always the most active participant. A typical day at Broadstairs, where he stayed repeatedly from 1837 to 1851, would see him writing hard all morning; racing down to the sea for a swim; taking a light lunch, and walking twelve or fourteen miles during the afternoon.

His travelling holidays were equally active. They could be businesslike – a whirlwind trip to Yorkshire with Knight Browne in 1838 to inspect the schools he would pillory in *Nicholas Nickleby*; a short visit to

Birmingham with Kate in 1840 extended on Forster's arrival for unplanned excursions to Stratford and Wolverhampton and Lichfield, until Dickens and Forster had to pawn their watches to meet the cash crisis; a visit to Exeter later in the year to settle his parents in their retirement cottage, on which he also explored Dawlish and Teignmouth, Babbacombe and Torbay. Holidaying in Cornwall in 1842, he scrambled up to the Logan Rock and went down mines; climbed St Michael's Mount and descended St Knighton's Kieve.

Kate Dickens was sleepy-eyed, languorous in manner and naturally clumsy. So it is remarkable to find her exerting herself adeptly on holiday with her brisk young husband. Soon after their marriage they toured northern France and Belgium with Knight Browne. In 1841 they toured Scotland. Dickens was hugely impressed by the Pass of Glencoe in torrential rain. But more impressive was his getting Kate across a flooded river at Black Mount, where the bridge had been washed away, and slippery wooden planks laid from rock to rock with an insecure handrail on one side made the only passage. Not only did Dickens cross the trembling planks in driving wind and rain, he persuaded Kate to cross with him. In Montreal she acted in private amateur theatricals at the garrison, acquitting herself so well that her husband awarded her eight exclamation marks on the programme he sent to Forster.

Kate and Charles were in Canada after their chequered visit to America in 1842. His first impressions were all he had hoped and more: a fairer society than England's:

> *There is no man in this … State of New England [sic] who has not a blazing fire and a meat dinner every day of his life. A flaming sword in the air would not attract so much attention as a beggar in the streets. … A man with seven heads would be no sight at all compared with one who couldn't read and write.*

But he was quickly annoyed by intrusive journalists and public functionaries; infuriated when his demands that America sign an international copyright agreement and stop pirating European writing provoked newspaper attacks on him; disgusted by mid-western table manners and universal spitting; and horrified by slavery and the hypocrisy and racism that sustained it. To his credit, he refused official honours from any city that supported it. But over all, his first American trip revealed a Little Englander who couldn't see why Americans resented his criticizing their manners for differing from his own.

AN ENGLISHMAN ABROAD

His residence in Italy, taken up in 1844 because the lower cost of living made it easier to support his growing family, revealed the same insularity. He enjoyed Italian confectionery and puppetry, but hated a priest-ridden society and generally tended to find foreigners funny for being foreign. He was one of a minority of English liberals who never applauded Garibaldi loudly. When he met Mazzini a few years later, it was not out of sympathy for the *Risorgimento*, but because a fraudster had used Mazzini's name in begging money from Dickens. And Dickens, characteristically, was not interested in radical Italian nationalism, but in the school for poor children Mazzini had set up in Clerkenwell.

Switzerland in 1845 proved preferable to Italy. A Protestant country, it had scenic grandeur such as always appealed to Dickens' romantic temperament. But generally speaking, for all the energy that led him to enthusiastic sight-seeing and inspecting institutions wherever he went, and excepting France where he spoke fluent French and came to feel quite at home on frequent long visits during the Crimean war, Dickens out of England was something of a fish out of water.

"THE NYMPH OF THE WATERFALL" MACLISE'S IMAGINATIVE INTRODUCTION OF GEORGINA HOGARTH TO THE SETTING OF ST KNIGHTON'S KIEVE, CORNWALL.

FAMILY AND TRAVELS

Before THE Public

T HE RETIRING parliamentary reporter who only made one real friend in the press gallery became a writer with an unusually intense feeling for his public and an obsessive need to approach them directly. He watched the sales figures which provided a thermometer of his popularity. Pickwick started at 4,000 and rose to 20,000. As sales rose with *Oliver Twist* and *Nicholas Nickleby*, Dickens wanted a larger share of the gross profits that enriched his publishers, and felt that both this and creative freedom might be won if he ran a miscellany magazine with essays, stories and an occasional serial. So he started *Master Humphrey's Clock*; a bad idea, as it proved. For the notion of basing the numbers around an "old file's" club of eccentric friends and the manuscripts hidden in his clockcase proved sterile. The introduction of Mr Pickwick and the Wellers was a failure. The characters fell flat beneath his pen. Readers didn't need to make comparison with Addison and Steele's Sir Roger de Coverley – Dickens' avowed inspiration.

Every month in *Blackwood's Magazine* Professor Wilson brought out "Christopher North's" conversations in Ambrose's Edinburgh tavern: far more entertaining gatherings, whose vividly bigoted discussions of current controversies and new literature made Dickens' interests look dull and artificial. His sales fell alarmingly, and it took the sensational sentimental success of *The Old Curiosity Shop* to bring back his audience and raise it to 40,000. It was a shock when *Martin Chuzzlewit* saw it fall to 20,000 again, and after the couple of years economizing on the continent, he dropped Chapman and Hall as his publishers and came to an agreement with Bradbury and Evans, their printers, that they should undertake publishing his work for the next eight years, taking only 25% of the proceeds. And he turned again to the prospect of secure journalistic employment.

FAME AND BLAME

The *Daily News* was founded in 1846 as a new radical journal with Charles Dickens as its editor. The paper was a success, the editor lasted a week. The repetitious stranglehold of feeding the presses daily was no longer work this free spirit could undertake. After *Dombey and Son*, he revived his idea of a miscellany. *Household Words* was a straightforward series of unsigned articles and short stories with a running serial, all "Conducted by Charles Dickens" though other contributors submitted material. For the rest of his life, Dickens would have at his disposal a regular vehicle in which he could editorialize to his heart's content. Which he did, liberally voicing his opinions on anything from policemen to painters. He didn't have to report the day's news, or discuss the week's unless something had happened on which he wanted to comment. But he enjoyed the outlet for his overflowing feelings, and he wrote such bright journalistic prose that his readers enjoyed them too.

He shared more of himself in his next novel, *David Copperfield*, which was unashamedly autobiographical in many respects. Not that the public could have recognized Micawber as John Dickens or Dora as Maria Beadnell. But the world knew that Dickens had been a shorthand writer and a parliamentary reporter and a novelist. When David embraced that career pattern and it was observed that his initials reversed his creator's, the novel was immediately seen as one into which the author had poured his heart very personally.

Seven years and three novels after *David Copperfield* Dickens went before the public in the most unfortunate way. Repeated child-bearing and post-natal depression had turned Kate into a fat, unlovely, gloomy helpmeet. Her sister Georgina, living with the Dickenses since their return from America, gave Kate help with the household and children; gave Charles that unerotic sisterly companionship he always valued. Now she seemed to him not only the effective housekeeper, but – he persuaded himself – a better friend to his children. To crown everything, he fell in love with a young actress, Ellen Ternan, who had been engaged to perform in some of the theatricals he loved to stage. Dickens made arrangements for a separation from Kate, making her a generous allowance and providing a house where she was to live, accompanied at first by their eldest son.

Unsurprisingly word leaked out, and the news that the great evangelist of hearth and home had thrown out

his wife provoked malicious gossip. This was heightened by Georgina's refusal to leave Charles' household. Her mother and younger sister were furious at this betrayal of Kate. Dickens was unreasonably enraged that he and those he loved should be criticized. He drafted an ill-judged, ungenerous and self-serving statement and demanded that all newspaper proprietors with any loyalty to him should print it. Bradbury and Evans refused to let it appear in *Household Words*, and Dickens, beside himself with misplaced righteous indignation, took his business back to Chapman and Hall, severed his connections with *Household Words*, and started a new journal which he had to be told had better not, under the notorious circumstances, be called *Household Harmony*! It became *All the Year Round* and was, in effect, *Household Words* under a new title.

At the same time he started another venture to bring himself before the public. First for various charities, and then on his own behalf to cover the expense of buying the large house Gad's Hill Place in Kent, he began a series of public readings. As the furious energy Dickens had always commanded was recklessly hurled into the intensely dramatic performances punctuating tiring travel schedules, his doctors and grown-up children felt some anxiety, but Dickens was adamant. These occasions brought him directly in touch with his public. He heard their laughter; moved their tears; needed their applause. Public reading tours – one a strenuous return to America in 1867-68 – drained his energy and left him gout-ridden and exhausted. Dickens in his fifties was a national institution. But a prematurely aged and visibly enfeebled one.

CATHERINE DICKENS IN LATER LIFE.

THE Last Years

DICKENS AND THE
HON. MARY BOYLE
ACTING IN "USED
UP": THE START
OF A LIFELONG
FRIENDSHIP.

OLD FRIENDS RETIRED and died. Young protégés, "Dickens' young men" who contributed to *All the Year Round*: flamboyant G.A.Sala, gossippy Edmund Yates, and the attenuated assistant manager W.H.Wills. The incense of younger men was more appealing than the reservations of contemporaries. John Forster, still designated Dickens' executor, had grown more heavy and "Victorian" – as had Dickens' writing. But Charles, increasingly close to the more Bohemian young Wilkie Collins, cooled a little toward his old friend.

Collins shared Dickens' love of travelling holidays. The two made the *Lazy Tour of Two Idle Apprentices* together. Collins offered the shallow ideal of serial writing as "Make 'em laugh; make 'em cry; make 'em wait", and, with a mistress and children as well as a wife and family, he encouraged Dickens to look at the erotic underside of Second Empire Paris without the melodramatic attitudes of guilt for sin which marred his writing about sex. Still, it is unlikely that Collins ever persuaded Dickens to join him in actual dissipation.

Wilkie's brother Charles Allston Collins married Dickens' younger daughter, Katey, in 1860. Possibly the marriage was to some extent precipitated by Katey's indignation at the way her father treated her mother. Certainly in later life she was willing to say of the marital breakdown, "My father was a very wicked man" and "Auntie Georgie was not quite straight". Nor was her marriage really successful. Collins' health was uncertain and he dithered between painting and writing in his career. It seems possible that he also proved impotent. His death in 1873 may have been something of a relief to Katey, who subsequently contracted a very successful marriage to the Italian painter Carlo Perugini.

Mamie, her elder sister, stayed in the Dickens household at Gad's Hill, sharing with her aunt Georgie the role of chatelaine. Dickens always felt her temper to be milder than her sister's, and he fondly tolerated her increasing love of the fashionable society he despised, renting London houses for "the Season" because she wanted it. He even declined to protest when she went to stay with county friends and canvassed with them in the Conservative interest. Mamie was enjoying the reward of uncritical devotion. She would remain unmarried all her life, saying that having lived with her father she could never contemplate sharing her life with any other man.

The two youngest boys, Henry and "Plorn" also stayed with their father. The lads continued to enjoy the life of exuberant household entertainment and theatricals he enjoyed. Their boyhood was punctuated by visits from distinguished friends who became courtesy "uncles". Mark Lemon, editor of *Punch*, and a beloved "Uncle Porpoise" to the Dickens children, dropped out of their circle, however. Dickens could not forgive him for refusing to publish his sanctimonious letter criticizing his estranged wife Catherine. The Danish writer, Hans Christian Andersen, who visited the family and who should have been a wonderful guest for children, was voted "a bony bore".

In many respects, life at Gad's Hill seemed an unbroken continuation from Dickens' earlier summer life in rural cottages. The house fronted almost directly onto the road behind a shallow sweep of drive, but to the rear a large field allowed for cricket and other private sports. Dickens' beloved Medway corner of Kent, to be vividly realized in *Great Expectations*, allowed those long country walks that were his almost daily delight. Only, like the demanding readings that took their toll of his health, the constant energetic exercise and unstoppable release of spirits seemed to be testing Dickens' constitution unreasonably. Forster remarks that readers who only knew the writer from photographs would think of his hair as grey and scanty. American observers were more struck by the vanity with which he curled the wings forward in 1867, just as they tut-tutted over the fresh buttonhole that arrived every day, testifying to an admirer. Actually the gift of the hon. Mary Boyle, whose completely platonic friendship with Charles dated to their acting together in amateur theatricals in the 1850s. But Dickens' hair had always drawn American attention; on his first visit, well-bred Americans were shocked that he once combed his hair at table.

Familiarity with pictures of Dickens always makes it seem surprising that he died before he was sixty; he looked to have passed that age by the time he was fifty-four. Many of the admirers who loved the vitality of his early comic writing also found the work of his middle age comparatively drab and heavy, despite grotesques as wonderful as Mr Venus and a mature interest in the effects of changing financial fortune on personality. Perhaps there was some survival of his earlier buoyancy in the surprising ease he felt at the end of his life in France's garish Second Empire or America's mercenary Gilded Age, while his own country's sober money-making zeitgeist was comparatively unappealing. Yet he himself had done much to recommend the virtues of

thrift, good management and a face of public respectability.

Those who felt his plotting was obvious or haphazard were left a posthumous challenge. The uncompleted *Mystery of Edwin Drood* has never been solved, but lies as mysterious today as it was when a stroke suddenly felled its author after a morning's creative work. He had wished to be buried without ceremony in his beloved Kent – either in the Rochester Castle moat graveyard, or in the country churchyards of Shorne or Cobham. It was not to be. The man who had exemplified and almost created his age was interred with national mourning in Poet's Corner of Westminster Abbey.

LEFT TO RIGHT: MAMIE, CHARLES AND KATEY DICKENS IN THE GARDEN OF GAD'S HILL PLACE.

THE LAST YEARS

THE POPULAR WRITER

DICKENS' EXTRAORDINARY SUCCESS and achievement are inextricably bound up with his being a self-educated man of defiantly "popular" tastes. To hostile critics he seemed lowbrow – even vulgar – but to a wide audience that was untouched by "Serious Literature", he had all the accessibility of the Newgate Calendars or broadsheet ballads despised by the intelligentsia. His secondary characters showed him fully alive to common folk's heroic and impressively virtuous capacities, as well as their entertaining foibles, even if his centre-stage heroes and heroines were always well-bred and educated, or, like Oliver Twist, uttered language of improbable propriety for a "workhouse brat".

Gray's *Elegy in a Country Churchyard* might recognize the possibility of innately talented yokels, but such "rude forefathers of the village" were doomed to insignificance and oblivion as the "village Hampden" or the "mute, inglorious Milton". Dickens could create an imaginary decayed, shabby-genteel alcoholic clerk, and feel so confident of his virtue, decency and essential reality that he constantly referred to him in conversation as "my friend, Newman Noggs". As if to compensate for the unreal Oliver, he raised to immortality an actual workhouse gal his family had employed in Camden, and justly celebrated the courage and survival-instinct that could blossom in the lowest "skivvy", when he turned her into the pert little "Marchioness" of *The Old Curiosity Shop*. Scott had created peasants and artisans of worth and merit, of course, but his creations were always to some extent exotic: either Scottish or historical or both. Dickens found flowers of human courage and

fidelity in the gutters of contemporary London.

By sheer chance, too, he was economically accessible to more readers than could buy the traditional "three-decker" novel, increasingly demanded by circulating libraries because it tripled their hire charges. Because Chapman and Hall invited him to contribute the letterpress to a set of monthly caricatures, Dickens was fortuitously committed to producing a story in twenty parts sold at a shilling (5p) each. A new novel of the same length, published in three volumes between boards, could cost five guineas (£5.25) a volume. The whole of *Pickwick Papers* could be the property of the reader for £1, laid out over a year and a half. The success of *Pickwick* was such that, apart from novels published in magazines – *Oliver Twist, Hard Times, A Tale of Two Cities* and *Great Expectations* – all Dickens' later novels stuck to the "trademark" appearance Chapman and Hall had established: monthly numbers in green covers with vignettes running around the central title and by-line.

Part-issue publication had hitherto been used to let the respectable and literate working and lower-middle classes hire-purchase *The Pilgrim's Progress* or *Robinson Crusoe*, or some such respectable lengthy uncopyrighted prose. The more raffish could buy Pierce Egan's illustrated tales of sporting low-life. Dickens established the principle that new, respectable popular novels might appear as original serials. Thackeray copied him, with bright yellow covers. Hardy wrote serials. Sherlock Holmes was born in *Beeton's Christmas Annual*, and was then joined by Oscar Wilde's *Dorian Gray*, as a *Lippincott's* serial.

DICKENS READING
IN PUBLIC, 1858.

Sensation

T WAS DICKENS' GOOD fortune to have an appetite for the sensational that matched his readers'. The nurse who regaled him with stories about the wonderful Bluebeard, "Captain Murderer" – who baked successive brides in pies and ate them, until one cunningly took a horrible poison of spider's knees which turned him blue and settled his hash when he gobbled her up – fixed little Charles' taste for gore and horror and nightmare frissons before he was six.

When he was nineteen he encountered his first real murderers. The publisher J.W. Fairburn apparently commissioned the young shorthand reporter to cover the trial of the Shoreditch bodysnatchers, John Bishop, Thomas

Horrible and Bar-bar-ous Murder of Poor
JAEL DENNY,
THE ILL-FATED VICTIM OF THOMAS DRORY.

TYPICAL BROADSHEET
WOODCUT OF
"HORRIBLE MURDER".

Head (aka Williams) and "Blaze-Eye Jack" May. Bishop and Head had drowned at least five people in their well after slipping them Mickey Finns of rum and laudanum. May helped them sell the body of, a Lincolnshire drover's boy called Cunningham. The trial gained pathos from the prosecution's erroneous belief that Cunningham was an orphaned Italian immigrant who exhibited white mice on the streets. Dickens noted an interesting truth at this trial, remarking:

> *There was nothing in the aspect or manner of any of them which betokened a predisposition to any thing like the outrage on humanity of which they stood convicted … May, who was the best-looking of the three, had a countenance which most persons would consider open and manly … but neither in him nor his companions was there the slightest physiognomical trait of a murderer, according to common notions of the subject.*

Now what on earth were these "common notions" of a murderer's face? Notions, in fact, drawn from lurid broadsheet woodcuts of killers, or from the popular stage villains, who snarled and skulked to the delighted boos and hisses of the audience. As a writer, Dickens was often at his best when he set aside the penny-plain truths of everyday life, and substituted tuppence-coloured fictions familiar from cheap theatres and "penny dreadfuls". Ikey Solomons, the most famous Jewish receiver of the 1830s, was a good-looking young dandy. Fagin is an obvious variant of a conventional Shylock. Carker of *Dombey and Son* is one of Dickens' most naturalistic villains. Yet his too-white teeth and feline smile mark him down as wicked to anyone who has ever watched a B-movie.

"Let other pens dwell upon guilt and shame", Jane Austen remarked. Dickens was only too willing to be one of such pens. Seduction, bastardy, prostitution, theft, fraud, suicide, horrible drunkenness, sadism, murder and opium-taking are among the guilty and shameful practices described in his novels. Nor is his work usually successful when it eschews such things. His 1846 Christmas book *The Battle of Life* – proper enough to content Miss Austen – is so bad that even the loyal Forster could only say "it had points not unworthy of him". Those great Victorian favourites *A Child's Dream of a Star* and "The Boots' Story" from *The Holly Tree Inn* are repellently mawkish. Dickens' imagination thrives on sensation, extravagance, exuberant humour, fantastic comedy, and his own emotional recollections. He can give us wonderfully funny flirts, coquettes and would-be gallants. But almost the only serious aspect of serious love he handles with conviction is a young man's easily aroused sense of immaturity and embarrassment. His active centre-stage second-lead women are sometimes melodramatic tragedy queens, all flashing eyes and heaving bosoms, and at other times pretty ickle things whose creator hovers nauseatingly around them saying things like "poor little fluttering heart …" and drooling over their timid helplessness or occasional terror like a horror-film fan going to "see the women scream". His ingenuée heroines are pretty, subdued, ladylike, and generally seen-but-not-heard. If his young heroes are not followed through childhood, they are usually well-groomed sticks, prone to flashes of stagey utterance in moments of passion. It would be a strange Dickens-lover who listed Nicholas Nickleby and Madeline Bray, Edward Chester and Emma Haredale, Martin Chuzzlewit and Mary Grahame, or even Lucy Manette and Charles Darnay among his favourite characters.

All this inartistic art proves Dickens a great popular entertainer. Would anyone have enjoyed Todd Slaughter more if a convincing Elizabeth Bennett and Darcy worked through the romantic sub-plot while Sweeney Todd shaved and slit throats? Do we want a Hammer Films

Jonathan Harkness to confront Count Dracula with the decorum of a Merchant-Ivory hero confronting bad taste? Who would have paid sixpence to see Theda Bara vamp, or a few dollars to see Bette Davis serve roast rat to Joan Crawford if those ladies had performed with studied realism and artistic restraint? Conventions and stock characters and melodramatics are as useful to lazy audiences as to lazy writers. Most people who go to the arts to be entertained don't want to exert themselves by the intellectual study of character. They want their attention grabbed and their obvious expectations satisfied. In writing sensationally, Dickens may be said to have known his job.

A BROADSHEET PUBLISHER'S INACCURATE IMPRESSION OF THE SHOREDITCH BODYSNATCHERS. DICKENS GAVE A BETTER ACCOUNT OF THE TRIAL FOR FAIRBURN.

Theatre

HE DICKENS THEATRE was the title of Richard Garis' contribution to the outburst of Dickens criticism and commentary around 1960. This rightly pointed to a central element in Dickens' imagination: as a child he loved pantomime; from his mid-teens he sedulously visited theatres, enjoying complete "turkeys" as much as the artistry of well-performed plays – are there any more enjoyable passages in his works than Mr Crummles' performances, or Mr Wopsle's? He didn't confess in *Sketches* to being one of the "low copying clerks in attorneys' offices" who haunted the private theatres of London – but he was. He didn't admit that he was recapturing personal observations when he described the amateur Richard III uttering Colley Cibber's show-stopping interpolation:

"Orf with his ed" (very quick and loud; then slow and sneeringly) "So much for Bu-u-u-uckingham!" Lay the emphasis on the "uck"; get yourself gradually into a corner, and work with your right hand, while you're saying it, as if you were feeling your way, and it's sure to do.

He didn't tell the world that before he was twenty he had probably acted alongside "lady performers" who – unlike the stage-struck young clerks – paid "nothing for their characters" and were "usually selected from one class of society". Nor did any but his intimates know that he might have become a professional actor had not the *Morning Chronicle* offered steady work at a regular salary. All London knew, however, that the amateur actor who exulted in performing with the garrison at Montreal in 1842 became stage manager, prime mover and leading performer in the company of amateurs drawn from literary and artistic circles who hired Miss Kelly's private theatre in Dean Street, Soho in 1845. They mounted a brilliantly successful production of Jonson's *Every Man in His Humour*; followed it with Beaumont and Fletcher's *The Elder Brother* in the same year; revived *Every Man* in 1847 with supporting farces to raise money to pay off Leigh Hunt's debts; revived it again in private performance at Bulwer Lytton's stately home, Knebworth, in 1851, and went public with Lytton's comedy *Not So Bad as We Seem* to raise funds for a new literary charity. This last was performed before the Queen and Prince Albert. Dickens continued to enjoy private amateur theatricals, setting up theatres in Rockingham Castle, the home of his friends Mr and Mrs Richard Watson, and in his own London home at

DICKENS AS CAPTAIN BOBADIE IN "EVERY MAN AND HIS HUMOUR".

Tavistock House to which he moved in 1851.

It was hardly surprising, then, that the man whom almost everyone except the Carlyles hailed as a magnificent actor should turn his love of appearing before an audience and parading his own creations into the vividly dramatic public readings with which he filled his own and his favourite charities' purses in the last years of his life.

It is surprising that it should have taken some time before Dickens the writer's huge debt to Dickens the amateur thespian and theatregoer should have been clearly recognized. Writers often talk a lot of humbug about their characters being "purely imaginary", especially if libel suits are threatening. In fact, for a character to become clearly formed in the mind's eye, most writers need to draw on observation and embellishment of individuals they know, possibly compositing two or three into one figure. Or else they must fall back on the "stock" characters created by others who have become familiar in popular representations on stage or page, or today, the large or small screen. We have seen that Dickens drew sensational villains from popular theatre; that Sam Weller was based on the comic servant actor Sam Vale – a vail being a tip in nineteenth century slang. We know that Dickens loved the solo performances of the actor Charles Mathews, and learned from him the use of eccentric speech rhythms to establish a character. It seems unsurprising that Dickens should have rushed to lookingglasses and tried out facial expressions and speeches in character while composing fiction.

The first descriptions of Mr Pickwick give us his beaming eyes, twinkling behind his glasses; his notebook, his telescope – all the paraphernalia of an amateur intellectual. But when Seymour, Buss and Phiz fixed Pickwick's appearance in everyone's mind, low-crowned hat, blue coat, tight trousers, gaiters and all, Dickens became aware that some characters could be usefully identified by their costume and props, just as if they were on the stage. So Bill Sikes becomes a dirty white hat, a belcher handkerchief round the neck, and a spot-eyed mongrel. Ralph Nickleby apparently never takes off his spencer jacket and wellington boots. The unconvincing figure of Rigaud Blandois in *Little Dorrit* seems adequately established for Dickens by repeated Mephistophelean mugging: "his moustache went up and his eyebrows came down". In the same novel, the servant Affery's equally stagey gesture of throwing her apron over her head when aware of something she doesn't want to know, is quite effective and the farcical minor figure of "Mr F's Aunt", exploding into hilarious irrelevancies to dislocate rational conversation, is far more entertaining than a realistic portrayal of an Alzheimer's victim would have been. It may seem odd to find the young Dickens trying to excuse his awkward plotting by appealing to a stage convention whose absurdity he recognizes. Yet it surely proves his committed theatricality, as we can see in *Oliver Twist*:

It is the custom of the stage, in all good murderous melodramas, to present the tragic and the comic scenes, in as regular alternation, as the layers of red and white in a side of streaky bacon. The hero sinks upon his straw bed, weighed down by fetters and misfortunes; in the next scene, his faithful but unconscious squire regales the audience with a comic song ... Such changes appear at first absurd; but they are not so unnatural as they would seem at first sight. The transitions in real life from well-spread boards to deathbeds ... are not a whit less startling.

CHARLES MATHEWS, WHO WAS DICKENS' FAVOURITE ACTOR.

BILL SIKES, WITH IDENTIFYING HAT, BELCHER, BREECHES, ANKLEBOOTS, CUDGEL AND DOG.

Ghosts

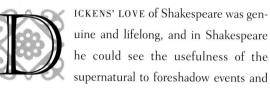

THE GHOST OF CHRISTMAS TO COME SHOWS SCROOGE HIS GRAVE.

ICKENS' LOVE of Shakespeare was genuine and lifelong, and in Shakespeare he could see the usefulness of the supernatural to foreshadow events and create moments of horror. But however much he enjoyed *Macbeth*, one cannot imagine Dickens joining

Shakespeare and James I in shuddering at witches. And one might feel that ghosts, too, should have squeaked and gibbered as a matter of mere stagecraft for him. This, however, was not the case.

At Pittsburgh I saw another solitary confinement prison … A horrible thought occurred to me when I was recalling all I had seen that night. What if ghosts be one of the terrors of the jails? I have pondered on it often since then … The more I think of it the more certain I feel that not a few of these men (during a portion of their imprisonment, at least) are nightly visited by spectres.

This is astonishing. Dickens, thirty when he wrote these observations home from America, gave very serious thought to prison reforms involving solitary confinement and produced some of his most mature social and psychological observations on the subject. Yet here he is, an intelligent grown man, quite genuinely shuddering like a schoolboy over possible spooks in the cells!

The common sense he was capable of bringing to bear on the question of ghosts showed up seventeen years later when the Christmas number of *All the Year Round* featured stories by various contributors, supposedly told by members of a house party sleeping in different rooms of a "Haunted House". The mature Dickens remarks that, alone at night, and imagining creaks and bumps, "You can fill any house with noises, if you will, until you have a noise for every nerve in your nervous system." Moreover he acknowledges the contributory presence of disturbed young people at the centre of poltergeist episodes and hauntings. A temporary servant starts the panic in "The Haunted House" by saying she has seen "Eyes", and becoming cataleptic with fear. Yet she and a village odd-job boy who is equally convinced that the house holds real phantoms, appear to be responsible for faking the mysterious sounds. Dickens as narrator comments sensibly that such hoaxing is "one of the first elements, above all others, rationally to be suspected in, and strictly looked for, and separated from, any question of this kind."

His own "haunted room" story introduces good ghostly shocks, as the narrator when shaving suddenly sees the face of a young boy or a strange young man in his glass, or wakes in horror believing the skeleton of the schoolboy supposed to haunt the room is beside him in bed. But the only ghosts accompanying him turn out to be memories of his own past, a concept prefigured in Scrooge's Ghost of Christmas Past, and still more in *The Haunted Man*, the Christmas book of 1847. And even while Dickens lightly frightens his readers in "The Haunted House" with the spectre of the supposed ghostly schoolboy "Master B", he makes the phantom's wailings a comic complaint about having being over-liberally dosed with calomel.

In fact, despite his apparent half-belief in supernatural apparitions – it seems likely that he is describing a genuine experience when, in the same story, he refers to having once "seen" his deceased father sitting silent and motionless in his room – Dickens was never a ghost writer like M.R. James, deliberately terrifying any susceptible readers who might pick up his books. Many children, joyfully introduced to Dickens through *A Christmas Carol,* have been really scared by the hooded figure of the Ghost of Christmas That is to Come, and its half-understood visions of Scrooge's corpse. Children, too, can share Dickens' tremor of fear when the ghost leads Scrooge to a sinister cemetery. But no adult could mistake the "all-a-dream" nature of Scrooge's four visitors, the wild inventiveness that gives a Ghost of Memory a giant candle-snuffer with which to repress itself and its painful recollections, and the comedy with which Marley's ghost is given the traditional ghostly chains and fetters, only they are made of the cash-boxes that obsessed him in life.

Above all, the glorious comedy of Scrooge's dyspeptic conversation with the ghost encourages the adult reader to agree that there's "more of gravy than of grave" about such visions.

The same linking of ghosts with indigestion is clear in the first two quasi-ghost stories Dickens published: "The Bagman's Story" and "The Story of the Bagman's Uncle" in *Pickwick Papers.* There is no frisson of fear as an old Spanish mahogany chair turns itself into an ugly old gentleman in the middle of the night, and shows bagman Tom Smart how to win the heart of a comely widow. Dickens leaves us in no doubt that punch rather than *psi* has brought the chair to life. The bagman's uncle rescuing a ghost damsel in distress from her ghost abductors in a ghost mail-coach is equally obviously sleeping off over-indulgence.

Yet as late in his career as *Great Expectations* Dickens could use a throwaway spectral vision to prefigure an incident he never, in the end, used. When the child Pip thinks for a moment he sees Miss Havisham hanging in Satis House, his creator surely intended a foreshadowing of the plot, and was not sure himself whether some such second sight might not exist. A man of his time, Dickens shared in the post-Romantic movement away from the Age of Reason which would have dismissed ghosts. He would have shared Dr Johnson's view that reason itself argued against ghosts, but human experience kept on reporting them. Agnostic and more than a little sceptical about ghosts by the end of his life, Dickens would surely have been an enthusiastic supporter of the Society for Psychical Research had he lived long enough, demanding that the tools of exact science and confirmed observation be brought to test all fascinating and thrilling accounts of hauntings.

"IN CAVERNS BY THE WATERSIDE … I'VE HAD A LOT OF PRACTICE" (OF HAUNTING). LEWIS CARROLL ENJOYS A ROBUST VICTORIAN LAUGH AT SPOOKS.

Misers

FROM THE ANCIENT ROMAN playwrights, Terence and Plautus, to Major Bloodnok and Gritpype-Thynne, lust and avarice have been two of the most successful mainsprings for comedy. Since Terence and Plautus they have often been combined in the figure of the old miser selected by the beautiful maiden's grasping father as an appropriate suitor for her. Classical comedy recounts the success of a handsome but impoverished hero in rescuing the heroine and her inheritance from the lascivious clutches of her rich admirer, whereupon the hero scoops the pool with the heroine thrown in as a part of the prize.

To disguise this disagreeable equation of lovely lady with lovely lolly, it is vital to make the opposition even more disagreeable. Hence the horrid old miser as heroine's father or anaphrodisiac suitor.

Dickens seems to have believed in such figures when he was young. Fagin, a Shylock-figure gloating over his stolen gems, hopefully describes himself as "just a miser" when he realizes that Oliver has seen him with the swag. Arthur Gride as a rival to Nicholas Nickleby has stepped straight from the stage. He drools horribly over

EBENEEZER SCROOGE
AS PLAYED BY
ALASTAIR SIM.

Madeline Bray, and is Dickens' most perfect example of that sadistic fantasy: loathsome lover wants terrified turned-off heroine. Quilp, salivating over Little Nell, is less horrible inasmuch as his genuine – if sinister – sexual vibrancy has been shown to attract older women in his wife's circle, and Nell's youth protects her from knowing what he has in mind. Quilp and Gride, like Shylock, traffic in bonds and lend money: the preferred occupation for stage misers.

Phiz's illustrations of Gride and Ralph Nickleby in the planning and catastrophe of Gride's intended wedding show how attractive this concept was. Previously Ralph was the unfeeling, capitalist hard man. A bully who neither skulked nor fawned. In court dress, introducing Kate to Lord Frederick, he is drawn with his head upright and jaw firm, while his hand and body sketch an apology for a bow. Like Thackeray's Lord Steyne, he is a powerful, dominating figure, even when pretending to courtliness. Once Ralph associates with Gride, however, Phiz pulls him into a stoop, creeping and snarling. The booted and spencered dominator declines into the conniving miser's confederate.

THE CASH NEXUS

In the characters of Anthony and Jonas Chuzzlewit, we see Dickens trying harder to combine the character of the hard-hearted Carlylean capitalist – "cash the sole nexus between man and man" – with the typical miser. They are textile merchants, not usurers. Anthony is a harsh realist like Ralph Nickleby, and says what we all want to say in calling Pecksniff a hypocrite. But his acquisitiveness is a matter of entrenched principle, and his old age gives him something of the miser's threadbare weakness. Still, in the end he and the son whom he has trained too well are so deeply entangled in Dickens' elaborate plot to make them possible victim and parricide that their miserly characters become secondary to dark hints about poison and possible suspicions.

It is with Scrooge that Dickens suddenly starts to *think* about this stock character of farce. One of the most perfectly named of this great namers' creations – scre-e-e-ewing money out of others, until it pops out like a cork from a bottle, or scre-e-e-ewing down a strongbox lid until it grips with a suck like a vacuum. One who is gloriously funny as Squeers and Pecksniff and Mrs Gamp were funny in their villainy and one who is given real pathos. First his sister reminds us that the most miserable old moneybags was a small boy once – and maybe was himself in some way abused. Then, through Scrooge's conversation with his intended, Dickens movingly observes the way in which society's respect for wealth can encourage the man with inadequate inner resources to drop other ambitions and built up a bank balance as a screen:

> *"This is the even-handed dealing of the world," he said. "There is nothing on which it is so hard as poverty; and there is nothing it professes to condemn with such severity as the pursuit of wealth."*

> *"You fear the world too much," she answered gently. "All your other hopes have merged into the hope of being beyond the chance of its sordid reproach."*

ABANDONING TRADITION

The Dickens who could perceive this truth underlying the Arthur Grides and Anthony Chuzzlewits was ready to abandon the traditional stage miser, and channel his concern about acquisitiveness into the study of greed and the dangers of unearned wealth which would increasingly occupy his attention. The "willing" Carter Barkis marks the turning point. His fear of anyone's

knowing how much money he has and where he keeps it is a foible, not a fault; an eccentricity which barely deserves the description of a neurosis. He is a decent man with miserly anxieties.

Only in his last completed novel would Dickens return to the subject of the pathological miser. And the historical examples named in *Our Mutual Friend* – Vulture Hopkins, Daniel Dancer, Blewberry Jones and the like – are just the reading matter, guiding Boffin's act and Wegg's deception. Boffin, we are to understand, was never truly tempted by avarice. He agreed all along with Rokesmith's characterization of misers as "abject wretches". The mature Dickens knew that, however they enthral readers of sensational biography, those men and women who hoard and hide behind property are as sadly mad as Howard Hughes, the barmy naked billionaire hiding his rebarbative personality from a society which despised it, and collecting his own urine in the absence of anything more worthwhile to amass.

Several eighteenth-century misers who starved themselves were capable of generosity to others. Far more dangerous, as Dickens knew, were the sane and rational financiers and bill-brokers. They lured the naive into speculation and borrowing. They justified their greed with prate about market forces and enlightened self-interest. They could hide their grasping cruelty behind Limited Liability and the screen of employees like Pancks or Riah who faced the public. The mature Dickens set aside the stage miser and the mad miser and looked squarely at the avarice underpinning civilization.

SHYLOCK, PROTOTYPICAL MISER—FATHER CARING EQUALLY FOR HIS DAUGHTER AND HIS DUCATS.

Madmen

THE POPULAR WRITER

BARNABY RUDGE, THE
INNOCENT MAD BOY
WITH HIS PET
RAVEN, GRIP.

Recognizing true miserliness as madness Dickens also developed his notions of insanity from the ridiculous "Madman's Manuscript" in *Pickwick* to brain-damaged Maggy in *Little Dorrit*. Today we feel impatient with young Dickens' silly belief that "madmen"

secretly know themselves to be "mad", and exult in their cunning. Yet we delight in the equally "incorrect" notions underlying the mad gentleman who courts Mrs Nickleby and Miss La Creevy:

> *Cormoran and Blunderbore! She is come! All the wealth I have is hers if she will take me for her slave. Where are grace, beauty, and blandishments, like those? In the Empress of Madagascar? No. In the Queen of Diamonds? No. In Mrs. Rowland, who every morning bathes in Kalydor for nothing? No. Melt all these down into one, with the three Graces, the nine Muses, and fourteen biscuit-bakers' daughters from Oxford Street, and make a woman half as lovely. Pho! I defy you.*

It is a spiteful authorial punishment for Mrs Nickleby's vanity to pretend that this surreal marvel anticipating Spike Milligan lost his senses "through evil tempers, and covetousness, and selfishness, and guzzling, and drinking"!

In fact, both the Madman of the *Pickwick Manuscript* and Barnaby Rudge show us that young Dickens was unaware of the distinction between congenital brain damage, hereditary predisposition to mental disorder, and mental disorder caused by stress. Barnaby is described as both lunatic and idiot, Dickens thinking the words synonymous. And, like the Madman of the *Manuscript*, Barnaby is supposed to be objectively aware of his condition and to prefer it to sanity. Since he is a sympathetic character, however, his pleasure lies in the hallucinatory forms he makes of clouds or a washing-line.

In fairness, we should note that Barnaby is part of the

great nineteenth century advance in humanity. Like Wordsworth's "Idiot Boy", he challenges that cruelty which allowed people to laugh at lunatics in Bedlam for entertainment. Like the Idiot Boy he focuses pathos on his mother. Mrs Rudge, like Betty Foy, is intended as a touching emblem of maternity, compelled to carry on as protectress long after her son is strong enough to care for himself. Dickens had already shown in *The Old Curiosity Shop* that he completely rejected the harsh old methods of treating lunatics – locking them up and shocking them with whips and drenchings. Fear of these things goaded the senile old Trent in his flight across England.

Still, Dickens made something rather interesting of Barnaby from the bald information that a madman was prominent among the Gordon rioters. He may do little to further rational understanding of either mental handicap or mental illness but as Barnaby became a favoured sentimental role for actresses, and the public accepted the fresh-faced, wild-eyed boy with colourful rags, a raven in a basket, and the innocent wish to grow rich and help his mother, he became a focus for the new idea of behaving kindly to the mentally disordered and the very challenging one of treating them, as far as possible, as beings having equal rights with ourselves and deserving as much respect for their moral worth. Backward and abused Smike, another favoured sentimental role for women, was similarly offered patiently respectful tuition by Nicholas Nickleby.

Dickens' next great madman carried this humanity even further. Unlike Barnaby, disordered from birth, Mr Dick is supposed to be a lunatic, driven out of his senses by the cruelty of his family. And Dickens has given him one central trait that could not be genetic: the monomaniac obsession with King Charles' head. Yet from his first appearance, smiling and winking at David from an upstairs room, Mr Dick's character is far more consonant with congenital brain damage than with induced mental illness. In fact, he shows all the sweet disposition, playfulness and willing helpfulness that one associates with Down's Syndrome, as, later, does Maggy in *Little Dorrit*, even though the case history Dickens gives her – fever at

the age of ten following which her hair fell out and she ceased to mature mentally – is more suggestive of brain injury caused by meningitis. There was no way Dickens could have known he was apparently describing a subdivision of congenital mental handicap: it was not until 1892 that Down proposed the term "mongolism" for the characteristics he had observed in "10% of all cases of idiocy". Dickens would only have known that when he perceived "idiots", many, like Maggy, had broad and "foolish" faces; and this group, smiled a lot, apparently meaninglessly.

What is truly impressive about Mr Dick is Dickens' admiration for Betsey Trotwood's treatment of him. She seems at least one hundred and twenty years ahead of her time in recognizing that some mental handicap is no bar to living in the community; that such a life can be of use and service to others, and will be the more so if it is praised and encouraged, "Mr Dick sets us all to rights!". Though such praise must not be misplaced to encourage unconstructive clowning or dullness ("Dick! Don't be foolish!").

How remarkably, too, Dickens restrains his account of Mr Dick's eccentricities. We never doubt that he is slightly "mad". Yet it would have been easy to overplay him as a necessary contrast to that eccentric firmness of Aunt Betsey's. Dickens, the madman's moral bookkeeper, blaming Mrs Nickleby's suitor's insanity on his wickedness, disappears in his maturity. Stroke or a breakdown, vividly observed in Mrs Skewton and Sir Leicester Dedlock and William Dorrit, may produce a senile dementia punitively reproducing the most undesirable aspects of earlier life. But characters Dickens genuinely thinks "mad" cease to be morally culpable, just as he stops presenting the misanthropic acquisitive lunacy we might call "Howard Hughes syndrome" as voluntary meanness.

ROY KINNEAR AS THE MAD GENTLEMAN NEXT DOOR IN THE 1968 TELEVISION ADAPTATION OF "NICHOLAS NICKLEBY". THIS PERFORMANCE WON A HUGE AUDIENCE OF CHILD FANS FOR DICKENS.

MADMEN

Murderers

WILLIAM PALMER, THE POISONER OF RUGELEY.

D ICKENS IS THE PRINCE of true crime buffs. He mentioned Bishop and "Williams" in the *Sketches*, and proved that the entertainer had taken over from the reporter by denying the truth he had seen at their trial. Bishop's head and features, he said, "might have afforded sufficient moral grounds for his instant execution at any time, even had there been no other evidence against him."

Nor did he forget this early exposure to the grave-robbers. The dummy books on his study door in Gad's Hill Place include *Burke (of Edinburgh) on the Sublime and the Beautiful*. The parenthesis shows that this is the most infamous of all resurrectionist-murderers, not the orator-philosopher. In *A Tale of Two Cities*, Dickens creates the comic resurrectionist Jerry Cruncher, and reveals his own ignorance of the craft. Like most people, he assumed coffins were disinterred. In fact the sack-'em-up men broke them open underground and dragged the bodies to the surface with a rope. Remembering mention of a gimlet at Bishop, Head and May's trial, Dickens gives Jerry "an instrument like a great corkscrew", although this was not a piece of grave-robbing equipment.

All his life Dickens followed the major murder cases. From New York in 1841, he facetiously compared

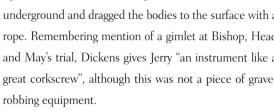

his own notoriety for demanding international copyright with that of John Colt, a scion of the millionaire gun-smiths' family awaiting execution for murdering his printer. Palmer the Rugeley poisoner of 1855 was such an "out-and-outer" – Dickens' favourite term for an irre-deemable villain – as to merit a piece in *Household Words*. Dickens' visit to Paris the following year found him fasci-nated by the Countess La Force's murder by her groom.

In Boston in 1868, the labora-tory where Professor Webster had murdered Professor Parkman was not to be missed.

The first murder in any of his novels shows him at his most realistic. Sikes battering Nancy to death in Spitalfields fictionalizes a commonplace occurrence. Until the 1870s, when Gladstone's licensing of night-houses restrained round-the-clock drinking, and Disraeli's Artisans' Dwellings Act started to ameliorate the festering slums, drunken men beat their partners to death with monotonous regularity. One such murder was reported every fortnight or so. The motives were usually trivial. The crimes were usually shocking in their brutality.

Dickens makes high melodrama of the confrontation between Sikes and his victim. "Bill, Bill, for dear God's sake, for your own, for mine, stop before you spill my blood! I have been true to you, upon my guilty soul I have!"

SIKES KILLS NANCY
IN "OLIVER TWIST".

cries Nancy. Which is grand *Guignolese* for, "No! Stop!! He-e-elp!!!!" Much as Dickens enjoyed such extravagance, and despite his success with the dramatized reading of "Sikes and Nancy" in the 1860s, he wisely dropped this tosh for the future. The murders in *Martin Chuzzlewit* and *Bleak House* take place off-stage. Bradley Headstone's murderous assault on Eugene Wrayburn is silent. Dickens focuses on the tension before and after murder.

This had already given him a useful chapter in *Oliver Twist*, as Sikes trudged around Hertfordshire before making his way back to Jacob's Island and his doom. Nature imitated art three years later, when Robert Blakesley stabbed his estranged wife and her brother-in-law in Eastcheap, and then evaded capture for five days, roaming around Hertfordshire until he gave himself up. Dickens' perception of murder was as something that might be planned absolutely but would still prove traumatic when completed. Sikes cannot drag his mind away from the memory of Nancy's body; he dies terrified of the vision of her staring eyes. Jonas Chuzzlewit dares not look back at the wood where he killed Tigg. Bradley Headstone runs over and over his murder in his mind, thinking of ways he might have done it better. And Dickens explicitly tells us that this is the experience of many murderers. Only Hortense, based on the ferociously impenitent

Swiss Mrs Manning, is untormented by her deed.

For Dickens, murder was self-evidently the worst sin, crime and aberration possible. The murderer's motive never enters his moral arithmetic. The enraged Sikes punishes Nancy for betraying the gang; Jonas and Bradley calculatingly kill blackmailers who know of their previous murder attempts. Those attempts were respectively motivated by avarice and jealousy. Hortense kills out of sheer bad temper when Tulkinghorne refuses to help her. He happens to be a disinterested quasi-blackmailer, but he has done her no harm. Dickens does not set one killer above the other.

Nor do the victims affect his judgment. Sikes kills a stagily golden-hearted whore. Headstone seeks to kill a flippant but queasy would-be seducer. Jonas' blackmailer is an entertaining confidence trickster; Bradley's a creepy riverside scoundrel detested by the residents of Limehouse Hole. It's all one to Dickens. Blackmail victim, raging drunkard, uncontrollable foreigner: a murderer is a murderer, the worst of all humans. Despite his opposition to capital punishment, Dickens has no regret for Fagin's impending hanging. The old man egged Sikes on to kill. It should be no surprise that once public executions were abolished and the gallows was reserved for murderers, Dickens' agitation against judicial killing fell silent.

Childhood

WILLIAM ORCHARDSON'S
PAINTING OF A BOY,
SAID TO BE DICKENS'
MODEL FOR PAUL
DOMBEY.

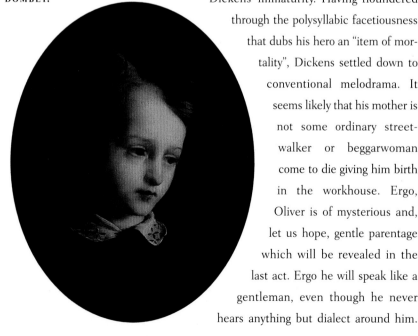

LIVER TWIST, LITTLE NELL, Tiny Tim, Paul and Florence Dombey, David Copperfield, Jo the crossing sweeper, Pip. For Dickens' contemporaries this gallery proved him one of the finest novelists of childhood. But since Oscar Wilde remarked caustically that one must have a heart of stone to read the death of Little Nell without laughing, they have seemed a more mixed bag. We should surely wish to discriminate between them: the beautifully remembered first-person studies of boyhood, David and Pip; the great tear-jerkers Nell, Tim, Paul and Jo; the inadequately realized cardboard figures going through the motions of potentially interesting situations, uttering the most correct drama-speak and never thinking an imperfect thought, Oliver and Florence. Oliver might be forgiven on the grounds of Dickens' immaturity. Having floundered through the polysyllabic facetiousness that dubs his hero an "item of mortality", Dickens settled down to conventional melodrama. It seems likely that his mother is not some ordinary street-walker or beggarwoman come to die giving him birth in the workhouse. Ergo, Oliver is of mysterious and, let us hope, gentle parentage which will be revealed in the last act. Ergo he will speak like a gentleman, even though he never hears anything but dialect around him.

Ergo he will knock down Noah Claypole as soon as he stands up to him. Ergo he will have genteel instincts, and shudder away from the "respectable old gentleman" and his ways as soon as he realizes he has been invited to join a gang of boy thieves. He is a figure from an inferior convention; another potential role for actresses to induce wet eyes in the audience rather than a model of boyhood from life.

But Florence Dombey is different. Her step-mamma is one of Dickens' most melodramatic characters: a fine cut of meat, too proud for the marriage market where she is sold. Florence's predicament, by contrast, is original and well imagined: the sensitive child rebuffed by a father who fears emotions, resents her capacity to evoke affection in others, and wanted to direct all his parental love into the tradition-sustaining channel of his sickly son. Bringing out this theme, Dickens uses two of those cameos of characters which so often illustrate his points like anecdotes in a sermon: one the fairly obvious orphaned girl Kate who feels as happy as any other child because her aunt brings her up with as much love as a mother; the other the more unexpected case of the widowed unemployed workingman John who spoils Martha, his ugly, sickly, ungrateful daughter and is gratified by her ungracious responses, knowing that he will not have her to love for long.

If only Dickens had understood that fully developed characters are more truly sympathetic if, like Martha, they are seen to have faults. Pip being loutish in Mr Wopsle's aunt's school, and David feeling patronage toward Mr Peggotty are more, not less appealing for their failings. If only he hadn't exploited children's innocence for those mawkish pieces of perfection, Nell and

Tim and even Jo, who never approaches justifying the nickname "Toughy". Jane Austen, consciously trying to create a morally perfect young girl for the only time in *Mansfield Park*, perceived the problem, and tried to make Fanny Price more real by making her unheroically timid. Dickens never realized there was a problem and was misled by public enthusiasm into believing that the laboured death of a saccharine saint was tragedy of the true kind.

The more credit to him for making something engag-

ing of Paul Dombey the "old-fashioned" child is also a splendid figure of innocent wisdom, whether he is discomposing Mrs Pipchin by witholding the complimentary remarks she expects, or flabbergasting his father with the question why good and powerful money couldn't save his mother. Paul, too, as an obviously dying child, convincingly brings out the best in other characters who were initially comic objects of satire: the Blimbers and Mr Toots are seen to be good people at heart. Miss Tox and even Mrs Chick are not unfeeling in his last illness. Only a monster of egoism like Major Bagstock is unaffected. Only the frozen figure of paternal pride cannot find a human way of expressing sympathy.

These are the child characters Dickens develops. We may deduce from those he observes more externally that despite his interest in the parental role, his mixed and intense memories of his own childhood, and the easy tears to which suffering children moved him, Charles Dickens was not really especially fond of children in the mass after infancy. The Artful Dodger may suggest to us Jack Wild, singing and dancing with Ron Moody to Lionel Bart's music but Dickens approved Cruikshank's very different drawings of a frightening overgrown lout. Street-smart wit and all, his creator had no hesitation in packing Master Dawkins off to transportation. David is pitied in Murdstone and Grinby's. Mick Walker and Mealy Potatoes must remain there and know their place. Large families of the poor are praised for their warmth and the, rather unconvincing, care larger children lavish on sick or little ones, the Cratchits with Tiny Tim, or, more strikingly, Johnny Tetterby lugging around the Infant Moloch in *The Haunted Man*. Large middle class families often offend the fastidious Dickens, Mrs Jellyby's brood or Mrs Pocket's. And over-managing teachers of the young give us comically aggrieved boys – the Pardiggles, Dr Blimber's pupils – but they never match the splendidly energetic and irrepressible complaints of a Huck Finn, or even a Just William. The Victorian adult world weighs down on Dickens' children. And, for all the vivid child's-eye vision sometimes granted him, we cannot acquit Dickens of being a Victorian adult.

A MAWKISH VICTORIAN IMPRESSION OF TINY TIM.

"LITTLE NELL", BY J.H.LOBLEY.

Love AND Marriage

"CHANGING HOMES":
G.E. HICKS' GENRE
PAINTING CATCHES
THE ALARMING STEP
OF VICTORIAN
MATRIMONY WITH
SOME SENSITIVITY.

IT WAS EARLY LAID DOWN that one plot-line of a novel should be the course of true love, culminating in marriage. Dickens was usually faithful to the notion that the hero or heroine must marry to round off the story. So we have the unmemorable tale of Emma Haredale and young Chester; the forgettable figures of Madeline Bray and Mary Grahame, Harry Maylie and Allen Woodcourt. Despite the comic successes of Dick Swiveller and the Marchioness, David Copperfield and Dora, Dickens' love stories are usually inert, unconvincing and boring.

This was by no means inevitable in Victorian novels, as witness those virgin daughters of the vicarage, Charlotte and Emily Brontë; the bluestocking heavy-moralizing "immoralist" George Eliot; the gloomy, guilty and confused Thomas Hardy. So why can't Dickens write well about love? Partly because his own falling in love did not meet with his own highest moral approval. He was essentially attracted by physical appearance as was most famously shown in his sudden infatuation for eighteen-year-old Christiana Weller when he was twenty-eight and married. Nor was this momentary and passing. He acted on

it. When his friend T.J.Thompson fell in love with her, he became a sort of aching-heart matchmaker, keeping up the interested friendship until their housekeeping in Italy turned him against them. The whole incident strongly suggests Arthur Clennam's "interest" in Pet Meagles, which, like David's love for Dora, is too simply based on ocular attraction for final approval. Arthur must appreciate the moral worth of Little Dorrit without any real trace of physical desire showing between them. The prime importance of appearance to Dickens is shown again in Flora Finching: the wonderful fictionalization of his disappointment on meeting his first love, Maria Beadnell, in middle age. "Flora," says the narrator, "always tall, had grown to be very broad, too, and short of breath; but that was not much. Flora, whom he had left a lily, had become a peony; but that was not much." Well, he *says* it's not much that the slim fair girl is now a stout, wheezy, red-faced woman. But he *notices* it before noticing her silly and inappropriately "artless" chatter!

The young Dickens can be arch about ankles. He admires a sparkling eye and a dimpling cheek, but only evil characters express open sexual admiration. Quilp's leering encomium upon Nell is disgusting given that she is a child – "what a nice kiss that was – just upon the rosy part! … such a chubby, rosy, cosy, little Nell …" This is the only strongly felt expression of sexual desire in Dickens.

Add to that his belief that women's nature "is ever, in the mass, better, truer, nobler, quicker to feel, and much more constant to retain, all tenderness and pity, self-denial and devotion, than the nature of men" (*Dombey and Son*). This popular codswallop allows angelic Agnes, pointing upward, to be a "truer" love than Dora. It allows the simplest conventional perception of marriages: hero and heroine will live happy ever after. Exemplary figures who have achieved this state are either Darby and Joan couples (the Garlands and the Boffins) or mutually supportive parents of large united families (the Micawbers, Cratchits, Tetterbys). Companionship lies at the heart of successful marriage in Dickens: even companionship in the absurdity of the Wititterlys or the Bayham Badgers or Barnet Skettleses. It evidently helps if a silly husband thinks

his ludicrous wife is something to boast about.

Unhappy marriages, as Tolstoy observed, take many forms. Dickens sarcastically calls Mr Punch a "'model of connubial bliss" in *Dombey and Son,* which centrally treats a very different sort of marital disaster: the proud and discontented trophy wife. In other novels, husbands harassed by their wives' incompetent housekeeping or parenting constitute one of Dickens' favourite and most personal versions of unhappy marriage. It was the excuse he used for his own marital breakdown.

Only once did he face what more probably lay behind his separation from Kate: discontent with her increasing age and girth. With benign memory extinguished by Redlaw's phantom, Mr Tetterby notices flatly that his wife is too fat and old "for him". She, conversely, notices that he is "commonplace", and she might have done better.

This last sense of marriage as a woman's "achievement" shows other features to be expected from Dickens. Matrimony *was* the conventional Victorian girl's conventional goal, and it was measured as more or less successful as the husband had more or less wealth, distinction or promise. Dickens, fully aware that this could lead to marriages that were morally no better than prostitution, still never questioned the convention. Saintly sisters like Ruth Pinch and Harriet Carker are rewarded with unexpectedly rich and reputable husbands. Ambitious spinsters are a joke. Tremulous Tony Weller and complacent William Dorrit confirm that eligible widowers are always in danger from designing women. And Dickens believes erroneously that women always dislike other more attractive women. It seems that being himself good-looking and intelligent, he never noticed that these qualities are always unfairly over-rewarded in just the same ways as inherited wealth or social status. It was another drawback to his attempts to write seriously about love and marriage.

DAVID AND DORA: EVEN JOHN FORSTER SAW HER AS A BETTER WOMAN THAN AGNES.

Autobiography

TARTING AS A REPORTER trained Dickens in accurate description. Proceeding to feature journalism encouraged him to add imagination and describe little-known places in new words – "Scotland Yard", "Seven Dials", "Monmouth Street". Going further, he drew upon general experiences that his readers might recognize – "Astley's", "Private Theatres", "Public Dinners". Ultimately, actual incidents were exaggerated and idealized – a genuine outing of young law-clerks

DAVID COPPERFIELD:
THE MOST
AUTOBIOGRAPHICAL
OF DICKENS' HEROES.

becoming "The Steam Excursion".

Sometimes Dickens' creative writing reveals his mind in ways that would otherwise be missed. The mature man found London dirty and depressing. He harked back to the Kent and the Medway towns as a Paradise Lost, to be Regained with Gad's Hill Place. The ambitious young Londoner had called Chatham, "Mudfog". One would not think from the Pickwickians' travels that Chatham meant more to Dickens than Ipswich. Their life and his centres on London; a place which he already describes with accurate street and place names, so that one can see from *Oliver Twist* that he was more familiar with Saffron Hill and Field Lane than with Whitechapel and Spitalfields.

Places more than people are drawn from life in the early books. *Oliver* shows off Dickens' knowledge of London; *Nicholas* was preceded by his tour with Knight Browne to Bowes and Barnard Castle, recceing the location of Dotheboys Hall. That tour supplied his first moment of pure autobiography, as he describes Nicholas's first stage to Grantham in the company of the Fieldingesque lady's-maid pretending that the coach which should meet her is her own. There had been such a woman on their journey, as well as a drunken Yorkshire schoolmistress who supplied matter for Squeers by sharing a silly parent's letter with her fellow-passengers. And in one sentence, Dickens describes exactly what he and Browne did, thereby excusing them from the fictional coach accident he has planned for the next chapter: "Twenty miles farther on, two of the front outside passengers wisely availing themselves of their arrival at one of the best inns in England, turned in, for the night, at the George at Grantham."

Recent travels are used again in *The Old Curiosity Shop*. Dickens joins practically every southern writer of the 1840s who saw it in expressing horror at the industrial landscape between Birmingham and Wolverhampton. In *Martin Chuzzlewit*, finding sales lower than he liked, and possibly provoked by continuing attacks on him in the American press, he used his American travels of the year before, and used them more satirically than he had done in the *American Notes*. The extraordinary lionization Martin suffers across the Atlantic would be truly perplexing and not necessarily unwelcome if thrust upon an unknown trainee architect. It reflected the treatment offered the genuinely popular author, who chafed at the humbug of this adulation being accompanied by the refusal of royalties.

Two novels later Dickens wrote his only fully conscious autobiographical novel, *David Copperfield*. It was not all or accurately self-revealing. He had no childhood sweetheart corrupted by a handsome schoolfriend and sinking to the streets. He did not marry a pretty little girl with no housekeeping ability who died; contracted no second marriage to a virtuous and upward-pointing sister-figure. Biographers may note the debt of David's entangled romance with Dora to Dickens' complicated affair with Maria Beadnell, but that led to no marriage. Dora is not like Kate and, tempting though it is to glance at Dickens' excuses for the breakdown of his own marriage seven years later, there was nothing at this period to suggest that Georgina – Agnes? – would one day be his perfect chatelaine. Nor did Dickens ever stay with the lady who believed donkeys should not use the path in front of her Broadstairs house, or ever know anyone who lived in a converted boat on a beach.

Dickens' public could see that David's adult career mimicked his creator's: from shorthand reporter, to fiction writer, to famous novelist. The public did not know – not even his family knew – that Murdstone and Grinby's warehouse recreated Warren's Blacking Factory. The public did not know that Mr Micawber's perpetual impecuniosity, orotund garrulity, and temporary accommodation in debtors' prison reflected John Dickens; that David, the lonely child in London lodgings reflected the most miser-

able months of Charles' life. From the start the public sensed the writer's deep involvement and inwardness with this creation. His friend Charles Kent told him late in life that he thought *David Copperfield* "incomparably the best" of all his books, and Dickens concurred.

The histrionic approach that led him to create characters by visualizing and enacting them in the mirrors around his desk made it easy for him to capture the sense of his own feelings as a child, either in his own or another's position. In Oliver's case, this had the unfortunate consequence of making Oliver middle-class and more than a little priggish. Florence Dombey shared the priggishness. But with David, Dickens was himself, without distorting the character. He recalls childish details that are instantly real to anyone with any memory: David "bolting furtive gooseberries, and trying to look unmoved," while his mother picks fruit; David joining Mr Murdstone and his friends in putting his eye to a telescope, and pretending he sees what they do, though he really sees nothing; David so frightened by the thought of Lazarus raised from the dead that he has to be shown the unmoving tombstones in the churchyard. These unheroic, unvirtuous moments breathe a life into David Copperfield that is hardly ever to be found in Dickens' stage-drawn heroes.

THE INDUSTRIAL
LANDSCAPE BETWEEN
BIRMINGHAM AND
WOLVERHAMPTON:
AN APPALLING SIGHT
TO MID-NINETEENTH-
CENTURY SOUTHERNERS.

AUTOBIOGRAPHY

CHAPTER TWO

Characters AND Originals

ELIZABETH DICKENS, CHARLES' MOTHER. LIVELY AND PERHAPS FLIRTATIOUS: CRUELLY CARICATURED AS MRS NICKLEBY.

THE USE of autobiographical material meant reproducing characters from life and memory and here Dickens was cruel though brilliant. His feelings for his parents mirrored Oscar Wilde's dictum perfectly: "Children begin by loving their parents; after a time they judge them; rarely, if ever, do they forgive them." Dickens forgave his father … just. He never quite forgave his mother.

Elizabeth Dickens bequeathed her son great gifts: easy sociability; precise observation and comic description; hilarious mimicry; a love for theatricals. From her and from his father's mother, the Crewes' housekeeper who was famous for telling stories to children, we can see the novelist descending. Yet her only full-length portrait in his books is the cruel caricature of Mrs Nickleby. Vain, silly, jealous, snobbish, impetuously logorrhoeac, the cause or intensifier of all her family's problems: Mrs Nickleby would be an uncharitable travesty of an enemy. Only Samuel Butler seemingly despised his mother more. Yet Dickens himself acknowledged the intention when he remarked that "Mrs Nickleby herself … asked whether [he] really believed there was ever such a woman".

Most commentators put this down to his bitterness that she had wanted him to go back to the blacking factory, which he said he never should or could forget. But the exasperatingly wrong-headed mother suggests still more strongly most adolescent or young adult children's difficulty in accepting a post-childhood perception of their parents. Fathers and mothers are either dowdy antiques, or overdressed mutton masquerading as lamb: there seems no happy medium. Jokes and family stories that delight in childhood are embarrassing when trotted out before friends whom we don't wish to see us as children still. Parents and offspring may find it hard to accept circumstances in which the young know more of the world than the old. The one-time authority still wants to be accorded Fifth Commandment honour, yet this is rightly begrudged as the fledgling starts trusting to its own wings. What is peculiar about Dickens is that he seems never to have outgrown his immature distaste for his mother's perpetual youthfulness, flirtatious love of dancing and belief that she might hold opinions differing from his. Even though rare moments like the creation of Clara Copperfield show some recollection of her early love, his usual attitude to his mother was distant contempt, moderated to detached and rather unsympathetic

THE POPULAR WRITER

PAGE 52

amusement when Alzheimer's made her last years absurd.

All of which advises us to be cautious about Dickens' occasional apotheoses of maternity, like little Paul Dombey's final vision of his angel-mother waiting for him on the bank of eternity. They are, alas, cant: the greatest of all satirists of cant could slip into it himself.

No doubt he learned it from his father. The man who tried to cadge money from his son's bank with the words, "Contemporaneous events of this nature place me in a difficulty from which, without some anticipatory pecuniary effort, I cannot extricate myself," was a worthy model for Mr Micawber. But the dignified pomposity concealed a father who forged his son's signature, and threatened all the time to overwhelm him in some financial scandal, as he had once sunk the family in the Marshalsea. It was generosity on Dickens' part to come to see this model for William Dorrit as "my poor father", and to recognize the honest and hard-working employee in the feckless and barely honest sponger.

These two were closest to him of all the people he put in his books. That he did so ruthlessly was an indication that others would not be spared. His mother's relative by marriage, Dr Lamert, was thrown rapidly into *Pickwick*, his name thinly disguised as "Dr Slammer". Kindly figures from childhood, like the family with whom he lodged in Lant Street while his father was in the Marshalsea, would be remembered as the Garlands; the Dickens family's friend Mrs Roylance who previously looked after him in Camden Town was an unhappier memory, and would be savaged as Mrs Pipchin. Relationships seemed to stick in his mind by names: Scrooge and Amy Dorrit, like Charles have sisters named Fanny: Amy's even has musical training while her siblings are left uneducated. Nell's and William Dorrit's brothers are called Fred, like the brother to whom Dickens was closest in youth, and Tiny Tim, too, was originally called Tiny Fred. In his earlier work, public figures were satirized under parodies of their own names: Mr Justice Gazelee tried the case of *Bardell v.Pickwick* disguised as Mr Stareleigh; Hatton Garden's unpopular magistrate Mr Laing nearly miscar-

ried justice against Oliver Twist under the name of Fang. Dickens didn't mimic Alderman Peter Laurie's name in Alderman Cute, but he openly boasted of having put the pompous ass into *The Chimes* when the alderman ignorantly claimed that Jacob's Island was not a real slum, but only the fictional creation of Dickens in *Oliver Twist*.

FAME AND DEFAMATION

Some quite extraordinary figures were recognizably based on living persons. Leigh Hunt's understandable distress at being identifiable as Harold Skimpole was matched by Walter Savage Landor's rage at being identified as the more amiable Lawrence Boythorn. It ended his intimacy with the younger man. Dickens was, perhaps, fortunate that only the dwarf beautician Mrs Arabella Hill had recourse to legal advice, and compelled him, through her solicitors, to turn Miss Mowcher from a wicked to a virtuous character. That earlier dwarf, Quilp, was said to have a known original in a squalid scrap-dealing wharf-owner from the Surrey shore. A careful study of old maps and directories strongly suggests that, quite remarkably, his is the one name to have survived from his period's jumble of privately owned stairs and jetties, and Quilp's Wharf was actually the original Butler's Wharf.

By the end of Dickens' life, some people hoped to have been immortalized by the Inimitable, and various canons of Rochester vied for their place in *Edwin Drood*. But too much has been made of the possibility that his mistress's postulated acquisitiveness coloured his last heroines. The similarity of the names Ellen Lawless Ternan and Helena Landless don't make them one and the same.

T.P. MCKENNA AS SKIMPOLE IN BBC TELEVISION'S "BLEAK HOUSE", 1984. A BRILLIANT CHARACTER: A CRUEL WRONG TO LEIGH HUNT.

Structure AND Unity

MONTHLY PART-ISSUE posed structural problems. The story was likely to proceed in jerks and the author couldn't go back and change something that didn't suit the denouement. Dickens took the obvious way out in *Pickwick.* He followed the picaresque form in which, originally, a picaroon or trickster travelled from one adventure to the next in different settings.

Dickens never completely abandoned the form. In all his longer novels the leading characters move between locations. While still moving the Pickwickians around, Dickens embarked on *Oliver Twist.* It was not at first intended to be a novel. It started as one of a projected series satirizing parochial mismanagement in "Mudfog". Only the success of Oliver's asking for more showed the possibility of a wider attack on the New Poor Law than could be sustained by one parish Board of Guardians. But as the novel moved, wider political satire fell away and the plot started to ramble. Oliver's repeated recapture by Fagin; the use of Monks to justify Fagin's continuing interest in a not-very-promising pupil; the plot denouement with revelations proving Rose to be Oliver's aunt – all these created a clumsy story awkwardly improvized to meet sudden needs. It would undergo improving simplification at the hands of dramatizers and film-makers. Unhappily the ending of *Oliver* satisfied Dickens' immediate audience, encouraging him to revert

again and again to the "long-lost relative" revelatory climax. So Smike turns out to be Ralph Nickleby's son, driving that stern villain to implausible suicide. Long-lost brotherhood explains the Single Gentleman's pursuit of Nell and her grandfather. An improbable blood link is established between Alice Marwood and Edith Dombey .

Unplanned monthly chapters had their advantages, however. Martin Chuzzlewit could be whisked away to America when Dickens felt like it. His story, like Nicholas Nickleby's, followed the *Bildungsroman* form in which the young hero seeks his fortune and makes his way in the world. Like the picaresque, it lent itself to monthly parts. Like the picaresque, it was adapted rather than abandoned by Dickens. In *Oliver Twist*, the first British novel to take a child as central character, that child is explicitly shown in a "Progress", like the hero of a *Bildungsroman. David Copperfield* is an unashamed *Bildungsroman.* Richard Carstone's progress in *Bleak House* varies the form by carrying the protagonist from early promise to well-deserved failure. Florence Dombey offers a novel female protagonist – the success of *Jane Eyre* the previous year made this timely, if it did not in fact influence Dickens. Pip is handed on a plate the financial security that usually crowned the hero's efforts; is denied the love of the heroine; and varies the form most interestingly by exhibiting growth in wisdom and morality rather than prosperity.

From *Dombey and Son* onward, Dickens planned the movement and content of the monthly parts with care, eschewing the cavalier reliance on his own creativity which bounced the earlier novels on so erratically. In his mature work, Dickens noted on regular *aide-mémoires* the inci-

THE POPULAR WRITER

dents and characters he proposed to handle in each number, even addressing to himself such notes as "not yet" when something inessential to the plot was to be included. He had main themes in mind from the start: that *Dombey and Son* was to be *Dombey and Daughter*, after all; that Pip was to be sadly mistaken in believing Miss Havisham to be his benefactress. The "revelation" that Nemo and Lady Dedlock were Esther's parents was intended and telegraphed from the outset of *Bleak House,* but not so obviously as we hindsighted readers may now imagine. Were Dickens as simple as that, there would be an agreed solution to the *Mystery of Edwin Drood.*

But plotting was not his sole source of unification. He told Forster that all the characters and incidents of *The Old Curiosity Shop* were intended to keep "the main purpose" always present. That "purpose" – innocent youth guiding misdirected old age through life – is lightly echoed in Dick Swiveller's redemption by his attachment to the naive Marchioness; in Kit Nubbles' leading his mother away from Little Bethel. Nell and her grandfather's wanderings are emphasized by the nomadic lives of the showpeople they meet. More strikingly still, the fixed and nameless characters underline the theme of youth and age: the old widow tending the grave of her husband who died when they were young; the furnace minder whose entire life has been passed keeping the fire alive; the old sextons whose awareness of other people's mortality never leads them to anticipate their own death.

Such thematic unification was more broadly attempted in *Martin Chuzzlewit*'s exposé of selfishness and *Dombey and Son*'s similar treatment of pride, though both vices encompass so many variations that they do not present themselves as continuously as Dickens hoped. In *David Copperfield* he returned to cameos, and the novel which ultimately turns on David's mistaken marriage to Dora and correct marriage to Agnes moves from one exemplum of matrimony to the next, from Clara Copperfield's entrapment by the maritally-speculating Murdstones to that prototypical spinster Betsey Trotwood's "grumpy frumpy story" of a dependent ne'er-do-well husband.

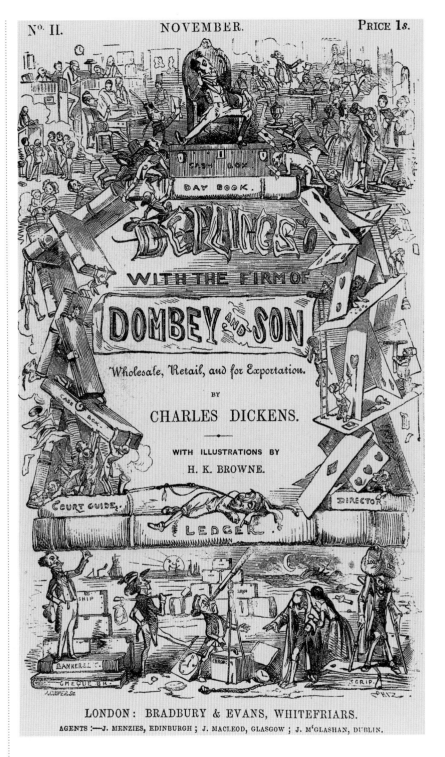

And in the darker, later novels, great overarching symbols given in the narrator's voice hold the works together: *Bleak House*'s weather moving between the fog of London and the rain of Lincolnshire; the real and figurative imprisonment of all the characters of *Little Dorrit*; the river, taking and restoring life throughout *Our Mutual Friend.*

THE COVER OF ONE OF THE PART-ISSUES OF "DOMBEY AND SON".

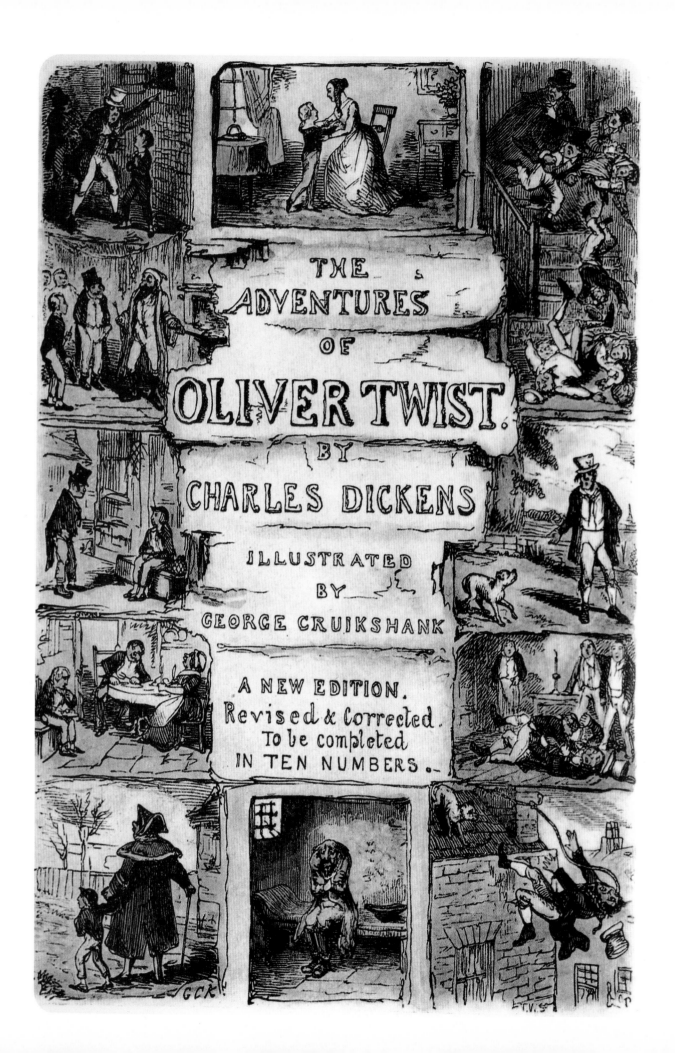

THE
ADVENTURES
OF
OLIVER TWIST.
BY
CHARLES DICKENS
ILLUSTRATED
BY
GEORGE CRUIKSHANK

A NEW EDITION.
Revised & Corrected.
To be completed
IN TEN NUMBERS.

THE NOVELS

THE WORD "'DICKENS" like the words "Shakespeare" or "Chaucer" stands for the man's works as well as himself. "I am familiar with Dickens" is unlikely to mean "I chat amiably with his ghost at seances". It more probably means "I have read all his novels; many of them several times over."

Conversations among Dickensians, at meetings of the Dickens Fellowship or gatherings at the various Dickens festivals or even chance encounters, are likely to take this familiarity for granted. The newcomer to Dickens circles may accordingly be intimidated. There are, after all, sixteen very solid novels to which he may hear easy reference. There are five short Christmas Books; a vast quantity of journalism, and pieces known best for their use in Dickens' readings. With literally hundreds of characters and settings comprising "Dickens", even an expert might be hard put to identify all the minor figures in the *Reprinted Pieces*. The following Dickensian "Trivial Pursuit" type questions may baffle many genuine aficionados:

WHO IS THE FIRST NAMED METROPOLITAN POLICEMAN TO FIGURE IN A DICKENS NOVEL?

A. Inspector Bucket   **B.** Officer Slyme
C. Sergeant Dornto

HOW MANY TIMES DOES REV. MELCHISADECH HOWLER APPEAR IN *DOMBEY AND SON*?

A. Once   **B.** Twice   **C.** Never

WHO LIVED NEAREST TO FASCINATION FLEDGEBY?

A. The Veneerings   **B.** Lady Tippins
C. Either the Lammles or Little Twemlow

   The answers are:

B. Chevy Slyme, surprisingly, appears heading the party sent to arrest Jonas at the end of *Martin Chuzzlewit*, having in his own opinion lowered himself by joining the police. We are not told his rank.

A. He is described, but does not appear when Mrs MacStinger's attachment to his preaching is first mentioned, along with the fact that he and his congregation once fell through the floor in the rapture of performing a sacred jig. But he only appears in person at Mrs MacStinger's wedding to Captain Bunsby where he is reported as offering up some "extemporary orisons" before the service.

C. The Lammles lived in Sackville Street, which is marginally closer to Fledgeby's apartment in the Albany than Duke Street, St James's, where Twemlow lived on the other side of Piccadilly. But we do not know how far down Sackville Street the Lammles were, whereas contemporary directories show that the livery stable above which Twemlow had his apartment was very near the top of Duke Street, putting the little diner-out hardly more than the width of Piccadilly away from the secret usurer.

If you answered all those with ease, you may certainly count yourself familiar with Dickens to a remarkable degree. But familiar or unfamiliar, there are few things more enjoyable than the leisurely critical consideration of a great writer's work, from start to finish. So looking at Dickens, one novel at a time – with a special glance at the Christmas Books – we can familiarize ourselves again or anew with the progress of his writing career and see just how he developed the natural talents and interests that made him the greatest novelist and classic representative of his age.

BOOK WRAPPER FOR "OLIVER TWIST".

Pickwick Papers

MR PICKWICK IN THE
WRONG BEDROOM,
THE WHITE HORSE
INN, IPSWICH.

I N SOME WAYS, as George Orwell remarked, we should all like Dickens to have gone on writing in the *Pickwick* vein for ever. This is the quintessential comedy of innocence, good humour and good cheer that catapulted the young writer to instant fame. This was the serial which led a dying man to say, in earshot of the minister "Well, thank God, *Pickwick* will be out in ten days anyway."

And yet, as Dickens himself was to note, the public of the 1850s would not have accepted another *Pickwick* from him. He grew beyond the strained alliteration and polysyllabism of that original title: *The Posthumous Papers of the Pickwick Club, containing a faithful record of the Preambulations, Perils, Travels, Adventures and Sporting Transactions of the Corresponding Members.* Edited by "Boz". His respectable readers would have censured the Pickwickians for coming home drunk from the cricket dinner and blaming it on the salmon, as Dickens' friend Potter was said to have done after one dissipation. The spinster aunt and the young ladies would have had it all their own way:

Mid-Victorians would not have been greatly amused by Dickens' good-humoured conviction, which never left him, that a smooth and seasoned villain's hypocrisy would usually deceive the conventionally virtuous. They would not have been approved had he repeated the over-indulgence in picnic punch which leads Mr Pickwick to wheelbarrowed humiliation in the pound. *Pickwick* is a book of William IV's reign. Albert the Good has not yet brought the bourgeois standards of Herr Biedermeier to his adopted country. Some eighteenth century robustness remains.

But, as Dickens knew, such robustness included barbarity. The first serious adventure in the book is Mr Winkle's near-duel with Captain Slammer. Already in the *Sketches* "The Great Winglebury Duel" had played on the truth that "gentlemen" tried in all seriousness to kill each other over trivial disputes. All credit to Dickens and Thackeray and the other representatives of stuffy "Victorianism" who drove this code of "honour" into the sewers where it belonged.

Dickens' cockney ignorance about pre-Victorian sport was another mark of civilization. The ignorance is innocently exemplified in Dingley Dell and All-Muggleton's cricket match where he imagines that bowlers are assigned to specific batsmen and that the fielding side should have scored at the end of their opponent's innings. Two generations later, no one who had passed through a post-Arnoldian public school could make such mistakes. But neither would educated sportsmen believe that setting dogs or cocks to fight to the death was fun; that betting on terriers killing sackfuls of rats was manly; that the height of sportsmanship was driving to an illegal meeting in the countryside to watch two barefist brawns batter each other to a bloody pulp until one collapsed completely. By restricting sportive slaughter to one shooting expedition and quietly abandoning Mr Winkle's sporting pretensions after the skating, Dickens declared himself out of sympathy with the brutish gamblers' delights that passed for sport until educators saw the value in disciplined exercise and team games.

But if sport be allowed its primary definition of "Amusement, diversion, fun" – rather than frightening and hurting and killing things and betting – then Dickens provides wonderful sport. Christmas at Dingley Dell is the first of his magical feasts. Wardle's traditional party opens with dinner and toasts and proceeds to country dances followed by another supper. Then there is kissing under the mistletoe; party games of blind man's buff and snapdragons; a wassail bowl to accompany forfeits and singing and storytelling until midnight and a toast to Christmas. It is glorious fun, and seems more akin to a Scottish Hogmanay

or a jolly wedding than our own supposedly "Dickensian" festivals of shopping and gift-giving and "sophisticated" social gatherings with cocktails and smalltalk, or hopping up and down in one place as a substitute for dancing.

With over one hundred and fifty named characters in fifty-six chapters, excluding figures in stories, and occasional ostlers or cabstand watermen addressed by christian names, it might seem that Dickens just jumped his comedy from one joke or pratfall to the next. But there is a little more planning ahead than that in his book. The first ten chapters of sightseeing and sport are linked by Mr Jingle's parasitism and elopement. "Jingling", incidentally, as Dickens may or may not have known, was miners' slang for cheating a collier by sending him to work an unprofitable section of the coalface. Then, after a single chapter reviving Mr Pickwick's antiquarian character with his refusal to accept BILST UM PSHI S.M. ARK, as an illiterate "Bill Stumps – his mark;" the unfortunately ambiguous remarks to Mrs Bardell about employing Sam

Weller lay the ground for Bardell vs. Pickwick matter, which is taken up at intervals until the trial twenty chapters later. The intervening travels burlesque Dickens' experiences in an election, provincial newspapers, provincial cultural society, and the provincial magistracy. Jingle and Job successfully embarrass Sam and Mr Pickwick, though Mr Pickwick wanders into a compromising situation without any assistance when staying at the White Horse in Ipswich. Before the trial, Dickens terminates the sporting interludes, and sets up the matrimonial hopes of Sam Weller and Mr Winkle, which interweave with the discomfiture of Stiggins, the exquisite satire on law, and the critique of penology, to lead to a denouement in which Pickwick plays matchmaking fairy godfather.

The amazing confidence that led the little-known journalist to call his protagonist "the immortal Pickwick" in the first sentence of the first number was justified by the last. Chapman and Hall's initial print order was a mere four hundred copies. Final monthly sales reached forty-thousand.

BARDELL VS. PICKWICK.

Oliver Twist

ESPITE THE SUCCESS OF PICKWICK, there were many who expected that Boz, having gone up like a rocket would come down like the stick. So when he took on *Bentley's Miscellany* it was not obvious that he would be the most prominent contributor. George Cruikshank the illustrator was twenty years older and famous. Two decades later he would claim that he devised *Oliver Twist*, citing in support his – undoubted – earlier sketch of the condemned cell at Newgate and – more dubious – claim that he had imagined Fagin and drawn him there before Dickens composed a word.

But internal evidence alone shows that the first eight chapters were entirely Dickens' work. The "New Poor Law" of 1834 was highly controversial, opposed by *The Times* and independent-minded radical Tories. But the facetious irony with which *Oliver Twist* attacks it and the parish officers administering it is purely Dickensian. Compared with the pathetic social commentary evoked by Mr Pickwick's incarceration in the Fleet prison, this is black comedy indeed, but so black and so comic that it remains the best known commentary on the scandalous new law and its workhouses.

Dickens' satire has bequeathed us the false impression that parish beadles were the worst and most officious executants of that law. Hatred of these spectacularly uniformed functionaries was a peculiarly Dickensian quirk: it opens the published selection of *Sketches*. Dickens attacks beadles at their most positive point: the care of poor and abandoned children.

Dickens must have known his own parish beadle's vital role in exposing and arresting Esther Hibner and her daughter for their appalling abuse and neglect of five orphan girls apprenticed to them as seamstresses in 1828. The beadle went to their house on a minor complaint from the impoverished grandmother of one of the girls, and immediately took the exhausted and starving little mites back to the workhouse where they were properly nursed and cared for. The Hibners were tried for the murder of Frances Colpitts who died of their treatment. And their evil sweatshop was in Pratt Street, Camden Town, just round the corner from Bayham Street, and a few blocks away from the Polygon Building in Somers Town where Charles lived with his parents in 1828.

Yet he gave us the ineradicable image of Bumble, the "parochial officer", siding inexorably with exploiting employers and baby-farmers against his charges, and ironic possessor of brass buttons depicting the Good Samaritan. Just once, in Chapter Four, Dickens almost relents, and gives the beadle "a husky manner" and an

excuse about a "troublesome cough" when Oliver's loneliness momentarily moves him. We don't easily think of Bumble without his beadle's uniform, though he has long been a workhouse master in civvies when he makes his most famous remark that "the law is an ass".

Bumble evokes and is angry comedy. However, the strength of the book, the matter which makes the first twenty chapters race the reader on at a breakneck pace, is the picture of the criminal underworld. Later Dickens was at pains to distance this book from its fellow "Newgate novels". Fagin and Sikes, he insisted, were unredeemed villains, not dashing or pathetic heroes like Bulwer Lytton's highwayman Paul Clifford and murderer Eugene Aram, or Harrison Ainsworth's Dick Turpin and Jack Sheppard.

Certainly Dickens hated criminals as criminals. Borrowing the Irish name Fagin from the kindest of the boys he had known at Warren's Blacking and bestowing it on the Jewish thief-trainer showed how deeply he felt Oliver's falling among thieves, relating it to his own most traumatic memory. Fagin was the character who lived in his imagination. He owes something to Peachum in *The Beggar's Opera*, shopping thieves when it serves him as well as receiving their stolen goods. But the character is transformed. Almost every sentence about him grabs our attention: his affected gentility and humility; the boys being trained in the den; the brilliant description of old Field Lane where stolen pocket handkerchiefs were sold; and Fagin's appropriately dazed passage through his trial and symbolically apt craziness in Newgate, believing that attachment to the one innocent being in his life might lead him out unscathed if Oliver would take his hand – like Dostoevsky's selfish woman being lifted from hell by the onion she once gave to a beggar. Only the twaddling plotting around Monks palls.

Only once does Dickens' naive ignorance of the real world of ragged thieves show through: "There's a pitcher of water in the corner by the door. Bring it here; and I'll give you a basin to wash in, my dear," says Fagin to the newly awakened Oliver. Of course he wants the boy's back turned so that he can hide his box of jewels. But who but fastidious Charles Dickens would have imagined that a filthy old fence in a vermin-ridden lair would think that a boy should wash as soon as he got up! He might as well have told him to brush his teeth and say his prayers! Rarely has the British middle-class' sublime assumption that everyone ought to be like them had such an exquisite exposition.

Sikes and Nancy start almost as effectively as Fagin. The Chertsey robbery is a brilliant nineteenth century exposé of criminal methods like *Rififi* or *The Day of the Jackal*. But Nancy's development from a louche Ratcliff girl into a stock "tart with a heart of gold" robs both of them of reality as she is increasingly associated with that vapid tribute to Mary Hogarth, Rose Maylie and the inert melodramatic plotting around Oliver's identity.

SIR HERBERT BEERBOHM TREE AS FAGIN.

JACK WILD AS THE ARTFUL DODGER AND MARK LESTER AS OLIVER IN SIR CAROL REED'S MUSICAL FILM "OLIVER!"

Nicholas Nickleby

"BOZ" STARTED HIS NEW BOOK with nervous facetiousness. With *Oliver* still running in *Bentley's Miscellany*, he doggy paddled up to the start of *Nicholas* rather than diving smoothly in. Feeble long-winded stuff about the United Metropolitan Improved Hot Muffin and Crumpet Baking and Punctual Delivery Company doesn't really lead anywhere. We reach the real starting point with the advertisement for Dotheboys Hall which gives us the true voice of Dickens. Mr Squeers' offer to teach everything under the sun, including "single-stick (if required)" gives a detached and original touch to those obsessive Victorian jokes about schools and canings – "Dr Swishtail's Academy", "Birchington Hall" and the like.

As Dickens would show when the novel reached Yorkshire, he actually regarded hitting a child with a stick as obscene.

Squeers is something new. Jingle had been an amusing con man, Bumble was a pompous jack-in-office. Fagin owed much to Defoe's *History of the Devil*, and Dickens' ability to draw comedy from him did not alter his central view of him as frightening and loathsome. Squeers is truly loathsome, but hilarious with it. We really do look forward to his return in the hope of some fresh outrageous remark, like "Here's richness!"

as he samples the watered milk he gives his boys.

Like the Poor Law satire of *Oliver*, the Yorkshire schools satire of *Nicholas* is drawn from a matter of public concern that had been discussed recently in *The Times*. And it is quite rapidly disposed of. Nicholas has thrashed Squeers and left Dotheboys with four-fifths of the book still to be written. Dickens was unperturbed. He had a good supporting character in Newman Noggs. He had Kate's career, paralleling Nicholas's, to give him an additional story line, with Mrs Nickleby as its exasperating comic engine. He used interpolated travellers' tales and introduced two lines that would become hallmarks of his creation: a spectral visitor made funny by casual colloquial conversation in "The Baron of Grogzwig", and extreme distaste for religiose self-denial and monasticism in "The Five Sisters of York." He had that imaginative fecundity which had crowded *Pickwick* and now brought Miss La Creevy and the Mantalinis into Kate's life, and would introduce the Kenwigses and the Crummleses and Mr Lillyvick and Miss Petowker and Miss Snevellici and Pyke and Pluck and the Wititterlys. And in these characters he used moral assessment which had already coloured the comic treatment of Mr Bumble and Mrs Corney. The caricatures in *Pickwick* were funny without moral judgement: the Leo Hunters and the rival editors of Eatanswill were squeaking and knockabout puppets rather than well-weighed commentaries on the provincial would-be intelligentsia. But even as we laugh at the pretensions of Mrs Kenwigs and Mrs Wititterly, we can see that Dickens invites us to consider the harmless affectations of the former as something adding colour and spice to a potentially dire

life on the margins of shabby gentility, and the vapid "silver fork" tastes of the latter as an indolent cover for inner emptiness, draining a securely prosperous existence of its potential satisfactions.

Dickens is learning, too, how far he can use a character. The Wititterlys are worth a chapter, and are quickly dropped. Likewise Mr Gregsbury MP allows the young writer to work off some irritation with parliament, and his very personal grievance that legislation doesn't protect authors' rights. But this leads nowhere, and the character is set aside.

The Cheeryble brothers point to the serious awareness of social and economic life that will come to make Dickens' later work much more than a sequence of comic characters ornamenting a melodramatic or sentimental love story. They are Mr Pickwick considered more realistically: fairy godfathers whose wealth is used with all the benevolence of Dickens' first protagonist, but who are related to the world of work, and offer Nicholas employment, where Mr Pickwick had lived in retirement on his investments and helped Mr Winkle retain his patrimony to live as a gentleman of leisure. In the Cheerybles, Dickens looked at the new world of businessmen and manufacturers and liked what he saw when he compared it with the idle aristocracy. He admired the hard work that enriched them, and he explicitly despised people who looked down on their humble origins and uneducated manners. He may have met the Grant brothers of Manchester on whom he based the twins. It is astonishing that everybody who knew them declared that Dickens' hagiographic portrait was a truly accurate likeness.

But Dickens would never again create self-made businessmen of unalloyed kindness and right judgement. He may have learned that the Grants were friends of Lord John Manners, whose sentimental "Young England" noblesse oblige Toryism seemed to him patronizing rubbish. He would not have been astonished, as Cobden was, when Manchester workingmen revealed to a parliamentary commission that the Grants used their powers as magistrates to retain all beershop licenses in their bailiwick for themselves, thus robbing thrifty foremen's wives of a recognized perquisite. The Grants were Quaker businessmen, and Dickens came increasingly to feel, like Marx and Engels, that Quakerism was hypocritical and businessmen would not be generous in an economy energized by competition.

So, with its mass of varied comic characters, with Smike for sentimental pathos, Squeers and his wife the first of the great evil comic grotesques, and the Grants the last capitalist benefactors to fill the role of deus ex machina, *Nicholas Nickleby* is the perfectly fulfilled example of "early Dickens".

THOMAS FORD'S PAINTING OF KATE NICKLEBY.

THE Old Curiosity Shop

"A TALE OF MASTER HUMPHREY": this, like *Oliver Twist*, was intended originally to comprise a couple of short magazine pieces. Only the realization that *Master Humphrey's Clock* was not selling led to its expansion. The pious pretence that its title looks forward to the old church full of memorial statuary, itself an image of Nell's overcrowded short life of experiences, is an example of the self-deception Dickens could impose upon his circle. The novel is stuck with an irrelevant title which might have done for a couple of chapters about Master Humphrey guiding a lost child to her strange home. It has no more to do with the development of the work than Master Humphrey himself: gone, soon forgotten, and never even recognized as a character by hundreds of readers who vaguely notice the novel's first-person opening without paying any attention to the narrator's disappearance.

Unlike most of Dickens' central child characters, Nell is firmly introduced through other people's vision rather than her own thoughts. Her youth and innocence are stressed. Master Humphrey is struck by her "very

small and delicate frame". She laughs with "childlike" hilarity at Kit but is quickly pulled back to put an arm round her grandfather's neck and hear his antiquated declaration of attachment: "Why dost thou sob? Is it because thou know'st I love thee?" In fact she sobs to tug at our heartstrings cheaply, not because she has any proper cause of intense emotion. When admonished not to forget her prayers, she answers priggishly: "No, indeed, they make me feel so happy."

Yet as soon as Master Humphrey is off the scene, characters express a very different attitude to her. Quilp asks her to consider becoming his second wife. Fred Trent urges Dick Swiveller to marry her. Little Nell's status as sexual object is so openly stated that we can appreciate Dickens' need for a sexless pair – the Old Bachelor and the Single Gentleman – to try unsuccessfully to be her fairy godfathers.

For Dickens and most of his readers, Nell's death was the greatest of tragic successes. Some apologists today urge the high rate of Victorian infant mortality in mitigation. Frankly, it just won't do. The laboured hints throughout the book don't amount to a plausible course of sickness. The little boy coming with the news that she is expected to become an angel before the spring signals a warning that we are in for more of the pasteboard angels with whom Dickens loves to surround deathbeds. And these won't even be introduced in the chaste prose which later masked the sloppiness of "A Child's Dream of a Star". Old Trent and his brother keep slipping into shoddy blank verse:

To be to you what you were once to him,
to repay your old affection, brother dear,
by constant care, solicitude and love.

It is a relief to turn to Quilp. The manifest success of the book, Quilp owes much to *Richard III*. But he goes further, to personify what Freud described as the Id. Quilp is unrestrained self-gratification. It's not only Dickens who felt a lot of himself in Quilp. Many of us would like to eat and drink and smoke whenever and whatever we liked. Many of us would like to scatter our enemies with fiendish howls and imprecations. Many of us would like to dominate any company we keep; attract the other sex at the same time as we terrified it into submission; leer at unsuitably young people we fancy; keep our own counsel rudely so that no one is ever too sharp for us. Most of us have our moments of wishing to be completely uninhibited.

Of course, we know we can't be. If we drank boiling rum, then, like Sampson Brass we'd scald ourselves. If we crunched up the heads and tails of shrimps, we'd choke. If we told everybody we disliked exactly what we thought of them, we should suffer social ostracism. But, goodness, it would be nice not to wait for a toddy to cool; not to have to peel shrimps; not to have to remain silent and polite when people annoy us. When we venture something like this, we are mischievous. And so the adjective "Quilpish", used, for example, by Galsworthy of George Forsyte, contains none of the overtones of horrible malevolence, ugliness and wickedness that are essential to Dickens' character. Yet it is true of Quilp, as of no other wicked character in Dickens, that we see our own "dark side" in him. And he makes us accept it and enjoy it and laugh at and with it.

Fittingly, he occurs in the book where Dickens takes good-natured leave of his own irresponsible youth, allowing Dick Swiveller to be feckless and untidy and self-indulgent and immature and all the things neat, tidy and responsible Charles Dickens gave up after he gave up clerking. Henceforth such characters would be criticized more or less severely in his work. But Dick is clearly on the side of light. While he was writing *The Old Curiosity Shop*, Dickens allowed himself his own last really mischievous, inconsiderate and Quilpish prank, holding his friend Eleanor Christian in the incoming tide at Broadstairs to the ruination of her dress and shoes, while she and his wife laughed and protested at his pretence of being so desperately in love that they must drown together.

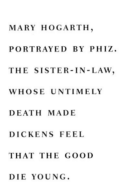

MARY HOGARTH, PORTRAYED BY PHIZ. THE SISTER-IN-LAW, WHOSE UNTIMELY DEATH MADE DICKENS FEEL THAT THE GOOD DIE YOUNG.

THE OLD CURIOSITY SHOP

Barnaby Rudge

F ALL DICKENS' NOVELS might be described as flawed masterpieces, *Barnaby Rudge* is probably the most flawed and the least masterly. It is the only novel he ever wrote suggesting "the school of Scott": the only one which seems to bracket him as a

**DOLLY VARDEN
BY W.P. FRITH.**

contemporary of Harrison Ainsworth and Bulwer Lytton. Indeed, Lytton apparently thought it was his finest artistic creation.

Bulwer was an impure stylist, or he might have seen bad blank verse blooming even more profusely here than it did in *The Old Curiosity Shop*:

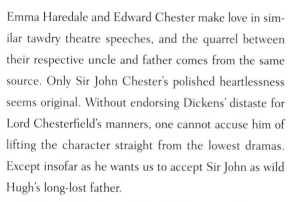

> *Begone! I curse the hour that I was born,*
> *The man I slew, and all the living world!*

Emma Haredale and Edward Chester make love in similar tawdry theatre speeches, and the quarrel between their respective uncle and father comes from the same source. Only Sir John Chester's polished heartlessness seems original. Without endorsing Dickens' distaste for Lord Chesterfield's manners, one cannot accuse him of lifting the character straight from the lowest dramas. Except insofar as he wants us to accept Sir John as wild Hugh's long-lost father.

If *Barnaby Rudge* and *The Old Curiosity Shop* seem to us less satisfactory than the earlier novels, it should be noted that both were written in weekly parts for magazine publication, which Dickens complained left him short of "elbow room". During *Barnaby* he also had his Scottish holiday and preparations to visit America contending for attention. He deplored his inability to make changes in previous sections, and sent Forster directives to alter or introduce material at the proof stages.

Nor was it an easy mental gear-shift to take up *Barnaby* within eight days of finishing the story of Little Nell. That tragedy had possessed him so intensely that he felt he was reliving the loss of Mary Hogarth, and undoubtedly truly complained that he had suffered more distress from Nell's death than any of his lachrymose readers. He was not to leave *Barnaby* with any such feeling of abandoning an old friend.

The great successes of the book are the riots themselves, and the servant characters of Miggs and Simon Tappertit. The riots are graphically described with all Dickens' sense of mobs as terrifying and London as a place. The city, he recognized, was closer to the country sixty years earlier, and more at threat from great assemblies of agitators gathering in the fields at its borders. But such a threat seemed to be looming again as the Chartists prepared their monster petition for parliament, and the Physical Force Chartists openly demanded revolutionary action to meet their ends. Dickens is very effective in showing the varying bands of men coming together to form mobs which storm and loot and sleep almost unpredictably, so that one hardly knows from one moment to the next whether intruders leaping down from the galleries of the House of Commons, or blazing fires with pools of molten lead and boiling liquor in the streets will prove the real climax. There is no doubt Dickens finds the gathering mob storm exhilarating, but even with Barnaby rushing along among the rioters it seems quite wrong to suggest that he is really in sympathy with them, any more than Bill Bruford's keen sensitivity to the excitement felt by football hooligans anticipating violence meant that he in any way approved their activities.

The rioters' cause was bad. Dickens, to be strongly anti-Catholic after his visit to Italy, was at this stage simply opposed to religious fanaticism. Miggs, and under her influence, Mrs Varden, take their place in the line of extravagant evangelicals, from Stiggins to Chadband, whom Dickens detested. The previous generation of radicals – Whig and Tory – had made the removal of Catholic and dissenting disabilities a central aim. Dickens loathed the unthinking Toryism that opposed them. He was at this time contributing radical squibs like his poem "The Fine Old English Tory Times" to Forster's *Examiner*. The "genuine John Bull" magistrate who threatens Barnaby

and his mother and refuses to believe him an idiot shows Dickens' mixture of fear and contempt for the traditionalists of "the stupid party". And to Forster's more orthodox Radical dismay, he was willing to go some way in sympathy for Lord George Gordon himself on the grounds that he was both touched and generous to the poor.

The treatment of Sim Tappertit and his United Bulldogs is funny, though one sees Dickens distancing himself from the absurd gallantry of youth which he had treated so much more sympathetically in Dick Swiveller. Linking Sim with Miggs, we may also note that he is no egalitarian friend to domestic servants. And, as was remarked earlier, he gravely mistrusts workingmen's unions and the secrecy forced on them by the suspicious drafters of the Combination Acts.

Dolly Varden was greatly admired by Victorian readers, and certainly her coquettishness is a vast improvement on Emma Haredale's or Madeline Bray's heroinely inertia. But her treatment, like that of every other woman in the novel, still shows that tendency to patronize which is always the true obverse of Dickens' general cant about women's moral superiority.

BARNABY RUDGE IS ARRESTED FOR HIS PART IN THE RIOTS.

Martin Chuzzlewit

MRS GAMP.

MR PECKSNIFF.

OSITIVELY THE LAST APPEARANCE of "Boz" as author of a new novel and positively the worst of his verbosely facetious titles: *The Life and Adventures of Martin Chuzzlewit, his relatives, friends and enemies. Comprising all his wills and his ways. With an Historical Record of what he did, And What Inherited the Family Plate: who came in for the Silver Spoons, And who for the wooden ladles. The whole forming a complete key to the House of Chuzzlewit: Edited by "Boz".*

The House of Chuzzlewit, as the opening chapter laboriously establishes, is the human race in acquisitive mood. Dickens also told Forster he intended the novel to expose selfishness. But the second chapter pushes such imperfectly planned "intentional" writing into the background as it leaps to the wonderful creation of Pecksniff.

Martin Chuzzlewit is astonishing for featuring not one, but two of Dickens' greatest caricatures. He would only repeat such glorious exorbitance once again, allowing Betsey Trotwood and Wilkins Micawber to appear in the same pages. But how, one marvels, could any writer ever have had so much abundant creative power to spare that while still delighting himself and everyone else with Seth Pecksniff, he should go on to invent Sairey Gamp?

The whole Victorian era looked hypocritical to Lytton Strachey's generation – family prayers coexisting with the seduction of housemaids, public philanthropy with intolerable factory and mine conditions, Christian missionary evangelism purveyed to imperially exploited natives.

Dickens anticipates Strachey with one economical sentence on Pecksniff:

Mr Pecksniff said grace – a short and pious grace, invoking a blessing on the appetites of those present, and committing all persons who had nothing to eat, to the care of Providence: whose business (so said the grace in effect) was to look after them.

It seems amazing now that those who went searching for originals behind Dickens' characters hit upon Sir Robert Peel as a possible model for Pecksniff. But Dickens' intimates had no doubt that Pecksniff's pious pomposities were copied from Samuel Carter Hall, editor of the *Art Monthly*. There was much private tittering fifteen years later when Dickens, rather cap-in-hand, invited the Halls to dine at Tavistock House during the scandalous separation from Kate. And with Pecksniffian perfection, the Halls responded that they were friends of Mrs Dickens, and would only come if she were hostess!

Dickens was, of course, affected by society's increased starchiness. Pickwick had been allowed to get drunk. Dick Swiveller was incautiously fond of "the rosy". But now drunkenness is made an occasional failing of Mr Pecksniff, as he persists in returning, trouserless, to Mrs Todgers' landing to harangue the company which has put him to bed. As the wind blowing him over at the beginning of the book showed, Mr Pecksniff was to be the butt of occasional slapstick moments.

Drink and glorious hypocrisy are keys to Mrs Gamp, too. Her ginny fragrance, like that of a passing fairy hiccuping on its way through a wine vault, is the funnier because of her constant pretence to virtue. She is as self-indulgent as Quilp, without his sadism; as histrionic as Pecksniff, but enacting a monoduologue, to paraphrase Charles Mathews, with the imaginary interlocutor Mrs Harris, whereas Pecksniff stage manages his daughters as his setting and foils. All the female side of human life, from marryins and births to berryins, is appropriate to Sairey the midwife-cum-monthly-cum-laying-out nurse. Her turns of phrase can be as unexpected as those of the madman in *Nicholas Nickleby*, yet they carry their own bizarre rightness: "But the words she spoke of Mrs Harris, lambs could not for-

give ... nor worms forget!" or "which fiddlestrings is weakness to expredge my nerves tonight." When old Martin finally adjures this miracle of comedy to try "a little less liquor, and a little more humanity" we feel almost as outraged as if Pecksniff had started pontificating at her. With her, we can only respond faintly, "Less liquor! – Sairey Gamp – Bottle on the chimley-piece, and let me put my lips to it, when I am so dispoged!" and fall into a walking swoon.

The fecund Dickensian imagination is still fully active in this novel, as Todgers' and its lodgers, Tigg Montague, Poll Sweedlepipe and young Bailey, and the American vignettes confirm. Young Martin's "selfishness" seems a rather flat characteristic, awkwardly tacked on to the standard Dickensian hero, and Mark Tapley's exaggerated good humour is hardly a satisfactory foil. One notices that for all the fuss Dickens makes about Mark's moral superiority in America, and Martin's reformed recognition that he deserves equality as the "& Co." partner, it still seems proper to the author that Mark should revert to secondary status as Mrs Lupin's husband at the Blue Dragon. Whatever Dickens likes to think he believes, virtue doesn't inevitably outweigh class in his mind, all things else being equal.

And in the treatment of Tom Pinch one sees the same thing. As a silently hopeless lover, Tom is not as effective as Hardy's passive heroes and heroines. As a virtuous model for Martin, he is too gawkily absurd to carry conviction. But it is interesting to see Dickens developing his authorial voice in the passages of commentary surrounding Tom and Ruth. He had always chatted amicably with his readers about his characters, now he starts attempting virtuoso passages without facetiousness: "Yoho for the moon," and "Blessings on thy simple head, Tom Pinch," and the like. They tend to be unbearably arch in this novel. But they pave the way for the powerful authorial voice that would contribute signally to *Dombey and Son* and *Bleak House*.

PAUL SCHOFIELD AS MARTIN AND PAULINE TURNER AS MARY GRAHAM IN BBC TELEVISION'S "MARTIN CHUZZLEWIT".

THE Christmas Books

ICKENS' DECISION to write a special novella for Christmas in 1843 had consequences beyond his wildest expectations. *A Christmas Carol* proved such a success that he repeated regular Christmas books until he started publishing *Household Words*, whereupon the special Christmas number became an annual consideration. And for the rest of his life "Carol Philosophy" would be his description of the moral outlook he wished to put before his readers. The story of Scrooge and his four ghosts is one of Dickens' greatest successes. Especially in the well-remembered opening when he growls "Bah! Humbug!" at cheery philanthropists and Marley's ghost alike. As the old skinflint refuses all demands on his benevolence, we rightly feel that Dickens is partly in sympathy with him. His own natural generosity was tempered when his old schoolfriend Dan Tobin turned out to be a hopeless scrounger, and proceeded from accepting charitable employment to requesting constant loans and assistance, until finally, with sublime impudence, he demanded the gift of a donkey to set himself up as a cheapjack, saying it should be left outside for him to collect the following day! This experience tempered Dickens' original willing response to all requests for aid, and led him toward that suspicion of begging letters and calls for charitable contributions.

MR FIZZIWIG'S BALL.

Readers with vague memories of sentimental little Tiny Tim at the heart of a glowing family Christmas are often surprised to discover the sensitive examination of Scrooge's childhood and development; the warning that the ragged orphans Ignorance and Want hide under prosperity's generous robe, and will poison society if their needs are not met; the chilling scenes of a miser's unlamented death held out by Christmas Future. And although Dickens devotes some of his finest descriptive writing to the shops and street markets full of produce and poultry, we should still note that from Fezziwig's ball to Scrooge's nephew's party, Dickensian Christmas jollification is a matter of dancing and games and high-spirited reunions, not an orgy of spending and acquiring.

The Chimes, written from Italy the following year would be, Dickens hoped, even better. He entered directly into current political events, satirizing Sir Peter Laurie, the magistrate who promised to "put down" suicide by imprisoning those who failed. Dickens described the angry rick-burners and Chartist crowds who had the middle classes worrying about the "Condition of England question". His lifelong distaste for the facts and figures with which Utilitarian intellectuals and political economists demonstrated that voluntary individual charity would never solve the problem of poverty was let loose in the portrait of Mr Filer, and until Forster persuaded him to be less specific and content himself with attacking "Good old days" sentimentality, he intended to savage the Young England movement out of which Disraeli and Lord John Manners ultimately developed one-nation Toryism. The

notion that the poor were seriously to blame for their own deprivation was something that few thinkers other than Malthus had ever endorsed, and Dickens is not very persuasive in making his ticket-porter hero Trotty Veck convict himself by coming to believe it. Nor does Trotty's lachrymose dream of the two young women he most cares for reduced to destitution, prostitution and suicide convey the harsh truthfulness that had informed the laundrywoman and undertaker's man robbing Scrooge after his death. The success Dickens scored by reading *The Chimes* to his friends owes more to its reflection of their current radical concerns than to its inherent merit. Its enormous sales owed more to readers' hope for another *Christmas Carol* than to favourable reports.

The Cricket on the Hearth the following year was less depressing, but still less validly related to the "Season of Goodwill" philosophy Dickens successfully attached to Christmas and the New Year. The idea of a friendly cricket in the home, chirping, chirping, chirping up the good and exposing social evils was one Dickens had proposed for a magazine. It came to nothing, as well it might: he may have enjoyed the night-song of cicadas during his year in Italy, but it would seem he had never experienced the utterly maddening noise of one of the little beasts indestructibly hidden indoors! As a sermon against marital mistrust, his new story was imperfectly suited to the ethos of familial contentment he was trying

to inculcate in his Christmas books. My own 7-year-old daughter protested irritably – but rightly – "too kissy!" when I tried to follow a successful nightly reading of *A Christmas Carol* with the apparently similar story of the Peerybingles.

The Battle of Life is a vapid love story no one in their right mind would read to children. Dickens' personal obsession with renunciation in love would find ultimate expression in the melodramas of the end of his life: *The Frozen Deep* which he coached Wilkie Collins to write for him to star in on the private stage, and *A Tale of Two Cities* in which he improved on the theme himself. It has no place in a Dickensian Christmas book.

Nor, perhaps, does the interesting theme of *The Haunted Man*, his last such creation. Though the Tetterbys, with their failing general store, overcrowded family, and humdrum life which easily converts to convincing marital discontent, are a real development from the Cratchits, they are less suitable for family reading in the festive season. The psychological theory lying behind the whole story is vital to an understanding of Dickens, and well worthy of discussion. Is it true, as he claims, that shared unhappy memories are crucial to cementing relationships; that our own experience of tears and sorrow lies behind our ability to extend useful sympathy to others? Whether Dickens is right or not, the serious belief makes sense of his willingness to make tear-jerkers of the poor and their children in so many otherwise sophisticated books. Dickens' "sentimentality", this story demonstrates, is something more important than enjoying a good cry out of self-indulgent soppiness. But whether he is right or wrong, this further rewrite of the instructive ghost or goblin story still fails to live up to the *Christmas Carol*. It was in creating Scrooge and Jacob Marley and Bob Cratchit and the three ghosts that Dickens stamped his impress for ever on Christmas.

CHARWOMAN, LAUNDRESS AND UNDERTAKER'S MAN SELL THE DEAD SCROOGE'S STOLEN GOODS TO A JUNK DEALER.

TROTTY VECK AND MEG.

Dombey AND Son

OMETHING ENTIRELY NEW. A novel planned from the start. From the outset: Paul was to die; Mr Dombey was to take against Florence and contract a loveless marriage with an aristocratic lady; was to be rec-

PAUL AND

FLORENCE DOMBEY.

Paul and Florence Dombey.

onciled with his daughter when that wife deserted him and humbled his pride.

Inevitably something was lost. Major Bagstock and Mrs Skewton are the only comic characters who fully live up to the great creations of the past, with their own instantly recognizable speech rhythms and extraordinary affectations. Captain Cuttle has attention lavished on him, but never repays it by evoking appropriate laughter. Only once is he perfectly farcical, when he believes he is taking a useful medical step by looking back and forth between the unconscious Florence's wrist which he grips and the watch in his hook, which will do its owner credit if set back an hour every morning and another quarter toward afternoon. The Reverend Melchisadech Howler has a wonderful name. But we never, alas, hear him grant the world two years' postponement of the doom he has prophesied for it, or see him lead his followers in a sacred jig.

Comedy takes a back seat in the planning of this book, even though the man who created Mrs Skewton and Cousin Feenix couldn't fail to stamp our minds for ever with his comic successes. All are morally placed now, of course. "Cleopatra" seems an ultimate paradox: false, from the heart. But her doddering noble cousin shows that the dilapidated aristocracy's absurd attention to surfaces and manners may cover a generosity and forgiving incuriosity about their neighbours' scandalous doings which middle-class prurient morality cannot emulate.

Toots, like the Blimbers, becomes touching for a fundamental decency which overrides the comedy of his presentation. His greedy parasite the Game Chicken seems to be the unique occasion when Dickens took an original's actual name and put him in a book under his own occupation. Probably, like most of the respectable public, he didn't know that 1830s prizefighter Henry Pearce's extraordinary nickname derived from the amiable shortening of his christian name to "Hen".

But death is at the heart of the writing. It is little Paul's inexorable doom after his mother has died giving birth to him. The waters flow for ever to the ceaseless waves of the ocean: this image is brought back and back to urge that life flows ceaselessly to death, even as life rolls on. Dickens had reason to be preoccupied with the topic. The previous year he had heard terrible news. His sister Fanny, his favourite sibling, was diagnosed consumptive. This was the fatal untreatable illness of the nineteenth century: the Victorians' equivalent of a spreading cancer or the AIDS virus. While writing *Dombey* on the continent Dickens returned home to see his sick sister. Though she and her husband Henry Burnett had become the kind of pious evangelicals he disliked, he did not forget his childhood love for her. As *Dombey* itself showed, the relation of sisterhood was still, as it always would be, one he cherished dearly.

Fanny's eldest boy, Henry, was a cripple who had been taken to Brighton for his health where, it seems, he made wry or droll remarks, old before his time. Dickens seems to have based Paul in part on this nephew. He experiments interestingly with showing the child's feelings in sickness, not quite as he suggested from the inside, but through Paul's subjective perception of others' objective reactions to him. One can only say it works and detaches the child from the sickening sentimentality that surrounded Nell's deathbed. I suspect that the only real childhood memory of Dickens' own mistreatment has been shifted to Miss Pankey and Master Bitherstone. If Mrs Roylance forced a sensitive child like Charles Dickens to go to bed without a candle or locked him in dark cellars as a punishment, she deserved every bit of abuse he showered on Mrs Pipchin. And the fictional treatment is, again, quite unsentimental.

So *Dombey* was planned under a pall. Although the happy ending of Florence's reconciliation with her father was always planned, and Dickens dropped a fleeting

notion of having Walter Gay go astray, hilarity drops out of the novel after Mrs Skewton's death. The writing concentrates on the lurid melodrama of Carker and Edith, and the worse melodramatic parallel between Mrs Skewton and Mrs Brown and their daughters.

The book's descriptive passages are magnificent. Its one real moment recapturing Dickens' proliferant exuberance is the brief inessential account of the Leamington dairy under whose tiles Mrs Skewton's page sleeps, and its shed in which her wheelchair is stored overnight "where new-laid eggs were produced by the poultry connected with the establishment, who roosted on a broken donkey-cart – persuaded, to all appearance, that it grew there, and was a species of tree." The sombre account of Dombey's empty house in Chapter Twenty-Three shows how the author, whose light-hearted descriptions held us for their own sakes in the *Sketches*, has reached the point that such descriptions can validly and poetically carry forward his serious moods. The personification of Day followed by Night followed by Day illuminating and darkening and illuminating the empty church in Chapter Thirty-One is something quite new; something unmatched in any other writer's descriptive prose until Robert Pirzig gave us the Spirit of New York as a real being in *Lila*. It compensates for the laboured and unsuccessful passages of "Let him remember …" authorial pontification thundered down on Mr Dombey's head. It reconciles us to the writer whose clumsy attempts at showing the railways and their alarming locomotives as a unifying force of destructive progress in this novel will be far overtaken by the descriptive narrative symbolism he creates in *Bleak House*. This is a writer who has achieved the best of its kind in a very individual form of comedy, and is pressing on to find new literary worlds to conquer.

"THE WOODEN MIDSHIPMAN": THE SIGN OVER A SHIP'S INSTRUMENT MAKER'S SHOP. USED BY DICKENS FOR SOL GILLS'.

DOMBEY AND SON

David Copperfield

THE LABOURED FACETIOUS TITLE declared that Mr David Copperfield the younger, never meant his personal history to be published. The final disclaimer was essentially true. The personal history of Charles Dickens was not something he intended to share with his public. Only Forster and Kate were told of the blacking factory lying behind Murdstone and Grinby's.

The use of memory gave Dickens something of a free hand. Did he know when he started writing that he would soon be describing the book about crocodiles which David reads to Peggotty, and which Forster marked "True" in the margin of his copy? Did he include other simple memories from childhood without specifically identifying them for his friend? Quite possibly. But it is more interesting to see the foundations for the fictional part of the book being laid in the first number. Betsey Trotwood makes such a wonderful opening impact, lashing out at Mr Chillip and storming off into oblivion, that it seems amazing that Dickens could restrain himself for another fourteen chapters before bringing her back on the scene. Yarmouth introduces Mr Peggotty's family, and Little Em'ly's symbolic daring in rushing out along the jetty overhanging deep water obviously foreshadows her future downfall. Especially as she has just expressed her heart's desire to become a lady and enrich her uncle. Her motive is like old Trent's. Her story and Daniel Peggotty's will be a sort of reversal of his and Nell's: reckless girlhood takes road to ruin for a generous cause, with devoted old intended beneficiary travelling hither and yon to rescue her.

Did the thought of his own self-supporting childhood in London evoke a strong wish in Dickens that someone might have cared enough to keep such track of him? Probably. He had sent Sol Gills around the world to find Walter Gay. Daniel Peggotty now does the same for Little Em'ly. Nobody looks for David, the deserted orphan Dickens had felt himself to be for those months his father spent in the Marshalsea.

Conscious cruelty to children, however, was beyond the capacity of any Dickens. Mr Murdstone and the deeply felt gallery of nameless Londoners who rob and terrorize little David owe much to the brutality of Benjamin Drouet, the Tooting baby-farmer whose misdeeds were being exposed in court as Dickens wrote. His name would appear next to "Burke (of Edinburgh)'s" among Dickens' dummy books. Dickens' angry journalism described his case at the same time as his angry fiction drew the ill-used David Copperfield.

By contrast, however much John Dickens' irresponsibility had damaged Charles' childhood, the man's amiability and good intentions could not be denied. His reward was to become Wilkins Micawber: orotund, mercurial, benignly patronizing with a charm that elevates the child David almost to an equal as "my friend Copperfield". If the second verse of "Auld Lang Syne" is ever sung again, somebody must surely quote Mr Micawber on its incomprehensible lallans dialect: "I am not exactly aware … what gowans may be, but I have no doubt that Copperfield and myself would frequently have taken a pull at them, if it had been feasible."

How early did Dickens decide that David's "undisciplined heart" and the consequent problems of unfortunate matrimony were to be a main theme of the book? Quite possibly from that very early moment when Mr Murdstone appears as a handsome gentleman with very black whiskers. As everyone has noticed, Clara Copperfield is as romantically irresponsible as her son. We can be sure that this is an intentional theme, because not only do the Micawbers, the Traddleses, Murdstone's continuing matrimonial plans, and even Betsey Trotwood's "grumpy frumpy story" give us parallel homiletic illustrations of marriage, but Dr Strong and Annie and Jack Maldon are the sort of completely flat and colourless characters Dickens is likely to give us at this period when a generalized theme or "main purpose" is taking precedence over vivid description or comic intent in his writing. And this is the period when he

declared "The world would not take another *Pickwick* from me now; but we can be cheerful and merry I hope, notwithstanding, and with a little more purpose in us." The cheerfulness he was about to introduce was Barkis. That character's "purpose" is obviously to show that a man of miserly character can, after all, be a good husband.

Cheerful and merry *David Copperfield* certainly is. Pecksniff and the divine Sairey, the great comics of

Martin Chuzzlewit had, in the end, been wicked people. Micawber and Betsey Trotwood are, in the end, virtuous. Miss Betsey advances that perception which had come to Dickens with Susan Nipper in *Dombey*: that the fierce and rather masculine women whom he normally found frightening – Miss Knag, Sally Brass, Mrs MacStinger – might, if they were not malevolent and repulsive, actually show a better and more useful way of feminine life than the self-effacing little dolls he naturally preferred. Goodness, wouldn't *David Copperfield* have been a better book if Agnes Wickfield had rather more of Susan Nipper and rather less of the rigid plaster saint about her!

DAVID COPPERFIELD
IN MURDSTONE
AND GRIMBY'S
BOTTLING FACTORY.

DAVID COPPERFIELD

Bleak House

WITH A SHORT AND SIMPLE TITLE, Dickens is at the very height of his powers. The wonderful prolix inventiveness is back. Readers who laugh aloud at his funniest moments find ourselves doing so at Grandfather Smallweed and old Mr Turveydrop and Chadband. Readers who admire Dickens' social observation are gratified with his sustained attack on the civil law.

The plotting is exemplary. Clues to Esther's parentage are unobtrusively present from the outset. Only the decision to weave Mrs Snagsby and Mrs Chadband into her story smacks of belated and unnecessary loose-end tying.

There is general social satire in the Fashionable Intelligence and the mob of poor relations. There is that appreciation of the weaknesses and strengths of the traditional gentleman that had been started in Cousin Feenix, brought to ripe perfection in Sir Leicester Dedlock's haughty indignation at any hint of social mobility, his rigid and unthinking integrity, his noble concern for Lady Dedlock in her exposure and shame. There is the revival of idealized lower middle class family life in Mrs Bagnet's birthday – not, perhaps, as brilliant as Daniel Peggotty's home in the boat, but still a fine advance on the Cratchits and Tetterbys. There is the first

full-length whodunnit, ten years before Wilkie Collins entered the field with *The Moonstone* – and which of us was not misled into expecting Inspector Bucket to arrest Lady Dedlock when he announced his expectation of the real murderess in Sir Leicester's room? And above all, there is the constantly wonderful narrative voice, opening with the mud of London and the imaginary megalosaurus climbing Holborn Hill, proceeding to the all-pervasive fog and the fine account of the Lord Chancellor's court in foggy Lincoln's Inn; breaking to the equally fine rain and lethargy of Lincolnshire; holding our attention thereafter whenever it turns to some living and breathing description of the flambeau extinguishers gaping at the ironwork on town houses or the light through the mullioned windows casting unexpected patterns on the pictures in Chesney Wold.

So why isn't *Bleak House* immediately recognized as Dickens' finest achievement? Because the instant he has established his power in the magnificent narrative voice of the opening chapters, he turns to the disastrous experiment which gives us one of his worst creations: the *fausse-naïve* voice of Esther Summerson. Dickens' view of an innocent young girl's mind seen from the inside is mawkish and self-pitying:

My dear old doll! I was such a shy little thing that I seldom dared to open my lips, and never dared to open my heart, to anybody else. It almost makes me cry to think what a relief it used to be to me, when I came home from school of a day, to run upstairs to my room, and say, "Oh you dear faithful Dolly, I knew you would be expecting me!"

This voice is maddeningly soppy in its expressions of friendship calling Ada "my pet", and "my love", and "my darling", and generally embarrassing the reader with perpetual verbal fondling at her golden hair and blue eyes. It is revoltingly disingenuous in reporting every compliment Esther's helpfulness is given, with some modest disclaimer that her friends must be engaged in a conspiracy to make her happy by pretending that she lightens their lives. Her accounts of the selfish or hypocritical people she describes are tainted by her narrative voice's assumption of artless uncertainty about their real motivation. Her description of Miss Barbary as "a good, good, woman", going to church every Sunday, frowning all the time and treating Esther coldly is vitiated when Esther says, "I never loved my godmother as I ought to have loved her, and as I felt I must have loved her if I had been a better girl." The man who created Mrs Pipchin and Mr Murdstone knew perfectly well that children detest people who treat them badly, and are not to be deceived into swallowing the adult world's self-deceiving assumption of virtuous motives for unkindness.

Critics who want the excellence of *Bleak House* given proper recognition sometimes suggest that Esther and her narrative must be admired because she exposes Turveydrop and Skimpole and Mrs Jellyby, who are never seen through the anonymous authorial eye, or because wanting Esther out of the way is just what the worst characters in the book want. This is to fall into the trap of treating the character as an objective person, not a set of words on the page. Esther's predicament is well imagined. But the words she uses to describe it suggest a real hypocrite, forever pretending that she is too innocent to be sure about the evils she witnesses or accept the gratitude her helpfulness elicits. This is not to say that she *is* a hypocrite, or that her innocence is a pretence. The real mind that describes what she perceives is Dickens'. It is his assumption of a voice for her that fails. His own critical awareness constantly breaks through her supposed simplicity, and the contradiction jars.

This becomes inescapably apparent when Esther is allowed a moment of cynicism and a cheap crack that Dickens finds irresistible, though it should never have occurred to the character he gives it to utter. Esther suggests to Miss Flite that titles and honours are never awarded for "peaceful services, however great and good". Miss Flite demurs foolishly that "all the greatest ornaments of England in knowledge, imagination, active humanity, and improvements of every sort, are added to its nobility". And Esther makes an observation that is pure Dickens: "I am afraid she believed what she said: for there were moments when she was very mad indeed." This has no connection with the intended character of Miss Summerson, who would never mock Miss Flite's dementia by equating it with political misjudgement. It epitomizes the flaw running through this very great book.

DIANA RIGG AS LADY DEDLOCK IN BBC TELEVISION'S "BLEAK HOUSE".

Hard Times

A NOVEL BESOUGHT BY Bradbury and Evans to revive the flagging sales of *Household Words*. So a novel written in the cramping format of weekly rather than monthly installments. A novel which did not allow the flight to a continental setting which was his ambition after *Bleak House*. That would have to wait for *Little Dorrit*.

A visit to Birmingham to address the Mechanics Institute drew his attention to the times' industrialization and its division of society into employed masses and employing middle classes. A long-running strike in Preston was in the news, and the editor of *Household Words* travelled north to see what it was all about, devoting about ten minutes of his visit to a strike meeting, where he decided that he approved of the working-men, but thought they were being misled by agitators.

Forster was overseeing work in progress by Mrs Gaskell, and thought her novel *North and South*

COUSIN FEENIX,
SEATED, LOOKS VERY
LIKE A PREMATURELY
AGED DISRAELI.

might do for *Household Words*. As she knew far more about mill towns than Dickens, he risked the charge of plagiarizing her idea and had to assure her that he would not write up the strike in his book. He also claimed unconvincingly that he had long intended a fiction dealing with industrial life.

Hard Times is, Dickens would have been furious to

learn, more interesting as a historical fact than a great fiction. It has fine moments, like Mrs Gradgrind's death or Mr Bounderby's "potent restoratives" for Mrs Sparsit's fainting fit. Or the magnificent description of Coketown with its dye-stained waterways, and the piston engine working up and down "like the head of an elephant in a state of melancholy madness". But too much of the book is laboured: the name "M'Choakumchild" for a teacher, for example, and the whole unconvincing lesson in which Gradgrind's conscientious attempt to stifle child-ish fantasy is saccharine-sweetly corrected by yet another too-perfect little girl's naïvety.

In attacking utilitarian philosophy, political econ-omy, statistically based abstractions, loco-foco politics, and fact-based learning scoured clean, Dickens was try-ing to absorb a new ethos that was still imperfectly understood. Sir James Kay-Shuttleworth, philosophical radical, educationist and enthusiast for industrialism had been an obvious political ally for the creator of the Cheeryble brothers. He and his ilk passionately believed in trade and the peaceful competition of the manufac-turing market as a prosperity-enhancing leap forward from the bad old society of would-be warrior aristocrats. But Sir James and his Benthamite allies objected to children being taught fairy tales instead of statistics. Carlyle, a radical thinker with instincts even more con-servative and authoritarian than Dickens, profoundly opposed their "Dryasdust" philosophy and economic insistence on cash as the sole nexus between man and man. The creator of Sam Weller and Mrs Rouncewell might well feel that things had come to a pretty pass when "honest working Men" not only replaced "loyal servants", but could be classed as the dead abstraction "organized labour". The admirer of Pickwick and the Cheerybles had to admit that the new self-made businessman was likely to be a Bounderby, boasting of his own self-promoting energy, rather like Dickens himself!, and firmly denouncing any working men who wanted improved living conditions. Give a capitalist an establishment larger than an office holding Tim Linkinwater and Nicholas Nickleby, and it seemed he might turn out as anti-egalitarian as Sir Leicester Dedlock.

Nor was it easy for Dickens to appreciate why a self-made manufacturing class should turn to the familiar sprigs of aristocracy for political representation. The London dandy James Harthouse could just as well be a Tory as a Whig. Dickens had once shared a platform addressing a workingmen's institute with Cobden and Disraeli, and must have doubted the seriousness of party divisions when the two vied amicably for the same sectional interest and the landed gentry's bizarre Jewish leader in the Commons, whose features seem to have been used by Phiz to represent Cousin Feenix, could associate himself with the cause of labour. Still more galling, the "progressive" Liberal leaders were all hereditary aristocrats: Lord John Russell, Lord Aberdeen, Lord Palmerston. Boodle, Coodle and Doodle. Buffy, Cuffy and Duffy.

"It's aw' a muddle", is Stephen Blackpool's uninspiring cry, as he is ground between the upper and nether millstones of capital and labour. And he speaks for his author. Dickens' treatment of Stephen shows that he desperately wants individualism to survive. But he has no more idea than anyone else how this is to be achieved when the factory system turns men into adjuncts of machines. The one hope he holds out is that popular entertainment may keep alive fancy for the masses. But he harks back nostalgically to the popular entertainment of circuses and travelling juggler and acrobats that he himself had enjoyed so much when he went to the races. Sleary, with his irritating lisp, is a dull spokesman for vitality and truth. But Dickens himself spoke thickly, if quickly, and was felt by some people to lisp or hiss his esses. And the times were sad and serious times. Drab frock coats had replaced colourful

swallow-tails. Light-hearted Pickwickian coach travellers were replaced by the empty dandy-seducer on the statutory Parliamentary train that had to run daily to London from every station when the House was sitting. Not that Mr Harthouse took his political duties seriously.

But Dickens the novelist and opinion-former took himself very seriously indeed. He hoped that Sleary and his plaster saint spokeswoman Sissy Jupe might counter the truth he perceived quite clearly in the Gradgrinds and Bounderbys and Sparsits: that cash as the bottom line with class pride as its only romantic alleviation, like self-interest checked only by its own enlightenment, must always lead to corruption, dishonesty and heartlessness.

A NINETEENTH-CENTURY CIRCUS POSTER.

Little Dorrit

IT IS WELL KNOWN THAT DICKENS' original intention was a novel called *Nobody's Fault*, whose central character should precipitate crises and disasters, blandly saying each time that it was a mercy that nobody was to blame. We know, too, that the shambolic administration of the Crimean war was much on Dickens' mind, suggesting that the blindly blameless perpetrator's role was taken over by the Circumlocution Office and the Barnacles. But they seem too complacent to notice crisis or disaster.

The character "Nobody" is introduced in Chapters Sixteen and Seventeen. But he represents Clennam's denial of his infatuation with Pet Meagles. And Clennam neither precipitates crises nor denies his own responsibilities. He is only in the loosest linguistic sense heir to the original "Nobody". Mr Meagles, pluming himself on his practicality when he is amiably sentimental, seems closer to the prototype. But he certainly does not cause the book's crises, and is barely criticized.

The truth is Dickens was, as Forster said, unsure of his creative touch at first. He flailed about for a subject and changed direction in ways he seemed to have outgrown with *Martin Chuzzlewit*. The Marseilles prison scene with which the book opens leads nowhere. Rigaud the assassin declines to a tuppenny-ha'penny blackmailer, living by his wits on the secret of one of those ridiculous wills so beloved in Dickens' plots. The mystery of Flintwinch's doppelganger established in Affery's "dream" turns out, in a rushed conclusion, to be a disappointing detail of the same bathetic plot strand.

Even when Dickens found his stride, with the Father of the Marshalsea giving him the chance to be far more critical of his own father than he had hitherto dared, he still made a change of direction on the spur of the moment, seeing correctly that he might do something impressive with the Dorrit family by bringing them into money after their years of debtors' prison. And even with that well in his sights he hadn't settled the shape of his book finally. He was approaching his twentieth chapter when John Sadleir MP committed suicide on the collapse of his brother's Tipperary joint-stock bank of which he was a director. John's huge and improper borrowings caused the collapse. As he was also chairman of the London and County joint-stock bank and a junior lord of the treasury, his death and the bank failure precipitated a wide-ranging scandal very similar to those that rocked the City and Westminster in the 1980s and 1890s. Sadleir was a rather colourless man whose lifestyle did not seem to explain his disastrous overdrawings. Dickens pounced and created Mr Merdle.

And at last, with the Barnacles, Bar, Bishop and Physician all circling in Merdle's marble halls, exchanging information and watching the political alliances of Lord Decimus with the Stiltstalkings, Dickens has created that informal but powerful amalgam of supposedly disparate powers that we know today as "the Establishment". And satirized it with brilliant prescience.

POWER AND CORRUPTION

Could powerful financiers be socially destructive criminals? Remembering the notorious banker Henry Fauntleroy, hanged for forging securities in 1824, Dickens points out that credit in the City may be used for personal enrichment sustained by fraud and leading to serious losses for smaller investors. How true today, we think, remembering Robert Maxwell and the Bank of Credit and Commerce and the fall of Baring's. Will anyone be held responsible for the failure of colleagues and regulators to perceive such frauds or anticipate such falls? Certainly not, says Dickens. The Barnacles, in and out of Parliament, will stick together and insist that no one could possibly expect them to deal with these unlooked-for instances of human incompetence and dishonesty. Their tried and tested methods should not be changed. How true today, we think, noting the public excuses offered on behalf of the Bank of England; the success of the Civil Service in regrouping after Mrs Thatcher's efforts to cut its wastage and improve its efficiency; the Cabinet Secretary's bland confession that "economy with the truth" was used to suppress *Spycatcher*. Social gatherings of jobbers and placemen, at Gowan's wedding as well as Merdle's banquets, ensure that Dickens' establishment will stand together till the last possible moment to cover up individual failings. How true today, we think, remembering Tom Driberg and Sir Anthony Blunt and Jonathan Aitken. A public school education, engendering amateurism and pseudo-diffident charm, produces *flâneurs* like Henry Gowan, confident that the world owes them a living. Have they disappeared from the scene today, even if they have to go through university and compete with

other candidates for entry to the Civil Service or adoption by parliamentary constituency parties? In its satire on self-satisfied legislative and executive rule by the entrenched educated classes, *Little Dorrit* was unmatched until *Yes, Minister*.

The non-satirical parts of the novel suggest that Dickens was facing a mid-life crisis. Forty-year-old Arthur Clennam is a muted hero, looking back over an unsatisfactory business without the energy to conquer new worlds. He loses effortlessly in his love for Pet Meagles. He is surrounded by spineless characters, notably the Marshalsea Collegians and their Father, who call abject failure enviable success.

Thus they mirror Mrs Gowan's empty grace-and-favour set in Hampton Court and the residents of uncomfortable Mayfair mews houses. London itself is tired and desolate. It is no surprise that the author of *Little Dorrit* was falling out of love with his wife and about to fall in love with a younger woman. Dickens gives his adored son Plornish's nickname to the innocent working class family of Bleeding Heart Yard. His nickname for himself – "Mr Sparkler" – is bestowed on a callow, susceptible fool who is at least harmless.

And in *Little Dorrit* herself, mothering her father and siblings, though only appreciated by poor mad Maggy, Dickens created one of his rare successes among the quietly active self-abnegating heroines he preferred. Her "party" in the cold London streets recaptures *Bleak House*'s descriptive power, and "sentimental" Victorian readers were surely right to be touched by her sleeping on the Death Register in the Borough High Street church vestry.

AMY DORRIT VISITS
ARTHUR CLENNAM
IN MARSHALSEA.

A Tale OF Two Cities

SYDNEY CARTON
COMFORTS THE
SEAMSTRESS IN
THE TUMBRIL.

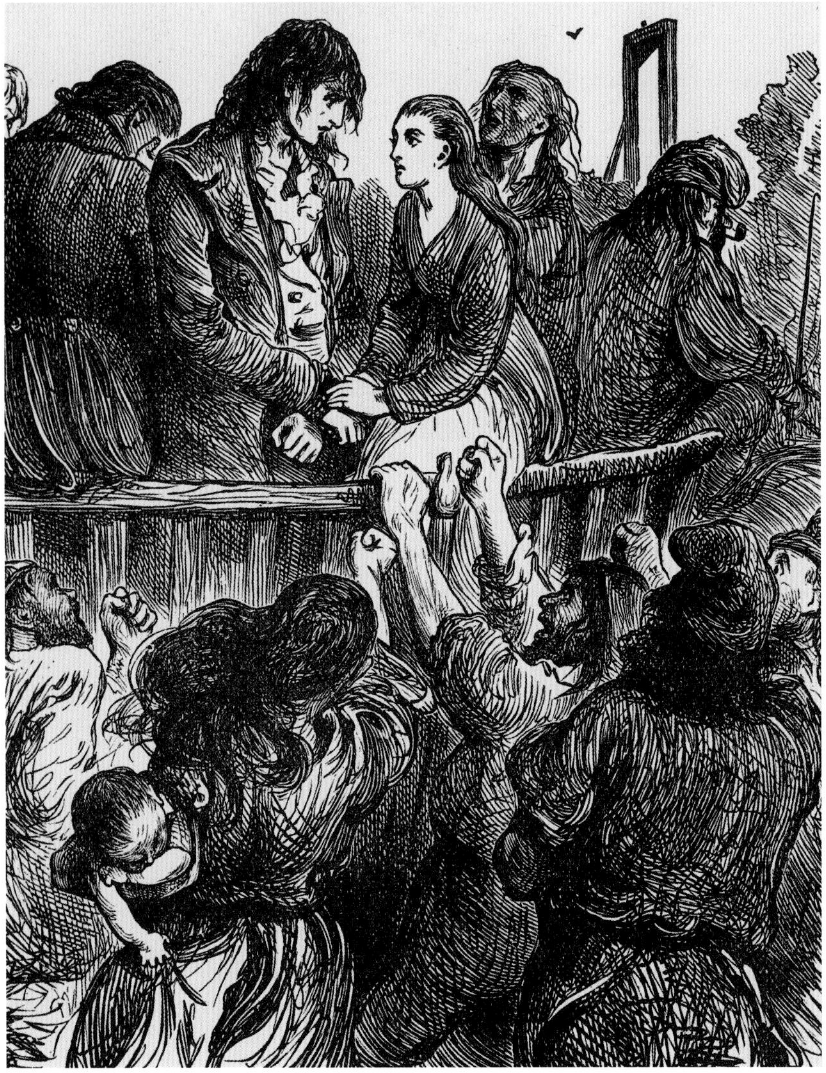

THE NEED TO GET *All the Year Round* off to a good commercial start forced Dickens to open it with a serial novel from his own pen. So he was back in the straitjacket of weekly rather than monthly parts, and complaining as ever of the want of elbow room.

Wrongly. After the diffuse rambling of *Little Dorrit*, *A Tale of Two Cities* was brilliantly planned and plotted. There is no laboured drifting to the love between Charles Darnay and Lucie Manette: Dickens knows from the start that he intends Sydney Carton's likeness to Darnay to precipitate a self-renunciatory tragic denouement. He had been plotting such a story ever since he enjoyed the stage triumph of a self-sacrificing hero's role in *The Frozen Deep*. The concept may have taken on greater intensity for him as he grimly and sacrificially repressed his desire for Ellen Ternan at the outset of his love for her. But the tragic plot is the point of *A Tale of Two Cities*, not the nature of unrequited or sacrificial love. Dickens couldn't have created an Emma Bovary or an Anna Karenina or a Hedda Gabler if he'd wanted to. But he could always imagine strong tragic predicaments, despite his inability to flesh them out realistically. Now he takes a predicament, and allows the "poetic justice" of the hero's being granted a final centre-stage to do its own work without the distraction of sentimental characterization.

There are no significant characters suddenly introduced on a whim or in response to topical events like Mr Merdle; no decisions with the novel under way to change course. Barsad and Cly are introduced from the start. Jerry Cruncher's bodysnatching reverts to a criminal topic that always fascinated Dickens – there are hints of it in *Oliver Twist* and *Dombey and Son*. But Cruncher's resurrectionism is purposefully planned. In itself it echoes that theme which almost became the novel's title, "Restored to Life". In the plot, it explains the sudden reappearance of the supposedly dead spy. Everything is ready to fall in place with the precision that had prepared Lady Dedlock as Esther Summerson's mother well before a suspicious Inspector Bucket was created to focus the investigation of mysteries in *Bleak House*.

And being firmly plotted, this book lacks the feeling of imitation-Scott that enfeebled its historical predecessor, *Barnaby Rudge*. *A Tale of Two Cities* is pure Dickens, but essentially a Dickens we have never seen before. This is a Dickens who has at last captured in prose fiction the stage heroics he adored. He has at last created a melodrama figure that any actor would gladly play. Nicholas thrashing Squeers and spouting hollow stuff about his love for Madeline Bray makes a dull workaday job for a juvenile lead. Edith Dombey "spurning" her own noble bosom – whatever that is supposed to mean! – would have been hard for Mrs Patrick Campbell herself to endow with the illusion of a third dimension. Sydney Carton carried Martin Harvey to a knighthood, as well the role might. "It is a far, far better thing that I do now …" is memorable as a finer and more original speech that "Wretch, touch him at your peril! … My blood is up, and I have the strength of ten men such as you!" (Nicholas to Squeers). Better still, Dickens writes Sydney Carton's final speech as thoughts. He has outgrown the immature tendency to let his characters indulge in tremendous soliloquies. He has left behind that inadequate sense of climax which allowed him to give Lady Dedlock a few lines of inappropriate blank verse when confronting her daughter for the first and last time. He uses the chaster prose which he has learned to apply to moments of high emotion, and yet gives his popular audience all the over-the-top heroics they may want in the basic story; all the tear-jerking self-gratifying sense that the slovenly, brilliant, dissipated lush, as unheroic as ourselves has proved the best man of 'em all in the end.

History leads Dickens back to the topic that always fascinated him and his generation: revolution, and the astonishing fact of the Terror taking place in Paris, the great centre of genteel civilization. Like Carlyle, whose advice he sought in writing the book, Dickens was sure the *Ancien Régime* brought its own destruction on itself. Like any humane person, he found the final form of that destruction nauseating. But the nausea was a lesson

from history. Ever since *A Christmas Carol*, Dickens had been warning that the underclass in Britain might pull down society in revolution if something were not done about their ignorance and want.

As a sensible novelist writing to entertain as well as instruct, he didn't bog himself down in historical paradoxes, like Robespierre, the incorruptible opponent of capital punishment, becoming the instigator of moralistic bloodshed. He never considered the possibility that bread shortages and foreign alliances stimulated each new turn of the revolutionary screw. That would have been a Gradgrind approach to matter that for him concerned justice and was best illustrated through personalities. So he gave scenes and cameos of a populace becoming justifiably enraged until its actions carried revenge far beyond the bounds of justice. And he gave Britain its classic image of the French Revolution: elegant young men in well-cut topcoats and skin-tight boots and breeches carried in tumbrels to the guillotine, while sinister harridans scream their delight as each head falls, and make knitting a threatening rather than a domestic occupation.

The writer who wanted to bring the classes together, and so refused to support strikers in Preston, now links the top and bottom of society in guilt. The worst of the aristocrats have brought their doom upon themselves. The Madame Defarges have insisted on carrying that doom to the innocent, visiting the sins of the fathers on a guiltless generation. The people in between are not represented as history's troubled or fanatical lawyers and intellectuals and time-servers who spoke in the Assembly and passed new decrees and went to the guillotine themselves. Their helplessness is personified in Dr Manette: buried alive by the old regime; "restored to life" and fêted as a Bastille victim, before being reduced to total despair as the Revolution spins out of control.

DIRK BOGARDE AS SYDNEY CARTON GOES TO THE GUILLOTINE IN BETTY BOX'S VERSION OF "A TALE OF TWO CITIES".

A TALE OF TWO CITIES

Great Expectations

HE WANING POPULARITY of Charles Lever's serial novel *A Day's Ride* threatened the circulation of *All the Year Round*. Once again Dickens had to write a novel in weekly parts to save his journal. Once again the result was tight plotting. He started with an idea he thought both grotesque and funny: that an orphan boy should accidentally befriend a convict, and inherit money from him under the impression that he had been adopted by a respectable member of society.

This basic plot and basic mystery is stronger and more central than any Dickens had hitherto devised. Not even the footling Compeyson subplot giving tension to the last quarter of the book can undermine it.

The well-conceived story of a young man's "great expectations" takes on great force because the topic had been of concern to Dickens all his life. Ever since Mrs Nickleby encouraged a nervous Mr Nickleby to "spec-u-late", Dickens had repeatedly suggested that unearned wealth was a danger and the hope or promise of it an absolute curse. Of all Dickens' novels, only *Pickwick*, *Dombey* and *A Tale of Two Cities* avoid the theme. There was nothing Dickens believed more firmly.

And there was nothing he was better fitted to examine. All his life he had spent or borrowed close to the limit of his earnings. Hardworking and moderate in his tastes, Dickens was nonetheless neither frugal nor thrifty, and he understood only too well the dangers of idle indebtedness.

His public was delighted with the new novel. Forster had been urging him to recover the humour of his early work. Dickens might well have asked whether Mr Turveydrop deporting himself and Mr Sparkler admiring every woman with no biggodd nonsense about her weren't fully as funny as two thirds of the characters in *Pickwick*. But the growing complaint that he had lost his old energy and fun really pointed to public discontent with the social satire of his mature work. Boodle, Coodle and Doodle; Bar, Bishop and Physician; the Fashionable Intelligence and the debilitated cousins were too challenging, too "political", and not farcical enough for readers who simply wanted to be entertained. Even *A Tale of Two Cities* was more of a grimly Carlylean history lesson than *Copperfield*'s warmest admirers wanted. The story of little Pip growing up to inherit unlooked-for wealth and class

JEAN SIMMONS AS
ESTELLA, MARTITA HUNT
AS MISS HAVISHAM AND
ANTHONY WAGER
AS PIP IN DAVID LEAN'S
"GREAT EXPECTATIONS".

had a Cinderella quality about it. The fact that he turns into the snob seems the personal matter of an individual character, not a problem challenging the whole of society. *Great Expectations*' real challenge to social assumptions and evaluations could easily be overlooked. Pumblechook and Wopsle are the obvious clowns of the book, and their rustic pomposity in the Medway parishes was humour that could be enjoyed without a qualm by the foppish and aristocratic and rich and powerful and wannabe-all-or-any-of-the-above society in the capital.

It was back to the Medway country for sure in this novel. Though Dickens doesn't name precise places, Cooling with its little cluster of child graves in the churchyard is obviously in Dickens' mind as Pip's country and Rochester is the old town. He is at home and he feels at home, even though the idyll is never as perfect as it might be. Mrs Joe is a cruel parent supported by the horrible social authority of Pumblechook. Orlick lurks around the forge, carrying out the blackest wishes of Pip's suppressed Id – striking down Mrs Joe, or making lewd gestures at Biddy Wopsle – but popping up again to take fearful revenge like the suppressed guilt created by every outing of the self's inner Quilp. And poisoning the heart of the childhood landscape lies the convict hulk and Magwitch.

The innocent guilt of that childhood theft of pie and file comes to be the centre of Pip's life. If Pip's money is tainted – and even had Magwitch's fortune not been forfeited, Pip makes it clear to the reader he could never accept it – then Pip's new-found class is worthless.

In fact, Dickens goes a long way to challenge his own class-bound conventionality in this book. We have seen that criminals were always his aversion and murderers were absolute anathema. Yet in *Great Expectations* he grits his teeth and makes Magwitch a fully sympathetic character. Both recall being cold and dependent on an indeterminate adult who had access to or took away the fire. Both live by their wits on the streets. Dickens, the narrowly respectable creator of *Oliver Twist* is almost comfortable with the notion that upbringing, or non-upbringing, has made Magwitch a "warmint".

Dickens the creator of unreal ideal Agnes and melodramatic destroyer Hortense, now acknowledges that a distantly cold and superior lady love may acquire all her gentility from a vengeful madwoman and all her heredity from a "warmint" and a murderess. It is a perception running even deeper than his willingness to eschew a happy romantic ending until persuaded by Bulwer Lytton to hint one in.

Our Mutual Friend

THE MYSTERIOUS WILL and missing legatee which seem vital to Dickens' plotting are introduced promptly in this novel. Though the legatee runs through such a confusion of names that the reader must be attentive to keep up with him. John Harmon's initials recur in Julius Handford. John Rokesmith looks like Handford's twin brother. Do we recall clearly that the drowned Harmon sought in Limehouse was the Man from Somewhere in Mortimer's interrupted and world-weary tale? Do we reflect that he might still be alive as Bella grumbles about having to wear mourning for a stranger she has been bequeathed to in another virtual stranger's will?

Dickens complained that commentators thought themselves very clever and imagined they had uncovered a secret when spotting that Rokesmith was Harmon. Whereas it was always his intention to let that be known. It is true that the evidence comes earlier and more suggestively than had been done for (say) the link between Nemo and Esther Summerson. He seems to have intended some difficulty in identification, too, to be met by some salvaged part of the drowned Radfoot. For in Book One, Chapter Seven Mr Venus the taxidermist and skeleton articulator says mysteriously, "I took an interest in that discovery in the river … I've got up there – never mind, though." Which suggests that he

MR PODSNAP.

has collected a bone for "miscellaneous working in" which will later prove that Radfoot could not be Harmon. It may have been exasperation with knowing commentators that led Dickens to drop the idea and reveal the full tale of Harmon in the dramatically preposterous soliloquy of Book One, Chapter Eight.

But with the original mystery to all intents and purposes solved, Dickens needed new sources of narrative tension. The reform of Bella's mercenary nature was obviously intended from the outset. Whether Boffin's miserliness was always intended to be a therapeutic act is not quite so clear. Despite his early comic naïvety, he suspects a confidence trickster after his money when Harmon seeks a mysterious interview with him out of the main road. And before Book One ends, while he is still the overt model of generosity, he has demonstrated a very mercantile attitude to his dust heaps: "Ay, ay … I may sell them … I ain't a scholar in much, Rokesmith, but I'm a pretty fair scholar in dust. I can price the mounds to a fraction, and I know how they can be best disposed of." So the miserly phase is not entirely unheralded, rapidly as it develops in Book Three, and certainly as it has been mentally written off by the time the noises near St Alphege's church organ almost give away the Boffins' presence at the Rokesmiths' wedding. True, the miserly appearance is only exhibited in the company of its confederates or their intended dupes. But once it has been introduced the plot never leads Boffin into any other company. And the acting capability it presupposes in both Boffin and his missus surpasses credibility. Can we really be sure that Dickens "knew all along" that Boffin's black countenance was feigned and Mrs Boffin's distress was merely caused by seeing Bella deceived? Was the actual partial corruption of Boffin briefly intended to be one strand in a novel which has so much to say about the corrupting interrelations of money and class?

The Bella–Harmon–Boffin plotting is interwoven with the Hexams–Eugene–Headstone plot in which class, money and respectability are manifestly central. Eugene and Mortimer are both cursed with that small unearned income which Dickens thought so much more damaging than poverty. Both must learn to work, and Eugene, in this decade of dundreary-whiskered sexual exploiters, must overcome the temptation to seduce Lizzie Hexam and accept that he loses no worthwhile caste by marrying the river-scavenger's daughter.

Lizzie herself has had her brother Charley educated above their station. Charley is one of the very rare instances of Dickens' using a variant of Charles or Dick(ens) as a dislikeable character's name. And the dislikeable brother of a good older sister, at that! Was he uneasy about his own social uprooting from a station in which, for example, he could never have kept a young actress in a house in Peckham as he did with Ellen Ternan? Is there suppressed self-hatred in Charley?

Or, indeed, in his master Bradley Headstone, whose real self-improvement and success in overcoming his distaste for Lizzie's background does him little good? This self-elevated member of the lower middle class endures supercilious taunts from the upper-class wastrel Wrayburn. His jealous and ultimately murderous wrath, is deeply felt and understandable. Yet Dickens shows him no sympathy. The dislike of schoolmasters which runs through his work is apparent. He does not show us who teaches Lizzie what at Eugene's expense to fit her for his companionship. Yet it is casually assumed to outweigh anything "mechanical" Mr Headstone can offer. And Bradley's painful and self-punitive passion may owe something to Dickens' self-contempt for his own sexual needs.

Perhaps reformably louche Eugene was always bound to beat tidy, somewhat Dickensian Bradley, given that Dickens' curious admiration for the "real" gentleman is

granted the climactic conclusion of the book when Twemlow endorses Eugene's marriage. Twemlow has no title: he is an aristocrat's hanging-on poor relation; a useless diner-out, unobtrusively exploiting his status with ambitious middle class hosts. He is not entirely false like Lady Tippins, but he conditions his hair with egg-yolk and may be caught looking like the flames on the Monument. Like "Hamilton" Veneering, "Melvin" Twemlow sports one

of the unfortunate Scottish surnames masquerading as christian names which Dickens evidently sees as incompatible with educated gentlemanly status – the masculine equivalent of the "Anastatias" and "Sophronias" disfiguring the women of this nouveau-riche circle. But the little diner-out is no echoic toady like Boots, Brewer and the Buffers. He has the genuinely diffident manners of a gentleman, and indeed, he and Mortimer are the only people whose manners are uniformly good in the Podsnap-Veneering circle. And so Twemlow can throw out, from the top of this book's class pyramid, the conclusion that all the bad characters, from Mrs Wilfer to Fascination Fledgeby need to learn: neither class nor money determines worth. Love and honour are all that matter. In his last completed novel, Dickens' simple values are still at bottom those he set out in *Nicholas Nickleby*.

ALFRED AND SOPHRONIA LAMMLES LEARN THAT THEY HAVE DECEIVED EACH OTHER.

THE Mystery OF Edwin Drood

THE LIMEHOUSE
OPIUM DEN DICKENS
INSPECTED, DRAWN
BY GUSTAVE DORÉ.

DICKENS' LAST NOVEL was planned in twelve rather than twenty monthly parts. *The Mystery of Edwin Drood* was as tightly constructed as *Bleak House*. As it needed to be. For it was indeed "A Mystery".

If he hadn't told Forster that it was about an uncle

murdering his nephew, we should be arguing to this day as to whether Edwin Drood was murdered or not; whether John Jasper was his killer or was going to bring the murderer to justice. For Dickens died exactly halfway through his story, with the mystery tautly established. And the solution? Well, clear enough in his own mind, as we can see from a multiplicity of clues. But far from revealed to us.

To grasp the problem we must, alas, laboriously summarize the plot. John Jasper, choirmaster of Cloisterham cathedral is guardian to his orphaned nephew Edwin Drood. Edwin is engaged by their parents' wills to Rosa Bud, the orphaned daughter of a friend of his father's. Jasper teaches Rosa singing, but she fears his near-hypnotic control of her which masks secret passion. To Cloisterham come twin orphans: Neville and Helena Landless from Ceylon. Their guardian, the self-important philanthropist Honeythunder, places Helena at Miss Twinkleton's Academy where she becomes Rosa Bud's friend, while Neville studies with athletic young Canon Crisparkle. Neville and Edwin take an instant dislike to each other. Jasper gets them drunk, and they quarrel. But Crisparkle and less willingly, Jasper, persuade them to dine at Jasper's on Christmas Eve and bury the hatchet.

Before Christmas, Jasper explores the cathedral at night with Durdles, a tipsy master-mason, taking the chance to drug him and borrow his keys for his own purposes. Edwin, meanwhile, receives a ring from Rosa's guardian, Grewgious, which her father left for the young couple to confirm their betrothal. Edwin promises to return it should he and Rosa break off their engagement. Which they almost immediately do to their mutual satisfaction and improved friendship.

On Christmas Day, Neville is immediately arrested. Edwin has disappeared after their dinner at Jasper's, and Jasper suspects Neville of making away with him. When Grewgious tells Jasper that Rosa and Edwin had broken their engagement, Jasper collapses.

Nothing can be proved against Neville who leaves Cloisterham for London where Helena joins him six months later. Rosa Bud, too, comes to London after Jasper has made unwelcome advances to her. An ex-naval lieutenant named Tartar with rooms next to Neville's turns out to be Crisparkle's former school fag, and he and Rosa fall in love. A mysterious figure called Dick Datchery turns up in Cloisterham – an obvious spy in a wig. He watches Jasper's movements, employing the stone-throwing urchin, Deputy, whom Durdles uses to see him home at night. He also discovers the "Princess Puffer", a London opium den keeper who has come to Cloisterham to blackmail Jasper.

And there Dickens died. In addition to telling Forster that the uncle killed the nephew, he said the body would be identified by a ring and the murderer would learn his murder had been needless. And he would unknowingly unfold the whole story himself. Tartar was to marry Rosa, and Crisparkle Helena. Neville would die. The ring is obviously the one Edwin had not yet returned to Grewgious. The revelation was pretty certainly to come about under the influence of opium or mesmerism, which Dickens believed to be energy transferring from one person to another, and which he probably thought similar to the telepathic communication between the Landlesses. Grewgious' clerk Bazzard might easily be Datchery – he saw the ring, was away from chambers subsequently, and is a would-be dramatist. Helena Landless, said to have dressed up as a boy to run away during childhood, has also been proposed. Helena's character owes much to Constance Kent, cleared of murdering her baby brother in 1860, only to confess to it five years later when she was twenty-one. Dickens suspected that she was covering for her father. But Datchery bears much likeness to Dickens' standard disguised policemen.

Clearly Dickens intended the body to be found in a grave or tomb: Durdles' obsessive discussion of the "old ones" he has found buried in the crypt shows that he will find Edwin's body somewhere. Probably by tapping a tomb he has installed and thinking he hears the echo of rubbish his men have left inside it – something he mimes to Jasper. It may be that auctioneer Sapsea's memorial to his wife was intended: Durdles used it as his example, and Jasper surreptitiously noted the weight and ring of its key when he held it. We may guess that the body will have been buried in the quicklime Jasper nearly falls over, and Rosa's ring will survive its action.

The murder is probably committed by pushing Edwin off the cathedral tower. Jasper's opium dreams, unravelled by the Princess Puffer, always start with a sinister "journey" and something "down there", before passing to exotic processions. And the book opens with the tower and an impaling spike in such a dream, preceding visions of dancing girls and elephants. Further details Dickens would surely have revealed had he lived, are the events at the Christmas Eve dinner – mysteriously never described. And the parentage of the Landlesses: the sort of thing invariably cleared up with some "long-lost" relationship. It may be relevant that Jasper has a "sister-in-law" buried outside the cathedral. This could mean a step-sister in Dickens' day. There can be little doubt we should ultimately have learned just how Jasper was related to Edwin.

Readers loved the serial. For two or three generations, the "dark" style of *Bleak House*, *Little Dorrit* and *Our Mutual Friend* was out of favour. Sapsea, Grewgious, Durdles and Deputy all suggested that harmless humourous Pickwicky Dickens was back. Although he privately called Sapsea a Tory jackass, the book doesn't describe his specific politics. Dickens satirizes bullying "do-gooders" in Mr Honeythunder, but clearly loves the public school sportsmen, Crisparkle and Tartar. So he ended his writing at ease with his times and popular with his audience.

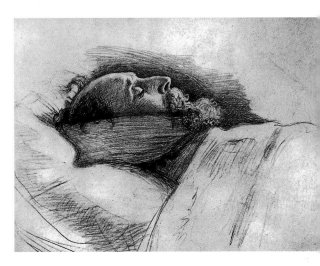

DICKENS ON HIS DEATHBED.

4 THE FRIEND OF THE POOR

IN HIS EULOGY AT DICKENS' memorial service, Dean Stanley did not start with praise for the humourist with the largest popular audience of any serious English novelist ever. He said, "He whom we mourn was the friend of mankind, a philanthropist in the true sense; the friend of youth, the friend of the poor, the enemy of every form of meanness and oppression." Dickens would have approved this being given pride of place.

It is this "true philanthropist" whom George Orwell accurately described as "worth stealing". By which he meant that Dickens' instantly accessible humanity makes him a valuable ally if he can be claimed as "really" a practising Christian, or "really" a Marxist, or "really" a traditional good-hearted Englishman. Orwell heroically resisted claiming him as "really" a democratic socialist, though he did make the mistaken claim that Dickens was not the sort of idiot who thought you can cure the spots by cutting them off. At the outset of his career, this is exactly the sort of reformer Dickens was.

When I was very young, an Instructive Aunt told me that Dickens "Always Put a Social Wrong to be Righted in Each Novel": thus, debtors' prisons in *Pickwick*, workhouses in *Oliver*; cheap boarding schools in *Nicholas*; bad nursing in *Chuzzlewit*. It's a good thing Instructive Aunty didn't go any further, or the list would have developed an appearance of rickety improvisation. As it is, I would today question the proposal that *Pickwick* makes a consciously philanthropic attack on imprisonment for debt, and positively demur at the suggestion that *Martin Chuzzlewit* played any significant part in replacing Sairey Gamps with Florence Nightingales. Of course, Dickens liked to suggest that he had made such a contribution, just as he – rightly – claimed credit for the ending of cheap Yorkshire boarding schools. But Gampish nursing was perfectly normal before the Crimean War; Mrs Gamp herself was loosely modelled on a woman hired by Angela Burdett Coutts, Dickens' wealthiest friend. Mr Brownlow hires "a fat old woman … with … a small Prayer Book and a large nightcap" whose mode of sitting up with Oliver is to go off "into a series of short naps, chequered at frequent intervals with sundry tumblings forward and divers moans and chokings", which cause her "to rub her nose very hard, and then fall asleep again." Years later, Dickens as the "Uncommercial Traveller" came across "an elderly, able-bodied pauperess" in a Workhouse Infirmary, and identified her regretfully as "a reduced member of my friend Mrs Gamp's family." This post-Crimean personage had the merit of turning a Gampish phrase, when she remarked of her charges' susceptibility to fits, "They drops with no more notice than if they was coach-horses dropped from the moon, sir."

So it appears that Dickens not only boasted of cutting the spots off, he sometimes plumed himself when, on his own evidence, the spots had survived his treatment for quite some time.

Still, warm admirers like Forster agreed with sceptical critics like Walter Bagehot that the early attacks on "remediable" social ills were preferable to the later critiques of society's way of institutionalizing ineradicable greed and heartlessness. Dickens saw the two as part and parcel of his same humane endeavour. He truly did hate all meanness and oppression whenever he recognized it.

A GROUP OF NINETEENTH-CENTURY STREET CHILDREN, RECORDED BY DR BARNADOS.

THE Poor Law AND THE Workhouse

THE POOR LAW, in the opinion of George Canning, was the reason England escaped revolution. Since Elizabeth I's reign, it had been the duty of parishes to feed and shelter their poor.

They could choose their own form of poor relief. Some built large Poor-houses where the indigent dwelt and contributed to their maintenance by whatever work the parish put before them. Others gave "outdoor relief": grants of money, or food, clothing and coals, to sustain paupers in their own homes. A system devised in the parish of Speenhamland linked outdoor cash relief to the price of corn, and ordered recipients to take any employment offered in the parish. This naturally depressed wages. Farmers weren't going to pay more than the going "Speenhamland" rate if that guaranteed them labour. Workers were trapped at bare subsistence pay.

Yet unrestricted outdoor relief seemed a drain on ratepayers, as Mr Bumble pointed out to Mrs Corney:

Why here's one man that, in consideration of his wife and large family has a quartern loaf and a good pound of cheese, full weight. Is he grateful, ma'am? Is he grateful? Not a copper farthing's worth of it! What does he do, ma'am, but ask for a few coals; if it's only a pocket hand-kerchief full, he says! Coals! What would he do with coals? Toast his cheese with 'em and then come back for more.

In 1834, Nassau Senior, Professor of Political Economy at Oxford, chaired a Commission on the Poor Law. Senior, a rigorous free market economist, recommended that outdoor relief should be stopped, as it "pauperized" recipients by encouraging them to depend on hand-outs. Relief must only be given in workhouses. Any parish without one must combine with other parishes to build a "Union" house where the standard of living must be kept below the minimum level that could be earned outside. Otherwise the poor would choose to live *gratis* off the rates. The New Poor Law enacted that this should be done.

There was a national outcry. The living standards of the poor were so low that prison might already be more comfortable than freedom. Now workhouses were to force the honest poor into worse conditions than jail-birds. Radical Tories were up in arms against this "progressive" measure. Justices of the Peace and members of Parliament in the north encouraged violent demonstrations against the new workhouses. Many parishes held out as long as they could and gave outdoor relief. The young Disraeli declared that in England

OLIVER ASKS FOR MORE: MARK LESTER IN "OLIVER!".

poverty was "now a crime". The grim Parish Unions were nicknamed "Poor Law Bastilles."

Dickens seized on the issue. Young and facetious, he started *Oliver Twist* by twitting the economists on their demand that no one should be more comfortable in the house than out, and pretended that the measured diets of small quantities of bread, meat, potatoes and broth, were limitations on the workhouse's imagined luxury. He went on to rather insensitive jocularity about one of the system's worst features: the rigid separation of men's and women's wings which cruelly broke up families:

[the Board of Guardians] were very sage, deep, philosophical men; and when they came to turn their attention to the workhouse, they found out at once, what ordinary folks would never have discovered – the poor people liked it! It was a regular place of entertainment for the poorer classes; a tavern where there was nothing to pay; a public breakfast, dinner, tea, and supper, all the year round... "Oho!" said the board, looking very knowing; "we are the fellows to set this to rights … " So they established the rule that poor people should have the alternative … of being starved by a slow process in the house, or by a quick one out of it. With this in view, they … issued three meals of thin gruel a day, with an onion twice a week, and half a roll on Sundays. They made … other wise and humane regulations … ; kindly undertook to divorce poor married people … and, instead of compelling a man to support his family as they had theretofore done, took his family away from him and made him a bachelor. There is no saying how many applicants for relief, under these last two heads, might have started up in all classes of society, if it had not been coupled with the workhouse; but … relief was inseparable from the workhouse and the gruel; and that frightened people.

Well into the twentieth century Albert Chevalier's song "My Dear Old Duch" wrung tears from audiences who knew this "divorce" as the separation of loving old couples. But with his mockery and Oliver's dramatic plea for "more" Dickens targeted hatred on the New Poor Law.

He was far from cutting the spot off, however. Progressive whiggism had introduced it. Peelite conservatism favoured it. Disraelian conservatism was out of power until the ruling classes were habituated to it. Dickens' own next glance at a workhouse, in *The Uncommercial Traveller*, took the system for granted, though he put his finger on one problem. The poorest urban parishes with the largest indigent populations could only levy the lowest rates. Wapping levied a sevenpenny rate; rich West End parishes could raise seven shillings. This inequity would continue until 1921, when George Lansbury led Poplar Council to jail in defiance of the government's attempt to make them cut rates by cutting benefits. Their protest forced London to redistribute rates income from richer to poorer boroughs, the reform Dickens had demanded seventy years earlier.

The workhouses, astonishingly, were not finally abolished until the Attlee government, after the Second World War. The more credit to Dickens, then, that in *Our Mutual Friend* he returned to sensitive awareness of the terror these abominable institutions held for the poor. In creating the character of old Betty Higden, dying and homeless, but proudly valuing her independence and running away from anyone who looks likely to bring her before a relieving officer, Dickens truly proved himself the friend of the poor and the enemy to meanness and oppression.

THE WORKHOUSE IN ST JAMES' PARISH, AS DEPICTED BY ROWLANDSON AND PUGIN.

Education AND Schools

C HEAP YORKSHIRE boarding schools were the one spot Dickens undoubtedly cut off and cured. Their value was a matter of debate. William Cobbett, proto-Dickensian travelling radical reporter, had attended one. Although this left him effectively self-

educated, he bore his Yorkshire schoolmaster no ill-will. Others felt differently, and the wretched standards of hygiene and nutrition in the schools often brought their proprietors before the courts. Dickens highlighted their boasted "No Vacations" which made them dumping grounds for unwanted illegitimate or step-children.

His wonderful grotesque creation of Squeers was instantly effective. Squeers had one eye: William Shaw of Bowes, no worse than many of his fellow pedagogues, was identifiable as the only one-eyed schoolmaster in Yorkshire. He was out of business and bankrupt by 1840. The public shame of having a child educated at anything like Dotheboys Hall became so great that

within eight years, the last of Shaw's competitors had ceased to advertise.

In theory, Dickens believed in education as the essential way to stop poverty from degenerating to crime. He visited Field Lane Ragged School – one of the first church sponsored elementary schools for slum children – and encouraged Miss Burdett Coutts to support the movement generously. He spoke and raised money on behalf of Mechanics' Institutes, convinced that self-education was of inestimable value to working men, and rightly respectful of those who travelled to lectures and kept up their reading after the grinding toil imposed by Victorian industrialism. But, as these four examples show, he found little to admire in actual teaching.

"Now, Dombey," said Miss Blimber, "how have you got on with those books?" They comprised a little English, and a deal of Latin – names of things, declensions of articles and substantives, exercises thereon, and preliminary rules – a trifle of orthography, a glance at ancient history, a wink or two at modern ditto, a few tables, two or three weights and measures, and a little general information. When poor Paul had spelt out number two, he found he had no idea of number one; fragments whereof afterwards obtruded themselves into number three, which slided into number four, which grafted itself onto number two. So that whether twenty Romuluses made a Remus, or hic haec hoc was troy weight, or a verb always agreed with an ancient Briton, or three times four was Taurus a bull, were open questions with him. "Oh, Dombey, Dombey!" said Miss Blimber, "this is very shocking."

He had been eight years at a public school, and had learnt, I understood, to make Latin Verses of several sorts, in the most admirable manner. But I never heard that it had been anybody's business to find out what his natural bent was, or where his failings lay, or to adapt any kind of knowledge to him. He had been adapted to the Verses, and had learnt the art of making them to such perfection, that if he had remained at school until he was of age, I suppose he could have gone on making them over and over again, unless he had enlarged his education by forgetting how to do it … To be sure, I know nothing of the subject, and do not even now know whether the young gentlemen of classic Rome or Greece made verses to the same extent – or whether the young gentlemen of any country ever did.

"Bitzer," said Thomas Gradgrind, "your definition of a horse." "Quadruped. Graminiverous. Forty teeth, namely, twenty-four grinders, four eye-teeth, and twelve incisors. Sheds coat in spring; in marshy countries sheds hoofs too. Hoofs hard, but requiring to be shod with iron. Age known by marks in mouth." Thus (and much more) Bitzer. "Now, girl number twenty," said Mr. Gradgrind, "you know what a horse is."

"Difference between he says and they say? Give it me." Mary Anne immediately hooked her right arm behind her in her left hand – an attitude absolutely necessary to the situation – and replied: "One is indicative mood, present tense, third person singular, verb active to say. Other is indicative mood, present tense, third person plural, verb active to say."

"Why verb active, Mary Anne?"

"Because it takes a pronoun after it in the objective case, Miss Peecher."

"Very good indeed," remarked Miss Peecher, with encouragement. "In fact, could not be better. Don't forget to apply it, another time."

It is revealing that Dickens perpetrates two howlers in his critique of academic education. He thinks there is a declinable article in Latin, and he forms the false past tense "slided". In fact, he positively preferred the "practical mode" travestied by Squeers' sending boys to tend horses or gardens. Dickens admired training in manual tasks. "N.B. Miss Peecher and Miss Peecher's pupils were not much encouraged in the unscholastic art of needlework," he complained. Even the ragged schools were a "jumble", wrongly linking the New Testament to book-learning by using it for reading lessons! He wanted boys drilled in marching and seamanship and mental arithmetic at part-time classes in workhouse centres! He wanted girls taught housework and homecrafts. And both told to be good Christian citizens. Yet he hated the uniformed Charity Schools which had long attempted moral education: he felt they created socially isolated prigs. He wanted commercially useful living languages to replace the classics; more modern history than ancient. But like many badly schooled, necessarily self-educated people, he really rather despised formal education.

Actually, the best teacher in Dickens is Fagin, whose pocket-picking classes offer pupils well-disciplined, enjoyable hands-on practice! Ironically the real thieves' kitchen training "kiddies" – originally slang for child thieves – was in Baldwin's Gardens, in the catchment area of Field Lane Ragged School.

DR BLIMPER'S BOYS.

YOUNG MEN FROM THAT BASTION OF BRITISH FORMAL EDUCATION, ETON.

Penology AND Prisons

A N EFFECT beloved of twentieth century dramatizers and film-makers is the sudden exposure of Mr Pickwick to the horrors of a dungeon in the Fleet Prison. The great prison reformer, it seems, felt as we do about half-naked convicts in chains and fetters, set against unglazed barred windows in dirty walls.

Which is all nonsense. Debtors' prisons were squalid. They further demoralized those who were already weak. But they were not dungeons. It is seedy, noisy fecklessness that drives Mr Pickwick, heart-sick, to the solitude of his own room: "Some were shabby, some were smart, many dirty, a few clean; but there they all lounged, and loitered, and slunk about, with as little spirit or purpose as the beasts in a menagerie."

Little Dorrit repeats the message. The "Collegians" came to the Marshalsea because they were irresponsible. The Marshalsea made them worse. Tidy-minded, purposefully-directed Dickens was disgusted. When Little Dorrit herself asks whether it is fair that her father should still have to pay the full sum owed, after he has lost so many years of liberty for it, Arthur Clennam notes this as the only taint of the prison about her. It is an ambiguous judgement, which invites us to ponder just what society should do about those who cannot or will not pay their just debts.

Dungeons, for Dickens, belonged to the past or foreign countries. (Both at once in *A Tale of Two Cities'* Bastille and *La Force*!) The only London "dungeon" he names as such is the sample condemned cell in Newgate described in the *Sketches* as:

> a stone dungeon, eight feet long by six wide, with a bench at the upper end, under which were a common rug, a Bible and a Prayer-book. An iron candlestick was fixed into the wall at the side; and a small high window in the back admitted as much air and light as could struggle in between a double row of heavy, crossed iron bars.

In *Oliver Twist* he remembers the iron candlestick and says the bench was stone. Cruikshank drew a truckle bed, with the sheriffs' order for Fagin's execution on the wall. Both men were abolitionists at this time, yet neither thought the cell a social evil in need of reform.

But Dickens was interested in penological reform aimed at stopping prisons from serving as Universities of Crime. In the *Sketches* visit he had seen a girl "Hardened beyond all hope of redemption" and a woman with " half-starved features twisted into an expression of careful cunning". Such people, Dickens knew, might well be irredeemable. So they'd better be segregated from those whom they might corrupt instead of sleeping in Newgate wards with up to twenty other prisoners.

Jeremy Bentham, utilitarian promoter of "the greatest good of the greatest number" whose optimistic philosophy underlay most progressive thinking in Dickens' youth, had proposed the "Panopticon" prison as "a mill to grind rogues honest." His plan for rehabilitation was separating prisoners from each other entirely, and giving them useful work, not mere oakum picking, to carry out in their cells. They should receive improving visits from the chaplain and magistrates inspecting the prison. Warders would bring their meals in. Otherwise they should see no one. Thus they would break their criminal associations and, in solitude, undergo complete reformation.

Dickens enjoyed the chance to examine this "separate system" fully, freely and without let or hindrance throughout the day he spent at the Eastern Penitentiary near Philadelphia. He was appalled. Uninterrupted solitary confinement led to lassitude, depression and in some cases complete lunacy. The few robust enough to survive did so with covert glee in their unregenerate criminality, disguised under the hypocritical pretence that they were glad to have been sent to prison to be reformed. This posturing was encouraged by the prison inspectors who persistently asked prisoners to say they were happy. With varying results, the miserable inmates tried to gratify such Benthamite optimism. When the system was tried at the new Millbank Prison in England, Dickens' protest was strongly registered in *David Copperfield* when Uriah Heep and Mr Littimer as the visiting magistrates' "pet prisoners" show themselves utterly unreformed and creepy humbugs.

Dickens far preferred the "silent system" which he saw in Boston, and which was adopted by his friends Lieutenant Tracey, governor of the Middlesex House of Correction and Mr Chesterton of Tothill Fields Prison. This was devised by the sadistic, corrupt but inventive American, Elam Lynds, who built Sing Sing prison with convict slave labour at no cost to the state. First and foremost, Lynds believed in the whip. He gave an exemplary ten lashes to the worst offender among each new intake of prisoners on their admission. He armed his warders with rawhides and ordered instant flogging for any prisoner found talking ever. He prowled the galleries at night, flogging anyone trying to communicate with his neighbour. He once administered a sentence of five hundred lashes.

He had experimented with "separate" imprisonment, using the lash to correct any infringement of any kind.

Of the first eighty prisoners he put in solitary confinement, only two were still alive and sane after two years. So he devised the silent system instead. Convicts slept in solitude, but worked together all day, and their labour was useful. They were not forced to wear the black hoods with which the separate system masked any inmate let out of his cell for any purpose but they wore striped uniforms lest they escaped. And woe betide them if they slacked or opened their mouths.

Though Lynds was ultimately sacked for corruption, he was much admired by reforming prison disciplinary societies. Chesterton and Tracey were not sadistic. But imprisonment in their institutions carried the added hardship that the labour was useless: picking oakum, or turning treadmills and cranks that did nothing but count the number of revolutions. Dickens was uncertain whether the disciplined quiet of treadmills and oakum compensated for the lack of stones dressed and goods manufactured under the American system. But he certainly wanted prisoners punished, not "reformed". Equally he didn't want them driven literally mad by solitary confinement.

ROWLANDSON AND PUGIN: THE FLEET PRISON, WITH DEBTORS PLAYING SQUASH RACQUETS — A GAME THEY INVENTED.

Poverty AND Prostitutes

ANGELA BURDETT COUTTS, HEIRESS AND PHILANTHROPIST.

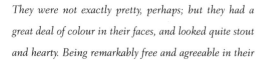

I N "THE PAWNBROKER'S SHOP" (*Sketches*) Dickens foreshadowed the probable fate of a poor girl pawning her last keepsakes at her mother's behest by describing, "In the next box," "a young female, whose attire, miserably poor, but extremely gaudy, wretchedly cold, but extravagantly fine, too plainly bespeaks her station, [and whose] practised smile is a wretched mockery of the misery of the heart," and "a woman in the common shop; the lowest of the low; dirty, unbonneted, flaunting, and slovenly." Dickens summarizes the daughter and the two prostitutes thus:

> *Who shall say how soon these women may change places? The last has but two more stages – the hospital and the grave. How many females situated as her two companions are, and as she may have been once, have terminated the same wretched course in the same wretched manner?*

Thus, very early, "the Friend of the Poor" observes that poverty can lead to prostitution which may mean misery, degradation and a pauper's grave. However, his first fictional prostitutes are introduced quite differently with satirical sarcasm:

> *They were not exactly pretty, perhaps; but they had a great deal of colour in their faces, and looked quite stout and hearty. Being remarkably free and agreeable in their manners, Oliver thought them very nice girls indeed. As there is no doubt they were.*

Nancy is still mocked when her consent to look for Oliver is put down to her recent arrival from "the genteel suburb of Ratcliffe" so that she is unfamiliar to local police and punters. But when Dickens changes direction and makes her sympathetic, he satirizes the respectable housemaids who disapprove of her being admitted to speak to Rose Maylie:

> *"It's no good being proper in this world," said the first housemaid. "Brass can do better than the gold what has stood the fire," said the second. The third contented herself with wondering "what ladies was made of" and the fourth took the first in a quartette of "Shameful!" with which the Dianas concluded.*

This was the first and last time Dickens satirized respectable women's self-righteous contempt for prostitutes. Rosa Dartle's jealous hatred of Em'ly is different, unfunny and personal. Yet overtly his attitude to fallen women became ever more sympathetic and earnest.

Never again did he describe a street-walker with the nonchalance initially afforded Nancy and Bet. Prostitution was treated as a social and moral problem. As is well-known, the most sustained practical social work Dickens ever undertook in person was advising Miss Burdett Coutts on Urania Cottage, her home for homeless and fallen women, and supervising its running with hearty realism and good sense.

So did Dickens, in the phrase he loved for his social commentary, "strike a blow" for poor prostitutes as he had for workhouse paupers and Yorkshire boarding schoolboys? The answer would have to be "yes, but not a very helpful one". He made it clear enough that respectable bourgeois marriage for money was in effect prostitution. But he displaced his prostitute characters from the reality he knew casually when he described them acting in "Private Theatre" performances; the reality he acknowledged with little apology when telling Emerson that he would be concerned if his son were unduly chaste; the reality he accepted as picturesque when letting Wilkie Collins show him the more lurid parts of Second Empire Paris; the reality with which he tempered Miss Coutts' pious expectation that her fallen women would all become penitent celibates; the reality he almost approved when, as Peter Ackroyd recently found, he invited his friend Maclise to stay with him at Broadstairs, holding out as a bait his discovery of the whereabouts of Margate prostitutes. Though we can't know for sure, Dickens' fastidiousness and prudery make it unlikely that he himself ever took advantage of prostitutes' services. But his powerful creation of guilt-stricken "unfortunates" contributed to the hypocrisy-driven hysteria which made of prostitution an insoluble "problem". If Charles expected Charley to be unchaste without becoming unbalanced, why did he pretend that women alleviating their poverty by catering to that unchastity must be given to "strange cries" and "haunted looks"?

Because, like Mr Gladstone, he mixed obsessive and perhaps guilty curiosity with benevolence and disapproval. The nightly presence of streetwalkers thronging the Haymarket annoyed respectable tidy-minded Victorians like Dickens, just as homeless street-urchins annoyed him and were pilloried as "young savages" and "vermin" in *Our Mutual Friend* and *Edwin Drood* and *The Uncommercial Traveller*. Street prostitutes disturbed Miss Coutts because she believed they endangered their souls. Gladstone shared this belief, but felt an obsessive attraction to the fallen objects which could lead him to seek out one especially pretty face repeatedly, and literally flagellate himself for the desire he knew vitiated his rescue work. Which anyway, as he also knew, had virtually no success. Dickens supervised Urania Cottage with a similarly obsessive interest, though the fifty percent success rate he predicted and almost achieved was satisfactory. The same obsession impelled him to introduce unnecessary and improbable scenes in his writing, like the prostitute who asks Little Dorrit to kiss her when she thinks she is a child, but flees on seeing she is a woman.

In the end, he failed to strike an effective blow for prostitutes, because he wasn't as deeply opposed to the trade as he felt he ought to be, and because the heart of the problem seemed to be insoluble poverty. Prostitution looked like a spot that could be cut off by charity and policing, as street arabs were cleared and sheltered by Barnardo and his imitators. But many women simply didn't want to give up the game. Dickens pretended they did, despite knowing that some women preferred the freedom of the streets to the comfort of Urania Cottage, or reverted to prostitution on the emigrant ships to Australia. He was a Friend to Poor Prostitutes as he was, sadly, never a Friend to Poor Street Children. But his lopsided friendship damaged them by encouraging the fog of visceral stigmatization, cheap sentiment and prurient curiosity which never attached to Doll Tearsheet or Moll Hackabout.

ACTORS IN A "PRIVATE THEATRE" WHERE, ACCORDING TO DICKENS, WOMEN'S ROLES WERE TAKEN BY PROSTITUTES.

POVERTY AND PROSTITUTES

THE Civil Law

LAWYERS CAME HIGH on the list of oppressors Dickens hated. Their fancy dress ("Wiglomeration") offended him, as did their forensic debating tricks, illogical courtroom conventions, and musty precedents. Dickens understood these well enough. In one celebrated exchange, he dramatised the prohibition of "hearsay evidence" with an example so exquisitely and deliberately off the point that it has become a lawyer's byword:

> *"Little to do, and plenty to get, I suppose?" said Serjeant Buzfuz with jocularity.*
>
> *"Oh, quite enough to get, sir, as the soldier said ven they ordered him three hundred and fifty lashes," replied Sam. "You mustn't tell us what the soldier, or any other man, said, sir," interposed the judge; "it's not evidence."*

How Dickens would have enjoyed the barrister's book on his supposed love life which indulges in copious unsupported conjecture, but fiercely reproves biographers who quote "hearsay evidence", sublimely unaware that the greater part of history is hearsay! He would surely, too, have been amused by the widespread misapprehension that circumstantial evidence is bad evidence, and the straight-faced assertion that there is "only circumstantial evidence" when circumstantial details actually corroborate the direct testimony of some witness who happens to be obnoxious to the establishment.

Legal training did not seem promising to Dickens. Rob "the Grinder", following the charity school education Dombey has granted him, makes repeated false starts at clerking in a lawyer's office. Richard Carstone,

educated into a charming lack of persistence by his public school, takes little harm from his failure to settle to medicine or the army. But he is destroyed by his experience of the law which leads him into the arms of Vholes and the toils of Jarndyce and Jarndyce.

Yet Dickens enrolled at the Middle Temple, ate his dinners from time to time, and nursed a longstanding ambition to be called to the bar with a view to becoming a stipendiary magistrate. No doubt Henry Fielding's success at Bow Street appealed to him, as did Putting Right the Wrongs he constantly felt he could perceive in magistrates' decisions on cases he hadn't heard.

Two of a TRADE can never AGREE

He never thought the law was a simple spot that could be cut off. Indeed, apart from campaigning strenuously for the abolition of public hanging, his normal demands of the criminal law were that its severities should be strengthened. He would have applauded punitive "Law and Order" speeches at modern party conferences. He particularly wanted the streets made comfortable for the middle classes. He complained that the police were not severe enough in moving on "roughs" or arresting stone-throwing urchins. He boasted of having made a citizen's arrest of a girl who was using foul language in the streets, and, to the astonishment of the police and magistrates, compelled them to apply an obscure clause of the Police Act and fine her £10. When he gave his name, the bench was particularly surprised that he expressly wanted her sent to prison. Who was now the Friend and who the Oppressor?

But the Civil Law was another matter. When Mr and Mrs Bumble face criminal proceedings for destroying evidence, Dickens approves. Bumble's famous objection is to the Civil Law.

> *"You were present on the occasion of the destruction of these trinkets, and indeed, are the more guilty of the two, in the eye of the law; for the law supposes that your wife acts under your direction."*
>
> *"If the law supposes that," said Mr. Bumble, squeezing his hat emphatically in both hands, "the law is a ass – a idiot. If that's the eye of the law, the law is a bachelor; and the worst I wish the law is, that his eye may be opened by experience – by experience."*

The joke is more a stock Dickensian gibe at matrimony than a satirical comment on the law. But a comment is there. A comment on Civil Law's attempt to define marital relations and responsibilities.

Civil Law was not so much a spot as a rash covering the body politic, as far as Dickens was concerned. He didn't give a button for its difficult task of trying to codify all the relative rights and duties of one man to another in a complex property-owning society. Rule of law for him meant disciplining thieves, robbers and people who were rude to him on the streets. It was always obvious to Dickens what was right and what was wrong. If the law quibbled and saw difficulties, the law was an ass.

Thus far Dickens was arrogantly wrong-headed with all the fervour of a demagogic populist. But when he came to traditional complaints about lawyers and the administration of the courts, he said things that had been valid since Tudor times and are valid today. "The law's delay," moaned Hamlet. Dickens labelled a shelf-full of his dummy books *A Short Suit in Chancery*. He wasn't being unduly cynical. Suits wherein lawyers' fees ate up disputed estates before the case was decided, were really known. Suitors could be dragged into law without wishing it and without having offended. "In chancery" was a byword for "in trouble": boxers used it to describe the pugilist being mercilessly bashed in a headlock. Dickens did not exaggerate to say that a house whose ownership was before the High Court of Chancery might go to rack and ruin before the court let anyone move in and repair it.

Lawyers' restrictive practices would not have surprised Dickens, either. We may object to paying two sets of overheads, for solicitors and barristers. Dickens faced an even greater array of restrictive and expensive lawyers: Serjeants, who were senior to Queen's Counsel, but equally incapable of performing without paid juniors; proctors who alone handled divorce, probate or admiralty law. He showed that Mr Pickwick pays for his solicitor Mr Perker, and his leading counsel Serjeant Snubbin and his junior counsel Mr Lowten, any one of whom could have handled the case alone. And when they have, lost it for him, he has their fees and those of Serjeant Buzfuz and Mr Phunky and Dodson and Fogg to meet. A thousand litigants are still angrier than Mr Pickwick, and agree that the law oppresses by falsely promising justice, and charging exorbitantly for it.

"THE LAW IS A ASS,"
SAID MR BUMBLE.

THE Poor AND THE Oppressors

"Y FAITH IN THE PEOPLE governing is, on the whole, infinitesimal; my faith in the People governed is, on the whole, illimitable." Dickens worried that his credo, heard without the capital P, led people to think he meant the masses needed to be governed and were not to be trusted with power. He meant the reverse. He meant "Down with the Ruling Classes! Up with the People!"

Yet, as we have seen, he was hostile to the destitute People when they were reduced to theft or begging on the streets. In his essay "Tramps" he damns all vagrants except peripatetic workers, and he disapproves of them if they take a break to watch other people working! His per-

oration on the death of Jo the crossing sweeper was justly famous for drawing attention to children dying of want:

Dead, your Majesty. Dead, my lords and gentlemen. Dead,
Right Reverends and Wrong Reverends of every order.
Dead, men and women, born with Heavenly compassion
in your hearts. And dying thus around us every day.

But Jo struggled to work, supporting himself by serving the middle classes, sweeping away filth and horse-droppings when they wanted to cross the street. He was respectfully servile to his betters and not street-smart enough to avoid being ripped off when he was handsomely tipped. Had he fought back, Dickens wouldn't have granted him such an epitaph, even though child thieves and beggars died all around, like Jo, every day.

Destitute women could escape Dickens' tirades by turning to prostitution. Some cross-gender consideration – call it sexism, call it gallantry, call it lechery if you like! – plays a part. The useful legend of the "ruined" and jilted woman forced onto the streets by a Carker or a Steerforth allows the question to be dramatized as upper class exploitation of the poor – "Victim o-o-orv a rich man's gime!" as the music hall song has it. More importantly, the starving prostitute, unlike the hungry thief, didn't threaten middle class men, so Dickens could allow her horrified sympathy. The woman who stole or begged still came under his ban.

As we have seen, he never supported

"THE BEGGAR" –
H.G. GLINDONI'S
IMPRESSION OF THE
ANCIEN RÉGIEME.

THE FRIEND OF THE POOR

workers who grouped together for collective bargaining. He praised "the combination of numbers" when applied to the independent "purchase and cooking of [workers'] food". He had no praise for such combination to negotiate with employers like Bounderby. He was unwilling to let a sympathetic fictional working man sympathise with "Moral Force" Chartism. Yet Chartists really did aim to bring the People responsibly into government; something Dickens also favoured, associating upper class patronage of the poor with treating the worker like a baby and telling him "that he must be goody-poody and do as he is toldy-poldy, and not to be a manny-panny or a voter-poter" ("The Boiled Beef of New England").

Patronage was a form of oppression Dickens felt deeply. Proudly independent himself, he loathed anyone who treated him with conscious superiority, which may explain his dislike of schoolmasters. He was only twenty-four when he reproved the Bishop of London for assuming he knew the wants and needs of the poor on their Day of Rest. "That a Prelate of your elevated rank has the faintest conception of those wants, and the nature of those necessities, I do not believe," wrote "Timothy Sparks". Dickens had already mastered that mock-modest courtesy which, like a committeeman's, "With respect, chairman… ", really means "Nevertheless, you"re a bloody fool!" And although he could himself patronize workingmen, servingmen, minor officialdom, and any woman who didn't look capable of biting him sharply where it hurt, he really did have a good sense of ordinary humanity's spiritual "need for fun". So he stood up brilliantly to killjoys who knew "better" taste. In this respect, the creator of Vincent Crummles, Mrs Jarley, Codlin & Short and Sleary was a true friend of those peripatetic poor who called down most puritanical disapproval, as well as their audiences. In "Dr" Marigold, the cheapjack whose first deaf-and-dumb child dies while he has to finish his patter, he combines an unpatronizing acceptance of "cheap and cheerful" tastes with a humane awareness that the cheerfully vulgar can suffer real personal tragedies and evince real domestic heroism.

Heroic domesticity, however, is usually seen at that level of home-bound poverty on the margin of (financial)

respectability which Dickens truly befriended because he belonged to it by birth. "Registrar-General's Class C: the lower-middle and upper-working classes" were the poor Dickens truly loved. The clerks and the mechanics and the small craftsmen. The Miss LaCreevys and Newman Noggses and Kenwigses and Poll Sweedlepipes and Mrs Todgers and Toodles and Captain Cuttles and Mr Snagsbys and Plornishes and Chiverys and Joe Gargerys and Wemmicks and Miss Abbey Pottersons and Jenny Wrens – the list goes on and on and seems endlessly varied. He knows these people fear the rent collector and the landlady and officialdom. He knows, angrily, that they are helpless before an administration which charges a poor inventor the huge total of £91

THE CHARTIST'S ATTEMPT TO FREE A PRISONER IN NEWPORT, WALES.

in fees after pushing him from pillar to post in search of a patent that doesn't even cover the whole British Isles. He knows they stand on their dignity with comical touchiness, not having a lot else to stand on. He pays them the compliment of allowing them imperfections and sillinesses and foibles and pretensions, without ever imagining that these things make them wicked. He pays them the further compliment of admitting that the class includes people who are both weak and wicked: Rob the Grinder and Mr Dolls and Bart Smallweed. Without the possibility of sin, there is no true humanity. Dickens truly saw humanity in the respectable, limited, modestly poor: a class normally despised and written off by the intelligentsia and the creative artists who know that a ten-classics library like John Dickens's won't help to make a living for Mr Superior Avant-Garde. Indeed, lower-middle class taste is likely to despise avant-garde work altogether, as Dickens despised the Pre-Raphaelites, and even declared himself opposed to "the whole school" of *Jane Eyre*!

But there are so many respectable upper-working and lower-middle class people with poor taste that the writer who cannot be a friend to them cants most horribly in claiming to be a friend of the human race. In this respect, Charles Dickens is a gloriously cant-free zone.

THE GREAT VICTORIAN

SIR ARTHUR HELPS, Clerk of the Privy Council, reviser of Queen Victoria's jottings, and acquaintance of Charles Dickens, once told Her Majesty that Dickens' name would "hereafter be closely associated with the Victorian era". Helps could not predict that Victoria would rule for another thirty years after Dickens' death and twenty-five after his own. So it seemed natural to memorialize Charles as the subject who would best characterize her reign.

Helps was right although the Victorian cultural ambience changed after he and Dickens left the scene. It can come as a shock to remember that Dickens missed the triumphalist imperialism ushered in by Disraeli's Royal Titles Act; or that he had but two years to live when Mr Gladstone first went to live in 10 Downing Street, and he never knew that moral firebrand as the "Grand Old Man" who would spend the next twenty-five years taking up and laying down the premiership. Charles Dickens was an early to mid-Victorian, dying in the thirty-third year of the queen's sixty-five-year reign.

He was also a child of his times who fitted and represented the shifting public persona of The Early Victorian, from romantic admirer of the young Queen, idolizing her at the time of her marriage, to respectable proponent of family values as championed by Albert the Good and his missus. Nothing is more Victorian about Dickens, however, than his final capacity to embrace two contradictory tendencies: the overt formalization of "manly" decency through the muscular Christianity espoused by reformed public schools, and the balancing covert increase in raffishness while the Widow of Windsor kept out of the public eye, and fashionable "celeb" London's old friend,

Louis Napoleon established a gaudy empire of gaming and *grandes horizontales*. The later Dickens admired the hearty model manliness of Crisparkle and Tartar almost at the same time as he enjoyed the reformable insouciant man-of-the-worldliness of Wrayburn and Mortimer. The creator of Sydney Carton may have liked respectability, but he loved, too, the disreputability that might cover fundamental decency and a broken heart.

In Dickens' very appearance and facial hair one can see him as a man of his time. He varied the use of his razor almost as often as Disraeli. Clean-shaven with long natural hair when the Queen ascended the throne, he grew moustaches after the fashion of the country when in Italy. Back home he shaved them off and presented an upstanding, lightly side-whiskered appearance for his first daguerreotype. Soon, like Thackeray, he was mocking those old beaux whose rouge and wigs and hair-dyes tried vainly to recapture the elegant past of Brummel. On his next Italian visit he repeated the moustaches, and then added the beard, which would distinguish all the well-known photographs of his latter life, and make him, like Tennyson and Salisbury, a hirsute model of mature Victorianism. Yet unlike them, he developed some "swell" characteristics as artificial as the centre-partings and dundreary-whiskers with which young fashionables signalled the naughtiness which would climax in the Nineties. In Dickens' case, the use of curlers and stiff, ugly forward-brushing on his thinning side hair, marked him as still the would-be dandy, the spokesman for middle-class Victorian respectability who nonetheless bowed to the impulses behind man-o'-the-world stylishness.

A PORTRAIT FROM 1867 OF QUEEN VICTORIA BY JACOB THOMPSON.

Party Politics

DICKENS WAS A RADICAL. He said so repeatedly, occasionally varying the term to Liberal at the end of his life. "Radical" was a loose general term equivalent to "progressive" or "left-wing", like "Liberal" in America today. There never was a formal Radical party. Dickens was born soon after death ended the rivalry of Pitt and Fox; he died as the rivalry of Gladstone and Disraeli began. It is easy to feel that the Radicals were the left wing of Fox's Whigs, metamorphosed naturally

DICKENS AND
DISRAELI AT GAD'S
HILL PLACE.

into Gladstone's Liberals, while Pitt's Tories changed into Disraeli's Conservatives. Easy, but wrong.

The party system as we know it solidified in Dickens' lifetime. Free and independent, and bribeable, MPs with "rotten borough" constituencies allotted them by great landlords yielded to party nominees controlled by party managers. The Reform Club was founded for pro-Reforming Whigs, and the Carlton for Tory loyalists. Disraeli initially hated this transition, despising party managers as unprincipled spin-doctors ("Tadpole and Taper"), and calling Conservatives, when he first heard the term, "Tory men with Whig measures". Yet Victoria's politicians made perpetual pragmatic U-turns. Peel quit Canning's Tory administration fulminating against Canning's adoption of Catholic emancipation and his wish to repeal protectionist corn duties; and then lost his Tory University seat for dropping his own opposition to emancipation, and split the Tories by repealing the Corn Laws himself. Lord John Russell fought for Catholic emancipation in opposition, and then as Prime Minister promoted anti-Catholicism with his Bill to stop the Pope appointing bishops in England. Disraeli blocked all Russell's attempts to extend the franchise, and then did it himself.

Nor were politicians consistent in their party affiliation. Palmerston, Aberdeen and Gladstone all entered Parliament as Tories, and all became leaders of the Whig or Liberal party. Disraeli called himself oxymoronically a Radical Tory at the beginning of his career, then, still with more sound-bites than solidity, denounced Radicalism as "pollution", overthrew Peel in a Tory revolt, and ended as the great icon of Conservatism.

William Lamb entered parliament as a Whig; served under the Tories Canning and Wellington; and reverted to being a Whig on inheriting the title Melbourne and taking his seat in the Lords. John Roebuck and Bulwer Lytton were Radicals in the 1830s, calling their faction "the Mountain" in defiant honour of the extreme French Revolutionaries. Both ended their lives as active Conservatives supporting Disraeli.

In this maelstrom of political inconsistency, Dickens' combination of self-proclaimed Radicalism with innate authoritarian conservatism seems less strange. The Radical principle he espoused unflinchingly was resistance to aristocratic pretensions. Lords had no innate right to rule. The landed gentry, and their beau ideal the Fine Old English Gentleman were fossilized admirers of a barbaric past. A belief in the Good Old Days was a belief in the rack and the stake and the block and the stocks and the gibbet. Touch your forelock to the squire today and his drunken son will break your windows tomorrow. In all this, Dickens was always consistent.

It should have followed that he supported the Reform Bill, giving power to the people. Parliamentary Reformers normally also supported Catholic, Nonconformist and Jewish emancipation. The disabilities imposed on non-Anglicans at the time included exclusion from Parliament and the Universities. Dickens however, disliked Lord Grey's manner and speeches, and Melbourne, Grey's successor as leader of the 1830–32 Reformers, was too much the traditional aristocrat he abhorred. As the Honourable William Lamb, Melbourne shared with the diehard Tory Duke of Wellington a scabrous starring role in courtesan Harriette Wilson's memoirs. Dickens did not admire the aristocrats' contempt for vulgar curiosity about their sex lives. He stood apart from all parties in the major political issue of his early adult life.

Personality muted his approach to the politics of emancipation, too. He and the Catholic Liberator Daniel O'Connell appealed to each other's sentimentality. O'Connell moved Dickens to tears with a speech, and himself broke down and threw the book from a train

window when he read the death of Little Nell. But Dickens disliked Catholicism's supernatural dogmas, monastic abnegation of the flesh and clerical tyranny. He loathed most dissent, making an exception of rational Unitarianism. And he was innately anti-Semitic.

He might have seemed Whiggish, for he hated the Political Economy of the Philosophical Radicals; followed Forster – a more doctrinaire Radical – in admiring Peel for scrapping the Corn Laws; and accepted Lord John Russell as the most consistent, and pro-literary, statesman of his day. But he could not follow Russell's Whig party line as this would involve endorsing Palmerston.

"The Twirling Weathercock", as Dickens called him, was really no more inconsistent than any other Victorian statesman. Continental conservatives dreaded him as a dangerous arch-Liberal. His proto-imperialist "gunboat diplomacy" had Dickens' wholehearted support when it authorized firm suppression of the Indian Mutiny or alliance with France against Russia. But Palmerston supremely exemplified hereditary Ruling Class skill with the traditional patron-fed bureaucracy. The Barnacles and the Circumlocution Office. Palmerston's private life, too, continued the aristocratic tradition of unabashed sexual freedom which Victoria and Albert and the middle classes wanted to stamp out. Dickens joined Roebuck and Layard's agitation for administrative reform when the Crimean War exposed aristocratic Civil Service incompetence. He never noticed that the war's greatest reforming success – Florence Nightingale's improvement of nursing – was deeply indebted to the administrative efforts of Sidney Herbert, a Barnacle of Barnacles from the old Ruling Class aristocracy.

He died finding both Gladstone and Disraeli acceptable dinner companions, while believing that he rejected their politics. Today we may feel that both implemented Dickensian demands, Disraeli improving living conditions and sanitation for the poor, while Gladstone struck at patronage and privilege in the public services.

MR GLADSTONE CARICATURED BY "APE" (PELLEGRINI), WORKING IN FRANCE AS "SINGE".

Riot AND Revolution

HIRTY-TWO YEARS before Dickens' birth, the night sky above London was lurid with the light from pillaged and burning houses and chapels. Citizens shut themselves in their houses, displayed blue ribands, and chalked "No Popery" on their doors, in the hope that the mob which raged almost unchecked for five nights would leave them alone. Finally the troops sent to end the anarchy killed over two hundred rioters and wounded as many more. Dickens' related to the Gordon Riots as an Englishman born in 1970 relates to the Blitz. He knew people who remembered the chaos; knew familiar places that were hard to imagine filled with flames and terror; knew that survivors reckoned it the worst thing to have happened to London since the Great Fire of 1666.

Twelve years after the Gordon Riots, and just twenty before Dickens' birth, political changes in France led to

MARIE-ANTOINETTE GUILLOTINED, OCTOBER 16, 1793.

instability of a kind western Europe had not seen since the worst days of witch-hunting. Committees of uneducated fanatics listened to the denunciations of spies and informers. Those denounced were given perfunctory trials, usually convicted, and sent to prisons to await allocation to the daily procession of farm carts taking victims to public execution. So many people were beheaded that a sinister new device came into use to expedite the slaughter. Dickens related to the Terror, as an Englishman born in 1960 relates to the Holocaust. The greatest political evil known in a modern civilized country had occurred within living memory. England had fought it. But guilt seemed to attach to humanity as a whole, not merely the perpetrators. If one nation's civilized beings, motivated by unrestrained political ideals, could behave like this, why should not another's?

Twenty-five years after Dickens' birth, a huge crowd assembled in St George's Fields to present a "monster petition" in favour of the People's Charter to Parliament. Which rejected it. Three years later, earnest and bookish William Lovett and Francis Place, principle draftsmen of the Charter, yielded control of the movement to the demagogic firebrand Feargus O'Connor. The Charter asked for six simple constitutional reforms: annual parliaments, equal-sized constituencies, no property qualification for parliamentary candidates, payment for members of parliament, universal manhood suffrage, and voting by secret ballot. All but the first two, not in themselves obnoxious, have now been granted. All should have been acceptable to Dickens but although he believed in significant extension of the franchise he never endorsed any of them. O'Connor's torchlit mass meetings alarmed him. The "Physical Force" Chartists threatening violence frightened him. The degeneration of some mass meetings into riots terrified him. And he wrote *Barnaby Rudge*.

O'Connor travelled the country preaching Chartism and organizing support groups. Dickens noted the similarity to Lord George Gordon's crackpot agitation against the Act of 1778, relieving Catholics of outdated prohibitions on their voting, holding public office, or inheriting landed property. Lord George had used the slogan "No Popery". O'Connor used the slogan, "Give us the Six Points". Lord George assembled intimidating crowds of uneducated men. So did O'Connor. Lord George amassed a threatening mob to support his presentation of their petition to Parliament. So did O'Connor. Lord George's Protestant Association was forwarded by mischief-making undercover conspirators. O'Connor's Chartists weren't, but Dickens didn't know this: like Disraeli and Mrs Gaskell, he feared that this was a resurgence of the crude revolutionary spirit which had led to the Cato Street conspiracy and occasional assassinations in the north. Lord George's failed petition had led to five days of terrifying riots. O'Connor's hadn't, but he was going to try again. *Barnaby Rudge* was an exciting, well-researched warning to the workers that populist movements were based on the lunatic ideologies of men who should know better. The People's Friend never deigned to meet the People's Spokesmen, Place and Lovett. He knew best. He told the people that risings meant failure and ruin, even if dilatory hesitation by the authorities let them do untold damage before they were suppressed.

But the French Revolution had succeeded. Dickens' 1850s landlord in Boulogne was a passionate Bonapartist, and Dickens, the friendly dining companion of Louis Napoleon during his exile, made no serious complaint against the first emperor, whose "whiff of grapeshot" had shown how determined authority might have put down the Revolution from the start. As the Lord Mayor and the militia and the magistrates should have put down the Gordon Riots before they got out of hand.

Moreover the French had grievances Dickens recognized as just. The aristocracy had treated the peasantry with contemptuous arrogance far outdistancing that which he detested in the English nobility. So he concentrated on the actions of the masses in *A Tale of Two Cities*. The storming of the Bastille was acceptable; the September Massacres of 1791 less so; the people's endorsement of the Reign of Terror, not at all. Political leadership never appears. There are no Girondins or Jacobins in the role of Lord George Gordon or Feargus O'Connor. Instead, the Jacquerie and the Defarges organize a conspiracy. "Jacques Three" is an inevitable agitator when he circulates the infamy of Monsieur le Marquis before Bastille day. He is an evil fanatic when he urges on the jury to convict in the Terror.

Again Dickens' account was well researched, with help from Carlyle. His main aim in *A Tale of Two Cities*, however, was the melodramatic love story. The course of events in the Revolution helped his plot: it was plausible that an *émigré* should return to Paris before decrees rendered emigration treason, and trapped him. But the politics determining such changes were unnecessary to the scheme, and would make an unhelpful distraction. So we hear nothing of the Assembly and the Tennis Court Oath and the flight to Varennes. Just the violence and horror as seen from the streets.

But this time, knowing that the Revolution had succeeded in establishing some valid principles, and that France had recovered, and above all, that the grievance was an arrogance he could recognize, unlike his own arrogant ignorance of Chartism, Dickens was able to offer a message more sympathetic to the violent masses. If any ruling class tramples the populace out of shape, deformed violence will be the result. Forget the demagogues' rallying cries. Beware the outcome of neglecting the poor.

THE GORDON RIOTS AS DEPICTED ON A CIGARETTE CARD.

LITTLE LORD RUSSEL IS PRESENTED WITH THE WORKING MAN'S CHARTER.

NOT SO *VERY* UNREASONABLE!!! EH?

THE Police

ICKENS WAS never more representative of his class and time than in his growing approval of the Metropolitan Police. They still were not formed until 1829, and remained deeply suspect for the next ten years. Englishmen feared political spies, like Fouché's notorious French police. But by 1838 Dickens expresses jocular contempt for the policeman who arrests Oliver: the last person on the scene, says Dickens, as is generally the case.

Until their disbandment a year later, the Bow Street Runners were more glamourous. They were the first detectives. In 1850, Dickens declared himself no "devout believer" in their memory, and suspected "a vast, amount of humbug about them". Blathers and Duff, the Runners called in to investigate the attempted robbery at Mrs Maylie's, prove that he had his doubts while the Runners still existed. Their correct, decision that it's an outside job by a London gang is vitiated by their concomitant incorrect decision that it must be the work of either Conkey Chickweed or "the Family Pet". Blathers' long story about Conkey supports Dickens' later contention that the Runners traded in mystery. His further contention that they were "far too much in the habit of consorting with thieves" shows his innocence about detective practice, though the implication that cultivating informants can lead to

corruption has, alas, been proved repeatedly.

The 1850 comments prefaced articles on "The Detective Force" in *Household Words*. All but two of the eight-year-old Detective Branch came to an informal interview over cigars and brandy-and-water, and Dickens gave fascinating pen pictures of them under barely disguised names: Inspector "Wield" (Field), and Sergeants "Dornton" (Thornton), "Witchem" (Whicher), "Mith" (Smith), "Fendall" (Kendall) and "Straw" (Shaw). He also met "Inspector Stalker" (Superintendent Walker of the Executive Branch) under the misapprehension that he, too, was a detective, which leaves one uncertain whether or not to praise Dickens' observation for remarking that one would never have known him as one!

Whicher, Field and Thornton reminisced about cases, in which they trailed suspects all over the country, examining the mails without actually opening them, and constantly pretending to be people they weren't. Gentlemanly liberals usually disapproved of such deceptions and infringements of liberty but Dickens was sure the police always harried the right quarry, and applauded their cunning. Field subsequently told Dickens three more stories, which may have tended to self-serving exaggeration. For example, he described the 1838 murder of prostitute Eliza Grimwood, saying he had labori-

The **TOWNS-END**.
Mr. Townsend, Police-Officer, Bow-Street.

ously traced, and cleared, a respectable man whose gloves were under her pillow. But the suspect in that unsolved case was Eliza's pimp, not any publicity-shy punter.

Dickens' best journalistic use of Field was a night "on duty" with him, and supporting constables and an Assistant Commissioner, visiting the worst criminal slums in the St Giles's rookery and Mint Street, Southwark, coming back by way of the Ratcliffe Highway and Whitechapel. As a finale, a sergeant waited near Baldwin's Gardens to show him that thieves' training school he had imaginatively immortalized as Fagin's den.

Outings like these contributed realism to *Bleak House* and *Our Mutual Friend*. Inspector Bucket is a portrait of Field, catching his affably domineering manner with layabouts; catching, too, that air of portentous mystery and easy familiarity with crooks which Dickens criticized in the Bow Street Runners! He knew that, like the Runners, Metropolitan plain clothes officers carried an identifying tipstaff: he calls it a "pocket-staff". He noticed the discomfort of the original uniforms, as the constable moving Jo on gives "a slight professional hitch of his neck involving its better settlement in his stiff stock". Those tall leather stocks were sheer torture to the old Peelers! And he has Bucket, in disguise, arrest Mr George with an affability that no doubt Field persuaded the distinguished writer was always his manner with "respectable" suspects! Bucket's rather obvious habit of innocently slipping his real questions into quite irrelevant lines of conversation suggests that Dickens the amateur conjuror felt the police used distractive patter like his own.

One can just, but only just, believe in Bucket's postponing Hortense's arrest because it will be icing on the cake if she leads him to the murder weapon. The deliberate wrongful arrest of Mr George to allay her suspicion is less plausible. Field must have murmured "If only…!" at Dickens' notion of a murderess lodging with a detective inspector to keep an eye on him, or the inspector's wife doing useful unpaid shadowing! One hopes he was horrified by Bucket's negotiating with blackmailers before recommending Sir Leicester Dedlock to pay them. These things are really bad policing.

Our Mutual Friend returns to the uniformed branch. Mr Night-Inspector in the docklands has a professional likeness to the detectives. He is imperturbable. He addresses his Reserve officer with authoritative benignity. And the habit of appearing under some guise to avoid unpleasantness is so ingrained that he persuades Mortimer and Eugene to pose as lime merchants when they go to arrest Hexam, though this is comically unnecessary once the snug door is shut on them.

All that is convincing. But Dickens also loves the deference policemen show to the middle class: even to Miss Abbey Potterson in her own realm. If you have status, "our policemen are wonderful". If you haven't, they'll control

you. Dickens is all in favour of their firm, authoritarian attitude to the lower orders. He doesn't blame them for "moving Jo on", causing his death and Esther's disfigurement. He wanted the Commissioner to discipline them severely when they warned the public of dangerous criminal "no-go" areas: it was their job to make places safe. The People's Friend rightly saw proper policing to maintain the peace as a huge blessing, but overlooked the curtailment of some of the People's Freedom that it entailed.

INSPECTOR BUCKET (RIGHT) MAKES HIMSELF AT HOME WITH THE BAGSHOTS BEFORE ARRESTING MR GEORGE (CENTRE).

Progress
AND Prosperity

ET THE GREAT WORLD spin for ever down the ringing grooves of change," wrote Tennyson. The bard was glorifying nineteenth century progress under the impression that trains ran in grooves! Dickens was a similarly ignorant adulator of the new technology but he was more cautious than Tennyson. When he didn't know, he covered his blankness with rhetorical fog. Engineering? Hugely important. Look at trains, "Away with a rush and a roar and a rattle!" Look at bridges above the earth and tunnels beneath! Look at beneficial innovations:

> ... an invention (involving a very curious secret process) of great importance to his country and his fellow creatures. I won't say how much money it cost him, or how many years of his life he had been about it, but he brought it to perfection a dozen years ago.

This is Daniel Doyce's great discovery. What is it? Dickens can't even imagine. In the "Poor Man's Tale of a Patent" he knows every exasperating step through the bureaucracy; every fee charged by some absurd entity like the Deputy Chaff-wax or the Deputy Clerk of the Hanaper. He understands, too, the Poor Man's pride of creation. But he hasn't a clue what he's made:

> I have been twenty year, off and on, completing an Invention and perfecting it. I perfected of it last Christmas Eve at ten o'clock at night. Me and my wife stood and let some tears fall over the Model, when it was done and I brought her in to take a look at it.

And that's all we ever learn about it. Blanks in Dickens' knowledge show up whenever he mentions engineering, although his brother Alfred was a competent civil engineer and his brother-in-law Henry Austin a very successful one. But Dickens has no idea what Edwin Drood will be doing in Egypt as an engineer. He was friendly with the greatest creative engineer of his day, I.K.Brunel. But in Daniel Doyce he describes the "quiet deliberate manner... which is often observable in mechanics who consider and adjust with great nicety," – a temperament utterly unlike Brunel's quarrelsome energetic obstinacy. Dickens can put before us an instantly recognizable lawyer, teacher, soldier, landed gentleman, or clerk, whether he approves of them as individuals or not. He is lost with the practical men he wanted his sons to imitate. He is the forerunner of those highly educated administrators C.P. Snow encountered who believed that the country needed more scientists, but didn't know the second law of thermodynamics and didn't think it mat-

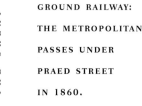

THE FIRST UNDER-
GROUND RAILWAY:
THE METROPOLITAN
PASSES UNDER
PRAED STREET
IN 1860.

tered! Dickens' uninterested ignorance of the technology he praises points the way to "the scientist' becoming one of the modern mystery-making "Medicine Men" whose influence he deplored.

He is ambivalent about the engineer as businessman. Doyce says, with a laugh, that "no inventor can be a man of business, you know," but makes clear that this is the opinion of businessmen. His books are in order and he seems competent. Yet he takes on Clennam to administer his affairs at the first opportunity, and Dickens doesn't seem to foresee the inventive capitalists, the Edisons and Fords and Nuffields, who would reap prosperity from technology.

But then, his own attitude to business was ambiguous. He had little more notion of what businessmen did than he had of engineers. Businessmen employed clerks and had desks and counting-houses. But what their clerks copied, what they wrote at their desks, what goods they made account of, were arcane mysteries. Dombey & Son deals "wholesale, retail and for exportation". Retailing and exporting what? Dickens has no idea. The *Son and Heir* is bound for Barbados. So it must be picking up sugar or rum, the sole exportable products of that island. But nothing suggests that Dickens knows this, or knows what it carries outward bound or where and how it will dispose of its cargo. Chicksey, Veneering and Stobbles is a "drug-house", appropriately situated in Mincing Lane where, indeed, great commodity brokers had offices and warehouses, close to the Customs Office. Rumty Wilfer has a stool in the counting-house. Mr Veneering has made the place handsome with mahogany and plate-glass since taking it over. And that is absolutely all Dickens knows about the business which has popped Mr Veneering into society with success and will drop him out with failure.

Like Rumty, Dickens was the son of a clerk in the public service and like many public servants and the traditional governing classes and professions, Dickens mistrusted "trade". In *Nickleby* it is either a swindle run by Ralph Nickleby, or greedy extortion in the hands of Squeers. "Never postpone business," says Squeers sen-

tentiously to his pupil, and receives ironical correction in the child's faltering "Never – perform – business." Part of Dickens always felt with Lenin that "buying cheap and selling dear" was despicable, and would have warmed to that inability to justify taking a profit that made Harry Truman a business failure. As for Shares – they were spec-u-la-tion: mere gambling! And 'Change, that centre of Victorian growth and respectability, was the unsavoury hang-out of Quilp!

Still, *Dombey and Son* moved on from the supposition that businessmen were all Montague Tiggs or Anthony Chuzzlewits or Scrooges. Business ethics caught Dickens' attention as he observed Mr Dombey's pride "showing well" in paying his creditors in full rather than escaping into "a composition with his creditors".

His own determination to make the maximum profit from his own work, and not see the lions' share go to his publishers, revealed a man who was starting to share Squeers' awareness of the account book lying behind the performance. And insofar as "businesslike" meant "tidy-minded and responsible" it appealed to his deepest middle-class instincts.

High finance was never forgiven. Mr Merdle leads the country in pursuit of paper wealth and swindles it. Dickens never seems to have understood investment as the means of financing production, and would have agreed with Keynes that the principle of the casino was the wrong way of going about it anyway. His vision of progress to prosperity was that of the hard-working, honest entrepreneur with vision and persistence working his way to the top. It became one of the most valuable legends of capitalism when the Enemy of the Oppression objected to profiteering or exploitation or swindling.

ROWLANDSON AND PUGIN: THE STOCK EXCHANGE

THE
Anti-intellectual

ARWIN'S *Descent of Man* was published just after Dickens' death, climaxing the debate over evolution and creation which was the most important philosophical question engaging Victorian intellectuals. Even before *The Origin of Species* (1859), Robert Chambers' *Vestiges of Creation* suggested that man might yet evolve further: an idea which interested general readers. G.H. Lewes, a journalist who specialized in expounding these problems to a wide audience, performed with Dickens' "splendid strollers". He could certainly have laid out for Dickens the philosophical debates of the day. *Household Words* and *All the Year Round* seemed made for such popular exposition. But Dickens was not especially interested. The expert on species he habitually mentioned, if his work required obeisance to such an intellectual, was Professor Owen: a relatively uncontroversial anatomist best remembered now for getting the Natural History Museum established.

Owen, like the geologist Lyell, was Dickens' occasional dinner guest. Geology proved that the world was far older than the 6000 years or so indicated by Archbishop Usher's calculation of Old Testament generations. The fossil record showed that huge and unimaginable dinosaurs once roamed the earth. Dickens decided that saurian times were muddy; imagined a

megalosaurus on Holborn Hill on an inclement day; and gave little further thought to Professor Lyell's difficulties with Biblical literalist theologians. One notable geologist found a place in his fiction: Professor Dingo – of European reputation! – who rendered himself objectionable in the North of Devon by chipping fragments off people's houses with his geological hammer, and under the same "ruling passion" for "the Temple of Science" passed away in a state of intellectual dementia, trying to chip fragments off the faces of his attendants!

Dickens' contempt for scientists was unconcealed at the outset of his career, when he had no Athenaeum-weight status of his own to conserve. The "scientific gentleman" in *Pickwick* is a farcical fool lacking even the misplaced intelligence of a modern comedy's mad scientist or back-room boffin. The astrologer in Dickens' pretty unfunny farce *The Lamplighter* is close kin, and his son's facetious forenames "Galileo Isaac Newton Flamstead" show that Dickens saw little difference between superstition and knowledge, and flaunted his ignorance!

In later life he would express respect for Faraday. But like most middlebrow contemporaries, he was not so much admiring of the great physicist's discoveries in electrolysis and electrodynamics as of the prince of analytical chemists. He proved to the Parliamentary Commission on Truck Shops – company stores where workers were compelled to take wages in kind – that Truck bread was adulterated with china clay. Analytical chemistry could detect the chalk in watered milk. It was as good as a conjuring trick and as acute as Mr Veneering's socially percipient butler! Let Dickens confront a piece of pseudo-science like phrenology, or human spontaneous combustion, or the "animal magnetism" explanation of hypnotism, and he would probably plump for the wrong side. He was mightily angry with better-informed people who challenged his ill-sourced evidence for spontaneous combustion.

Perhaps Dickens' mind was more taken up with the social than the physical sciences? Not a bit of it. He joined the semi-educated generality in howling them down. "Political Economy" was the forerunner of modern economics. But it was detested as "the Dismal Science": partly because the classical economists thought that any ameliorating interference with the free market in hard times would make distress worse, which seemed to prohibit charity; and partly because Malthus's Principles of Population demonstrated on statistical and economic grounds that people must inevitably outgrow resources, and so humanity would starve to death unless the poor stopped having babies. Dickens' generation found this shocking and funny at the same time. Dickens coarsely described Kate as "conducting an anti-Malthusian experiment" when she was pregnant. And his general distaste for political economy and its popular explicators like Harriet Martineau led him to satirize the philosophical radicals and theorizing philanthropists who were his natural allies against reactionary oppression. Inexorable reality itself oppressed humanity, some intellectuals felt, only Dickens thought he could make it go away by shouting at it!

Shouting at problems was rather the philosophy of Carlyle, whom Dickens respected more than any other contemporary. Son of a stonemason; beneficiary of Scottish education rather than snobbish Oxbridge; familiar with, though critical of, rigorous German philosophy as well as the classics, Carlyle was really a moralist drawing lessons from history and not an original

philosopher. Yet this made him more accessible than the scientists or the Benthamites. His humble background made him a declared radical. His belief in heroic personalities determining events was hugely attractive to the creator of fairy godfathers and active heroes. Like Dickens he would have been a natural Bonapartist had he been French. But he despised mere entertainment and both men would have been flabbergasted to learn how far Boz's reputation outweighs the Sage of Ecclefechan's today.

But not as an intellectual. Even in "Fancy", which he so often opposed to the dead hand of Gradgrind Utilitarianism, Dickens' discrimination could be abysmal. His musical delight was playing Home Sweet Home on the accordion. Mr Morfin of Dombey's cello playing in amateur quartets is almost an eccentricity; his whistling accurately through "Beethoven's Sonata in B" reduces the highbrow to farce. And in his own literary sphere, Dickens uttered misplaced private criticism of Hawthorne's characterization in *The Scarlet Letter*, while thoroughly enjoying and even borrowing from the semi-pornographic pseudo-social novels of Eugène Sue and Paul de Kock.

DUMMY BOOKS, MOCKING INTELLECTUAL PRETENSIONS, INSTALLED AT GAD'S HILL PLACE.

THE ANTI-INTELLECTUAL

Religion

THE OLD CHURCH AT
LEIGH: THE KIND OF
RURAL CHURCH
DICKENS IDEALIZED.

N THE MIDDLE of his career, Dickens developed the odious habit of breaking into capitals whenever he invoked the name of GOD. This lends a feeling of canting religiosity to any passage calling on GOD, and contrasts unfavourably with his casually irreligious curse, "may God reward the worthy gentlemen" who wish to keep the dwellings of the poor miserable. (*Dombey and Son*)

It is surprising that Mrs Nickleby's creator succumbed to orthographic humility. She is gloriously unchurchy as she rattles on about Devon, the place where "frogs used to get into the rushlight shades when one stopped all night, and sit up and look through the little holes like Christians." And the effect is repeated in *Barnaby Rudge* when Mr Parkes says the wind is "howling like a Christian".

Christians who howled were likely to be Methodists (who actually groaned). Dickens first attacked them in "The Bloomsbury Christening" by describing Nicodemus Dumps' misanthropical donations to, "two itinerant Methodist parsons, in the amiable hope that, if circumstances rendered any people happy in this world, they might perchance be rendered miserable by fears for the next." Gloomy evangelicalism was something Dickens always hated, and he ceased to find it funny when he considered the effect of upbringing by a Miss Barbary or a Mrs Clennam on children. George Eliot, whose agnostic commitment to Duty could make her as forbidding as any preacher, concurred, in *Silas Marner*, that the unforgiving joylessness of urban nonconformity was horrible. Yet in recalling her own Methodist aunt

when writing *Adam Bede*, she created the wholly sympathetic lay preacher Dinah Morris, and showed an understanding of working class religion far beyond the grasp of the Friend of the Poor. Dickens, like Dr Johnson, would not take a woman's preaching seriously.

Extempore prayer and preaching was, in fact, a nonconformist habit Dickens disliked. Every nonconformist with a sense of humour must forgive him with tears of joy on reading Chadband's hilarious homilies:

> *If the master of this house was to go forth into the city*
> *and there see an eel, and was to come back, and was to*
> *call untoe him the mistress of this house, and was to say,*
> *'Sarah, rejoice with me, for I have seen an elephant!'*
> *would that be Terewth?*

I am irresistibly reminded of a preacher of my childhood, who lugubriously vetoed "The lerve of lahfe", always preferring "The Lahfe of Lerve". Dickens, who thought the Love of Life central to spirituality, would have damned him as a humbug. For he quickly slipped into the lazy assumption that Dissenters are hypocrites. Stiggins turns up drunk to address the Brick Lane Grand Junction Temperance Society. The genteel would-be cook at the employment agency (*Nicholas Nickleby*) turns down a post on hearing that the Wrymug family is "Serious" until she learns that there are three "Serious" footmen, and the Cook will be expected to accompany one of them to Little Bethel Congregation every Sunday. Whereupon, it is clear, she will affect religiosity in the hope of catching a husband. Quilp sits, a pious fraud, among the congregation at Mrs

Nubbles' Little Bethel. Chadband, like nearly all Dickens' nonconformist ministers, is principally interested in squeezing food and drink out of his, largely female, admirers.

But what really annoyed Dickens about nonconformity was that, like Catholicism, it took its theology and public observances seriously. Nonconformists were "born again," and like Tony Weller, Dickens longed to put them out to severe nurses. They pledged total abstinence from liquor, which affronted those who could enjoy it in moderation. Some of them preached non-violence on religious grounds, and Gabriel Varden had observed, "Shouldn't I be a nice sort of Christian if I crept into a corner of my own chimney, and looked on while a parcel of whiskered savages bore off Dolly?" Dickens' ideal layman was Captain Cuttle, wrong in all his citations of the Bible and catechism, but believing in them; privately reading the burial service for Walter Gay; attending an unpretentious church which flies the Union Jack. The nonconformist objection that people like Cuttle couldn't understand their ritual prayers merely annoyed Dickens, who felt the traditional beauty of liturgical language and made himself believe, against all the odds, that dying Jo would appreciate the beauty of the Lord's Prayer on hearing it for the first time.

Not that Dickens was a churchgoing formalist. The Church of England annoyed him when it indulged in theological disputes. He knew gloomy city churches as the haunts of beadles and tip-hunting pew-openers. He found Mrs Milvey's mild proselytising tendency inferior to her husband's tolerance of other faiths. For a short period he attended a Unitarian church, whose pastor echoed his own non-dogmatic social beliefs.

Which were, as he constantly said, simple New Testament Christianity. Meaning Gospel Christianity. St Paul's subtleties, let alone the barmy Revelations granted St John the Divine, meant little to him, though he agreed that "the letter killeth but the spirit giveth life". And the spirit lay in Jesus. It was, to Dickens, obvious, and he explained it in the *Life of Christ* he wrote for his children. This was so untheological that his Catholic

admirer G.K. Chesterton despised it. But it was not, in fact, Unitarian, Dickens did not think Jesus was just the best man who ever lived. He believed in the miracles: he himself would undoubtedly have cured any sick sufferer if he had the power. And he believed in the Resurrection. For belief in an afterlife was evidently real to him, and we should take him at his repeated word, and accept that he thought angels gathered to "fall upon the people's necks, and kiss them tenderly" as they died ("A Child's Dream of a Star"). He wondered, briefly, when looking at the idol on a Chinese junk in Greenwich, whether Christianity might not have frozen in outdated beliefs like the Chinese, but shook off the doubt with the reflection that Christianity was the historically progressive faith. He came to accept Canon Crisparkle's hearty, muscular Christianity as an ideal.

So was Dickens content with goodwill and daily swimming and shadow-boxing? Was he really a religious man? Committed theologians, dedicated atheists and agnostics, usually feel he wasn't. But he urged his children to pray when they left home, saying he did so himself night and morning, and had never imposed this on them. And in his will he urged them, again, to "guide themselves by the teaching of the New Testament in its broad spirit," after committing his soul "to the mercy of God through our Lord and Saviour Jesus Christ". Why doubt his and many other Victorians' sincerity?

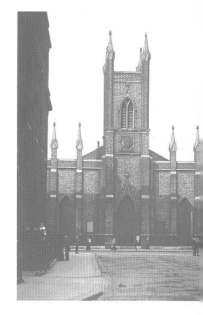

SEYMOUR STREET
CHURCH: THE KIND
OF CITY CHURCH
HE DISLIKED.

MR CHADBAND
PREACHES AT JO.

Race
AND Jews

BLACK AND BROWN RESIDENTS in Dickens' London were so rare that they can almost be identified individually to this day. Likewise Major Bagstock's dusky servant is the unique Hindu in Dickens; an exotic trophy of the Indian adventure most Englishmen thought silly until 1857.

Up to his visit to America, Dickens' view of black men hovered between the Trusty Black "Quanko Samba" in the West Indies (*Pickwick Papers*), and the kneeling slave in chains over the famous Anti-Slavery Society slogan "I am a Man and a Brother". Both views were patronizing.

In America, Dickens encountered black people for the first time, and didn't much like them. Though unlike Thackeray he retained his hatred of slavery, he made no

friends of black freemen. The hypocritical Sing Sing prisoner he most disliked was black. And Dickens' self-reported success in flooring every pro-slavery remark put to him seems too good to be true. One wonders whether he really did say he would never trust the Bible again if it supported slavery?

Likewise, one wonders whether he really felt that a dignified Indian chief was the only true gentleman he met in the prairieland of chaw tobacco and spittoons. If so, the impression did not last, for he was soon describing Indians as painted savages with tomahawks. His essay "The Noble Savage" was unabashed Eurocentric racism. While he may have disliked Rousseau-esque cant about simple primitives, he goes far beyond correcting this in his contempt for African kings and Ojibway Indians. His view of a touring party of the latter as an exotic freak show missed the scientific interest of the Anthropological Society that brought them over. Fortunately Dickens was unaware that the tour's organizer was the intellectual anatomist Dr Knox who had been drummed out of Edinburgh for buying the bodies murdered by Burke and Hare. He would surely have made hay of this fact had he known it!

Once chattel slavery was over, Dickens, like Carlyle, seems to have regarded the black man as "Quashee" the sub-human labourer, who should be forced back to work with the whip if he chose to enjoy his freedom in idleness. When Paul Bogle led a rising of poor black labourers in Jamaica which killed a tyrannical magistrate and several planters, and Governor Eyre put it down with military severity amounting to a massacre, Dickens joined Kingsley in supporting the governor and opposing

the outcry from those Englishmen who knew that Eyre had seized the opportunity to hang a mulatto political opponent. But Bogle and the politician Gordon were Baptists. Their cause was taken up by Exeter Hall, the headquarters of progressive nonconformity. And Exeter Hall lay behind Mrs Jellyby's "telescopic philanthropy", sending useless missions to "Borioboola-Gha", in itself an extension of "sending flannel waistcoats to the little niggers" who, as Tony Weller said, didn't want 'em.

The highly visible racial minority of Dickens' England was the Jewish community. We have seen that "Jews" were listed with "chalk and shrimps" among the principle products of the Medway towns on the Pickwickians visit. The anti-Semitic note was probably quite invisible to young Mr Dickens, who would indignantly say that soldiers, sailors and officers were also catalogued.

The creation of Fagin, too, seemed justified by the fact that London's genuine controller of boy thieves was Jewish. Dickens went so far as to attach his name (Barney) to Fagin's ally at The Three Cripples. It never troubles Dickens that giving Barney an exaggerated nasal accent – "Hush! Stradegers id the next roob," – and having Fagin repeatedly use the insinuating tag "my dear", when addressing men, not to mention calling Fagin "the Jew", "the Jew", "the old Jew" over and over again, could grate on people. But Dickens cannot plead ignorance that the word "Jew" easily took on an opprobrious overtone. For when good Jews come to pray with Fagin in his cell, and he drives them away, they are described as "Venerable men of his own persuasion…" These are the only actively good Jews Dickens created before Riah in *Our Mutual Friend*, and the only ones who weren't introduced as vulgarian local colour or bailiffs' men.

He was disingenuous in assuring Mrs Eliza Davis, the Jewish lady whose husband bought Tavistock House from him, that Fagin was historically accurate as representative of his race and not his religion, and Jews were unduly touchy if they felt affronted. But then, Mrs Davis had no idea that in private he called her husband "a Jew money-lender"! It could be complained that Dickens, as reporter of Bishop and Head's trial, knew that

an honest Jewish clothes dealer from Fagin's Field Lane ran all the way from his home to the court because he could not take a cab on the Sabbath but would not fail in his civic duty to testify against the murderers who bought smock-frocks from him.

Riah was created to placate the ill-feeling Mrs Davis reported. A saintly old man with beard, gown and staff like a prophet, talking archaic theatrical English, and unwillingly fronting for a nasty young Gentile bill-broker into whose clutches he has fallen: this was a peculiar figure to make amends to assimilated ladies and gentlemen who spoke good standard English, and who, if they were financiers called Rothschild or Henriques or Mocatta or Montefiore or Quintana, would not be very impressed by the gentility of dapper little Mr Dickens! The Jewish journals of opinion, *The Voice of Israel* and *The Voice of Jacob*, printed a good deal of correspondence arguing whether or not Jews should lend money, given the obloquy brought on the race by Christians' insistence that they become the official usurers of Europe. Moneylenders defending their trade often signed themselves "Riah", which was not quite what Dickens intended!

Dickens was, in fact, a standard unthinking Victorian, loosely assuming his own ethnic superiority, just as Disraeli defiantly trumpeted his. Pseudo-scientific ethnic evaluation was in its infancy. Its English proponent, Alexander Walker, had some influence on the intellectual Darwin; none on the anti-intellectual Dickens. Had either man lived to see racial inferiority enshrined in laws and prohibitions, they would have objected as Dickens did to slavery. He was racist, like almost all his contemporaries. But neither he, nor even Carlyle, prophet of the füehrer-prinzip, were proto-fascists, any more than the unthinkingly anti-Semitic D.H.Lawrence or T.S.Eliot were complicit in genocide.

COPE'S CIGARETTES

FAGIN

A CIGARETTE CARD VERSION OF FAGIN.

England, Home AND Beauty

E.F. SAVILLE IN A
TYPICAL POPULAR
THEATRE PATRIOTIC
THRILLER ROLE, AS
"UNION JACK".

S OMETHING REMAINED WITH DICKENS from his childhood aversion to the "Radical banditti". Of course as an adult he endorsed Radical contempt for the Prince Regent and didn't think the salaries drawn by the Barnacles were money well spent. But he never wanted

the army and navy abolished. Quite the reverse, like Gerard Manley Hopkins he was inclined, seeing a soldier, to love him, and to love our sailors and our tars. Not the middle-aged officer-class of his youth: the duelling Dr Slammers and boastful Major Bagstocks. The late Captain Swosser RN is mere comic matter in the mouths of the Bayham Badgers. But officers of the younger generation like Lt Tartar are warmly admired. Private soldiers and NCOs like Mr George and Mr Bagnet are praised so highly that one rather questions Kipling's reputation for rescuing Tommy Atkins single-handed from universal contumely as "the licentious soldiery". Dickens particularly respects pensioners, especially when they are visibly battle-scarred. The one-armed Greenwich pensioner who marries Mrs Mitts (with a one-legged Chelsea pensioner as best man) and takes her out of "Titbull's Alms-Houses" brings the Uncommercial Traveller as close to the world of *Cranford* as Dickens would ever come. Old "Gruff and Glum", the pensioner pegging away on his two wooden legs "as if he were scoring furiously at cribbage", becomes the splendid solo chorus to Bella Wilfer's wedding in Greenwich, and rounds it off admirably with a salute and "the gallantry of a man-of-wars-man and a heart of oak".

Patriotic pro-militarism could outweigh political ideals. Dickens never questioned the justice of the American Revolution. He admired Washington as he did not admire George III. But there is nothing grudging in his respect for Joe Willett when he returns, matured and short of an arm, from "the defence of the Salwanners, in America where the war is". Joe has been maimed in the service of King and Country, which makes him a brave man with good cause, no matter how bad the King's policy.

N.º 44   *London Pub by REDINGTON, 208, Hoxton, Old Town.*

Mr E.F. SAVILLE, AS UNION JACK.

Dickens might well have echoed Carl Schurtz's excellent corollary to Stephen Decatur's "Our country, right or wrong!" – "When right, to be kept right; when wrong, to be put right!" But put right by those educated to do it. Much as the abuse of the private soldier in the Crimean war offended him, he could feel without irony his friend Tennyson's restriction on the power of the rankers sent to their death in the Charge of the Light Brigade: "Theirs not to reason why. Theirs but to do or die."

The troopers were the heroes. Stay-at-home educated civilians like Dickens and his friends would do the reasoning for them, and try to see that politicians less brittle than Aberdeen and Palmerston appointed commanders less bone-headed than Lucan and Cardigan in future.

Patriotism even spread to religious ideals, as we have seen. Captain Cuttle seems only to have commanded a "dirty British coaster", though his lost hand hints at Royal Naval service. However that may be, he "was punctual in his attendance at a church in his own neighbourhood which hoisted the Union Jack every Sunday morning". and the church is the better for the Union Jack as the Captain is the better for the church-going. Still, the Captain's devotion, like his church's patriotism, is discreet and decent. He doesn't travel out of his way in search of exotic nonconformity. His church doesn't parade its loyalty every day of the week. And Dickens, too, rations his purple patriotic effusions, and seasons them so tartly with criticisms of Britannia, that they are easily missed. We shouldn't forget that they are there, and that he could not have won his immense popularity and retained it throughout the High Imperial period had he been incapable of occasional silly flag-waving, as in *Little Dorrit*:

In truth, no men on earth can cheer like Englishmen, who do so rally one another's blood and spirit when they cheer in earnest, that the stir is like the rush of their whole history, with all its standards waving at once, from Saxon Alfred's downward.

Yet there is an opposite tendency, too, in later Dickens. Mr Sapsea explicitly represents the provincial Tory jack-

ass. His patriotic toasts are anti-French relics from the Napoleonic wars. As an auctioneer, he thinks he knows the world without having seen it:

If I have not gone to foreign countries, young man, foreign countries have come to me. I see a French clock. I never saw him before, in my life, but I instantly lay my finger on him and say 'Paris!'

And no doubt he thinks of Paris as did that London Common Counsellor who offended Dickens in 1850 with the bland assertion "that the French are a frog-eating people who wear wooden shoes".

For Dickens, after spending summers in France, knew that the supposedly inferior foreigners did some things better than the British. They put abattoirs outside city bounds, instead of having a stinking blood- and dung-filled cattle market like Smithfield ("A Monument of French Folly"). London was shabby, "as compared with Paris, Bordeaux, Frankfurt, Milan, Geneva – almost any important town on the continent of Europe," and, "the mass of the London population have a secondhand look which is not to be detected on the mass of the Parisian population." ("The Boiled Beef of New England"). The general gloom of London derives from "the national dread of colour". (*Our Mutual Friend*)

All this anticipates the counter-tendency at the heart of High Imperialism to jeer at English insularity, English complacency and Englishness in general. Wilde and Shaw were key representatives. But it found its place, too, in Arnold Bennett and even occasionally in the arch-imperialist Kipling. Dickens was, as ever, a weathercock of changing cultural patterns, holding to the would-be Johnsonian patriotism that underlay late Victorian Imperialism, but leavening it with his old social satire and new hints that England might gain from more cosmopolitan tastes.

POTTERY FIGURES OF JOE WILLETT BIDDING DOLLY VARDEN FAREWELL BEFORE LEAVING FOR THE WAR IN AMERICA.

Prudery
AND Priopriety

NGLISH PRUDERY WAS NOTORIOUS before Victoria came to the throne. Goethe complained of it. But it visibly increased after her marriage to Albert, and became a straitjacket against which there was some reaction. In this, as in so many other respects, Dickens moved easily with his society, giving an admirable display of the general tendencies.

There might have seemed reason for censorship by the 1820s. Gillray's influential cartoons had made fairly gross depictions of statesmen's natural functions. Rowlandson's caricatures of social grotesques coexisted with direct erotica. However pretty the buxom maids he depicted in all their naked glory, his orgiastic scenes would have been considered indecent (if enjoyable) by Charles II and Rochester. And those witty rakes would have found no humour in the literary equivalents: the scatological "satires" produced by the Wych Street (Aldwych) publishers. These cheap booklets told quite filthy stories about the supposed doings of the Prince Regent's raffish circle, Fox and Sheridan and the rest. Clods of excrement held in the breeches of famous names were supposed to be extremely funny; showers of urine lacked the specious elegance Rowlandson cast over them in some of his drawings. Dickens seems to have known these distasteful productions, since he used

SUSAN NIPPER, AN EXAMPLE OF A STRONG AND DECOROUS DICKENS FEMALE CHARACTER.

the title of one of them – "The Golden Dustman" – as Noddy Boffin's nickname. And Boffin's wealth derives from mounds of literal filth.

Nobody who remembered such books ever wanted them back. Some of the praise Dickens received for avoiding indecency was well deserved when it is remembered that his earliest forte was extravagant, slapstick caricature, and his immediate predecessors in the form had been simply disgusting. What a relief to extract farce from the opposite extreme of squeamishness, as Mr Watkins Tottle is enraptured by Miss Lillerton's propriety in leaving the room when a gentleman dares to mention a flannel petticoat! Dickens is gloriously – and inoffensively – funny with Mr Mantalini's lascivious mind, as he swears never to arouse his wife's jealousy, "Not for twenty thousand hemispheres populated with-with-with little ballet-dancers!" (*Nicholas Nickleby*) It is delightful to hear Fanny Squeers' crude father rescue her from the embarrassment into which linguistic prudery plunges her:

"This … deceitfulness …, lowness …, falseness …, made
me blush for my – for my –".
"Gender," suggested Mr Squeers.

This is funnier for us than it was for Dickens' audience, because the word "sex" really did mean "gender" to them, and only suggested copulation if used in some compound phrase like "sex organs". But with this family, Dickens allowed himself mild double entendre: Squeers responds to Snawley's sententious invocation of Nature as a holy thing with:

"I believe you … I should like to know how we should ever get on without her … Oh what a blessed thing, sir, to be in a state of natur!"

There is one more double entendre before Propriety Closes Down. And it reveals Propriety breathing very hard indeed as Dickens makes heavy weather of Mr Willet calling his servants "whores" in *Barnaby Rudge*:

Mr. Willet, in his consternation, uttered but one word, and called that up the stairs in a stentorian voice six distinct times. But as this word was a monosyllable, which, however inoffensive when applied to the quadruped it denotes, is highly reprehensible when used in connection with females of unimpeachable character, many persons were inclined to believe that the young women laboured under some hallucination caused by excessive fear; and that their ears deceived them.

EXPRESSING INEXPRESSIBLES

We are entering the decades in which Dickens abandoned the word "breeches" except for the lowest classes. Gentlemen wear smallclothes, smalls or shorts. He completely gave up "trowsers", except to clothe the humblest labourers. Respectable folk wore "inexpressibles". Dickens does not go so far as to clothe furniture legs, and, indeed, I know of no contemporary evidence that this was ever done, unless in the decorative spirit that added bows to picture frames. In fact he enjoys an English laugh at American prudery, avoiding the hackneyed insistence on carving "turkey bosom" which Captain Marryatt ascribed to American ladies, and American writers ascribed to genteel freed slaves. "The naked eye" is the phrase with which Martin Chuzzlewit offends a New World bluestocking.

In some ways excessive delicacy suited Dickens who was, as we have seen, extremely fastidious. There is a certain charm in his indicating Susan Toots' (née Nipper's) pregnancy, through her bashful husband's concern that she should not frighten or exert herself

(*Dombey and Son*). But by the end of his life the intelligentsia were turning against the exaggerated code of propriety, and without becoming improper, Dickens turned too. Gentlemen wore trowsers or pantaloons once more. Mr Podsnap's pompous concern that nothing should be allowed which might bring a blush to the cheek of a young person was offensive to his creator, who had only been able to hint in the most distant way that Miss Wade's attraction to Tattycoram might be lesbian.

We simply don't know the exact nature of Dickens' relations with Ellen Ternan, though we know that one observer felt that he crudely flaunted his accompanying a young lady to whom he was not married when crossing the Channel. We know that he generally kept her out of sight while he lived, producing her suddenly as the first legatee in his will. We know, too, that his friendship with Wilkie Collins did not entail disapproval of the man's Bohemian life, any more than his pre-Albertian offer to show Maclise prostitutes in Margate had done. His salvation of Eugene Wrayburn is a new approach to the would-be seducer, who had to expiate his offence by death when he was Sir Mulberry Hawk. Though he would never have forfeited popularity by charting dangerous waters, as Hardy did in *Jude the Obscure*, Dickens floated in a cultural current whose extreme avant-garde subsequently risked Aubrey Beardsley's art, only to race back into the cupboard with Oscar Wilde's débâcle.

ROWLAND'S DRAWING OF DR SYNTAX INNOCENTLY VENTURING INTO A BROTHEL IS MILD COMPARED TO THE CRUDE CARICATURES OF NAKED AND URINATING WOMEN HE SOLD UNDER THE COUNTER.

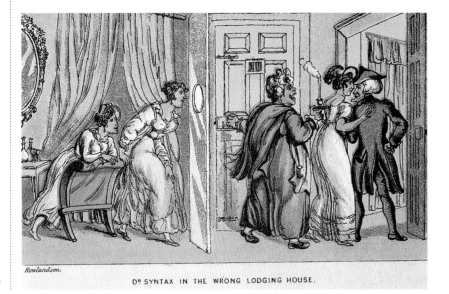

DR SYNTAX IN THE WRONG LODGING HOUSE.

Good Cheer

BOB CRATCHIT TRIES TO WARM HIMSELF AT A CANDLE.

IN SO MANY WAYS DICKENS was Victorian. What do we mean when we call the Victorians Dickensian?

The Enemy of Meanness and Oppression would have been saddened that the adjective is commonly attached to wretched social conditions and grim institutions that he wanted to reform away. Only the great gloomy single-celled prisons of the late nineteenth century stand as "Dickensian" memorials to his having "struck a blow". And although we overcrowd them scandalously, he would have made them even more "Dickensian". For it was with regret that he abandoned corporal punishment. He would have used the whip on criminals with the greatest of pleasure, but for its abominable tendency to spread. Whipping lunatics and children, he perceived, was a worse evil than not whipping convicts. So to save the children, villains must be spared. He regarded fines as medieval punishment that should be done away with like trial by combat. Incarceration with hard labour and a strict bread and water diet was his preferred regimen. All our prisoners today would be overfed, over-entertained, underworked "pet prisoners" in his view.

But readers who love Dickens will feel instantly that it is wrong to link him to iron bars, stone walls, and harsh discipline! The pleasure of Dickens is the celebration of life and laughter. His emblem is the cornucopia, not the restricted dietary. He shares with Shakespeare and Chaucer that immense range that led Dryden to say "Here is God's plenty!" Like his great predecessors, he risked over-ambition in being so plentiful. Shakespeare tried to fill the two-hour traffic of the stage with all

human life talking the highest blank verse and the lowest prose in situations where words alone had to conjure up any setting from bloody battlefields to ships at sea. Not surprisingly, some people, especially formal classical French critics, thought he failed. Not surprisingly his impassioned admirer, Dickens, who carried his works with him on all his travels and took great pride in living on

the hill where Falstaff conjured up men in buckram, has struck tidy-minded formalist critics as a clumsy failure, especially as compared with, say, Jane Austen.

Dickensians can't dispute the unwieldiness of the long serial novel or the unevenness of the Inimitable's creation. But they can dip into God's plenty, as in *A Christmas Carol*:

> *In came a fiddle with a music-book, and went up to the lofty desk, and made an orchestra of it, and tuned like fifty stomach aches. In came Mrs Fezziwig, one vast substantial smile. In came the three Miss Fezziwigs, beaming and lovable. In came the six young followers whose hearts they broke. In came all the young men and women employed in the business. In came the housemaid, with her cousin the baker. In came the cook, with her brother's particular friend the milkman. In came the boy from over the way, who was suspected of not having board enough from his master; trying to hide himself behind the girl from the next door but one, who was proved to have had her ears pulled by her mistress. In they all came, one after another; some shyly, some boldly, some gracefully, some awkwardly, some pushing, some pulling; in they all came, any how and every how.*

The rhythm of this prose congeries sweeps the reader forward. The repeated "In came …" phrases prepare the way for the old fashioned country dance which is about to follow, with each couple performing the figure at the top and skipping down the line to make way for the next couple repeating it after them. The writing encourages us to join in.

Dickens' good humour makes us join in things that could be sad: "The clerk in the tank applauded. Becoming immediately sensible of the impropriety, he poked the fire, and extinguished the last frail spark for ever." There's nothing very funny about a cold clerk in a small room accidentally putting out his tiny fire. But Dickens has made us complicit in "enjoying" Bob Cratchit's plight. He told us previously that the room is "a dismal little cell … a sort of tank". Now, in a characteristic jump, the odd

hyperbole of the tank goes beyond the metaphor of the cell and swallows up the original room. Which becomes a tank, just as Johnny Tetterby's baby brother, exhausting his time and energy becomes the infant Moloch to whom he is sacrificed, and Veneering's butler becomes the Analytical Chemist before he is himself swallowed up in yet another Dickensian trick, his epithet consuming its substantive, so that "the Chemist" becomes "the Analytical". And again, Dickens has made us complicit with him in sharing a secret: that "the Analytical" is Veneering's… butler, as "the Inexhaustible" is Bella Wilfer's baby. Dickens hugged his friends to him to share his enjoyment of the snuff-box his old schoolmaster William Davis gave him, inscribed to "The Inimitable Boz". By calling himself impersonally "The Inimitable", Dickens accepted the compliment but took off the curse of boasting or patronage.

The Inimitable is a founding father of Victorian and literary fun and gaiety. Could Gilbert have been as funny if Dickens hadn't mixed wild fantasy with social observation? Could Sherlock Holmes always have solved the case if The Inimitable hadn't decreed that Fairy Godfathers always make things right in the end? Could James Joyce have created a novel in which the reader savours each paragraph of Bloom's day if The Inimitable hadn't shown that prose can be enjoyed like poetry and the story doesn't suffer? Could Tom Robbins have celebrated glorious life triumphing over misplaced morality if Dickens hadn't waved a magic wand over Martin Chuzzlewit and Ebenezer Scrooge and Mr Toots and Eugene Wrayburn? The Happy Ending may not match our experience of the *Nine o'Clock News*. But we wish it did and think it should, and Dickens buoys up our optimism and encourages us, as he encouraged his own generation, to go on striving for it.

"THE EXERCISE YARD AT NEWGATE PRISON", BY GUSTAVE DORÉ.

GOOD CHEER

THE BEST=LOVED
MOTION PICTURE OF 1935

Touching scenes be-tween mother and son that you will never forget.

Prepare your heart for an experience never to be forgotten! The world has waited for this great motion picture. For two years it has been in production, the mightiest undertaking of Metro=Goldwyn=Mayer. Highest praise has preceded it, but your own tear=dimmed eyes, your own thrilled heart will tell you best how wonderful, how exciting, how tenderly moving it is! Directed by George Cukor, whose previous film success was "Little Women". A Star Cast of 65 players, bringing to life each immortal character. Its gayety and its heart=stab=bing drama await you... exactly as Charles Dickens might have wished for his greatest story.

"Barkis is willin'!" You'll enjoy the love-lorn Barkis, too timid to pop the question.

Agnes' heart almost stopped beating as David announc-ed to Aunt Betsy Trotwood, his forthcoming marriage to Dora.

The villainous Uriah Heep little suspect-ed the trap be-ing set for him.

David feels the wrath of his cruel step=father, Murdstone.

Produced by
DAVID O. SELZNICK

Directed by
GEORGE CUKOR

A
Metro-
Goldwyn-
Mayer
PICTURE

"Something will turn up!" There are laughs and tears in the lovable char-acterization of W. C. Fields, as Micawber.

The love of David for Dora is one of the sweetest ro-mances of all your picture days.

Charles DICKENS'
DAVID COPPERFIELD

W. C. FIELDS · LIONEL BARRYMORE · MADGE EVANS
MAUREEN O'SULLIVAN · EDNA MAY OLIVER
LEWIS STONE · FRANK LAWTON
FREDDIE BARTHOLOMEW
ELIZABETH ALLAN
AND YOUNG

6 THE IMMORTAL REPUTATION

"THE IMMORTAL MEMORY" is the toast of the Dickens Fellowship. That memory was literally alive when it was founded at the beginning of the century. Henry Fielding Dickens was well embarked on the distinguished legal career that would bring him a knighthood. He accepted chairmanship of the society, as his descendants have done since. He would live till 1933; his sister Katey predeceasing him in 1929. Aunt Georgie, with even longer memories of the great man, lived until 1916, and was readily available to enthusiasts who wanted to know what he had said and done about this or that. Happily for the old lady, whose feelings for her brother-in-law, were near-idolatrous, most early researchers concentrated on tracing out originals for characters and places in the novels – a more useful occupation than their supercilious successors often realize, as it can tell us a lot about Dickens' creative methods. She would have been appalled to face the prurient curiosity about his relations with Ellen that followed the deaths of his immediate family.

Many of the writer's lay admirers were equally appalled. For a hundred years there were those who refused to believe that the great artist of hearth and home featured discreditably in his own marital breakdown. I have written on unattractive topics, like Jack the Ripper and controversial topics like Kipling's politics, but I have only once received anonymous hate-mail, and that was in response to the popular illustrated life of Dickens I wrote for the centenary of his death. Many people were outraged by the simple facts simply reported. One lady sternly told me that Charles Dickens had married Angela Leath and they had eight children and I should be more careful what I said, as Charles's grand-daughter Monica Dickens wouldn't like it! This baffling misinformation was finally tracked down in a Dickensian byway when I realized that the good lady had taken as factual autobiography the first-person fiction framing the 1855 medley of Christmas stories, "The Holly Tree Inn", in *Household Words*.

What other writer would have his life staunchly and battily defended by the impassioned reading of one of his slightest fragments!

Not that his fame ever went completely unchallenged. There were always some readers who thought him frivolous or vulgar or in some way undeserving of serious attention. But the steam press and the spread of elementary education created a mass readership in his lifetime. It is easily, though wrongly felt that, at any given time since *Pickwick*, Dickens has invariably been the most popular English author. In fact, sensational hacks like G.W.M. Reynolds and Thomas Peckett Prest (of *Varney the Vampire* fame!) outsold him in his own day as Ian Fleming does in ours. But the Dickens Fellowship, with 6000 members is three times the size of the James Bond 007 Society, and half as large again as the Trollope Society; twice as large as the Brontëans; three times the William Morris and Jane Austen Societies.

So Dickens, it seems, remains the most popular classic? Apparently not. The Hardy Society declares an astonishing 14,000 members! Even so, we may be sure all of them know what Mr Pickwick looked like and quite possibly more of them could quote Dickens than Hardy from memory.

MGM'S MAGNIFICENT 1935 PRODUCTION OF "DAVID COPPERFIELD".

THE "Best Possession"

"**I** HAVE HAD STERN** occasion to impress upon my children that their father's name is their best possession," Dickens wrote self-importantly to Frederick Evans. And the family concurred. Mamie and Henry wrote glowing memories of their father. Mamie and Georgie published a collection of his letters, with all embarrassing references expurgated. They ensured sixty years of almost unblemished praise after the burial of the national treasure in the Abbey.

Within two years, the official picture of Dickens' life started to appear. John Forster was England's first professional biographer. He wrote lives of the major seventeenth century statesmen, and a life of Landor. He produced a massive biography of Goldsmith, almost swamping his subject with background anecdotes, and calling upon Leech and Maclise and Cattermole to illustrate the book. His life of Dickens appeared in three volumes between 1872 and 1874. It was his masterpiece and is still the essential full-length description of its subject.

Forster had known him intimately for over thirty years. He was Mamie's godfather: the first sponsor drawn from outside the family for one of Dickens' children. He was trusted by Dickens to receive and correct proofs in his absence, and even to insert sentences at his own discretion when some detail had to be added. His advice was sought and accepted as serial plots developed. He felt, before Dickens did, that little Nell would "have to" die. Conversely he saved Edith Dombey's life, suggesting that she should live to refuse Carker her sexual favours after their elopement, rather than disappointing him by dying as Dickens at first intended.

Did Dickens cool toward the man on whom he modelled Podsnap? Certainly he expressed violent amusement when Forster unexpectedly married in 1856, and may have resented the loss of his easily available bachelor companionship. Forster didn't really mind a laugh at his own expense. He printed "'Mrs Gamp's" description of himself catching a train: the "resolute gent … with the tight legs, and his weskit very much buttoned, and his mouth very much shut, and his coat a flying open, and his heels a giving it to the platform." He didn't recognize his own mannerisms in Podsnap – just as Leigh Hunt, revered by the Duke of Devonshire as the only man who ever repaid him a personal loan, couldn't recognize himself in the unscrupulous sponger Skimpole. Podsnap's insular conservatism was so far from Forster's hidebound Radicalism that the pomposity and characteristic gesture of sweeping distasteful subjects behind him quite escaped the original.

But however much the middle-aged Forster's self-importance irritated Dickens, he trusted him implicitly. He trusted him with the story of his early life. And his trust was not misplaced.

The Warren's Blacking episode astonished the world and created exactly the picture Forster wanted: the Friend of the Poor who had known poverty; the Friend to Children who had suffered as a child; the Social

MAMIE DICKENS AND GEORGINA HOGARTH.

Reformer who had almost been crushed by society. In addition Forster's mass of quotation from Dickens' letters exhibited the writer with boundless creative energy and the man who carried that energy into the exuberant activities of his life. The man who walked his huge dogs ten or fourteen miles every day. The entertainer of dinners and parties, whose vitality never left him, though photography never captured it in the rigid stillness of long exposures. And the paintings by Frith and Ary Scheffer that tried to show that sparkling animation which Maclise had caught in the "Nickleby" portrait, simply failed as portraits. Scheffer's was a bad likeness; Frith's, Dickens thought, made him look as though he was rejoicing at the news that a hated neighbour's house had caught fire!

Forster set a firm critical tone. Like many Victorians, he rated characterization as the highest literary achievement and judged each novel by its "memorable" creations. Rightly, he gave pride of place to Dickens' humour and comedy but he also saw the failure of some seemingly very "Victorian" heroines. He knew exactly what was wrong with Esther Summerson, and found Amy Dorrit insipid. He had no doubt that pretty, silly little Dora was a better creation, and a better woman, than inertly angelic Agnes. Had he not joined the chorus weeping for Little Nell, Forster would suggest that sentimentality was a personal Dickensian quirk which his contemporaries rejected.

Respectability was something Forster nailed to his friend's memory. Ellen Ternan was never mentioned in his text, popping up unexplained in Dickens' will. The marital breakdown was treated under the unrevealing chapter title "What Happened at This Time". The broken friendships that ensued were not described. The long lists of dinner guests put Dickens securely in the centre of decent

A DICKENS FELLOWSHIP OUTING, IN FULL COSTUME

society. The Greatest Man of the Age, known to all the other Great Men.

In 1902 the Dickens Fellowship was formed. The practice of dressing up in period clothes for Pickwickian outings or Dickensian celebrations started. As well as that of meeting to try and solve *The Mystery of Edwin Drood*. G.K. Chesterton headed the critics who loved the humour of early Dickens and disliked the "darkness" of *Bleak House* and *Little Dorrit*. The Dickens Fellowship acquired the house in Doughty Street for its headquarters and a memorial museum. It noted "Dickens Houses" in Broadstairs, where Miss Mary Strong had tried unsuccessfully, like Betsey Trotwood, to stop donkeys from passing in front of her door, and Took's Court, Cursitor Street, where the building is in the wrong position for Mr Snagsby's house, from whose back Guster could see the spunging-house on the corner. Fort House, where Dickens had so often stayed in Broadstairs, renamed itself Bleak House, though it had no connection with Mr Jarndyce's home. The Fellowship tried unsuccessfully to expose the pretence that "The Old Curiosity Shop" in Portugal Street was Dickens' original. The spurious claim dishonestly inflated the building's value, though paradoxically the painted lie has rescued the only surviving Tudor shop-dwelling in London from destructive slum-clearance.

So, a national monument of decency and merriment, remembered in the buildings he knew and described: this seemed Dickens' secure position in 1934 when the scandal suddenly broke.

FAGIN, MAGWITCH AND SYKES AT THE ROCHESTER CARNIVAL.

THE "BEST POSSESSION"

Scandal

ELLEN TERNAN.

HERE WERE HINTS of a hidden scandal in 1928. A pseudonymous novel by "Ephesian" described the breakdown of Dickens' marriage and ascribed it to his love for Ellen, whose unexplained name had been before the public ever since Forster printed Dickens' will in 1874. The author, barrister Bechofer "Khaki" Roberts, would claim in 1946 that events had justified him.

In 1928, too, Mrs Thomas Whiffen's reminiscences recounted the story that Dickens bought mementos for the cast of *The Frozen Deep*, and a jealous scene followed the jeweller's mistakenly sending a bracelet intended for Ellen to Catherine. Mrs Whiffen described Ellen as Dickens' god-daughter and said that she and her mother had been with Dickens in the Staplehurst railway disaster of 1865 when part of the boat-train plunged off a viaduct that was under repair, and Dickens climbed out to help the injured and dying. These revelations caused consternation among Dickens' idolaters. J.W.T. Ley, secretary of the Dickens Fellowship, denied them outright in the Fellowship's journal *The Dickensian*, and wheeled out Sir Henry Fielding Dickens to say he did not know of Miss Ternan being his father's god-daughter and she and her mother were certainly not in the railway disaster. Sir Henry was sixteen in 1865, and it seems that his father never told him of Ellen's presence. For she was there, and her mother may well have been the older lady who was also with him. Charles wrote to the station master at Charing Cross asking whether a gold watch-chain and charms with a seal engraved "Ellen" had been found in the debris.

In April 1934 Thomas Wright published a story in the *Daily Express* under the laboured title "98 Years Ago Today Charles Dickens Began His Honeymoon". Sir Henry Fielding Dickens had died the previous year, and Wright felt it would now hurt no one to repeat what he had heard in 1897 from Canon Benham, a former vicar of Margate. Benham, like Wright, was a Dickens fan, and he had given public readings from his works, sometimes in concert with Mrs George Robinson, the wife of a local schoolmaster. Mrs Robinson was the former Ellen Ternan. She had married George Wharton Robinson in 1876. He was twelve years younger than she and was preparing to take Holy Orders at Oxford when she met him. There were two children of the marriage, Geoffrey and Gladys, and Ellen, according to Wright, had confessed to Benham that Dickens persuaded her to become his mistress shortly after he separated from Catherine. Wright said she had been reluctant and was finally induced to consent by vanity and the hope of financial security.

She certainly secured the latter from somewhere. In 1901 she sold the lease of her house in Ampthill Square, declaring that she had purchased it from her mother and sister in 1860. She retired from the stage around the same time. Over the last ten years of Dickens' life, when she was close to him, she never worked and he withdrew several large unexplained sums from his bank or consols. Some of this, it is reasonable to speculate, may have gone to assisting Ellen.

In 1935 Wright enlarged his charges in a *Life of Dickens*, which the idolaters attacked vehemently. His plea that he could not decently publish the story until the immediate family were all beyond being distressed cut no ice. He was accused of printing evil unsupported forty-year-old gossip, having deliberately sat on the lies until everyone who could have refuted them was dead. Interestingly, though, Ellen's children did not utter the absolute refutation passionate Dickensians wanted. Geoffrey refused to comment at all. Gladys abused Wright, but defended her mother's character against the charge of being mercenary. If, there had been a liaison, she suggested, Ellen would have been motivated by pity for Dickens' loneliness.

Wright hit back in an autobiography. He produced the new claim, based on local oral tradition and the ratebooks, that Dickens had lived with Ellen in Peckham in 1867, using the pseudonym Tringham. This was promptly dismissed as idle and improbable gossip, but subsequent research by Felix Aylmer and oral traditions reported by Miss Gladys Storey and J.C. Reid not only support it, but suggest that as "Tringham", Dickens had previously maintained Ellen in a cottage at Slough.

Miss Storey's recollections, published as *Dickens and Daughter* in 1939, were of the highest importance. She had been Katey's companion in her last years, and recorded her unhappy memories of her father's behaviour when his marriage collapsed. Miss Storey also confirmed that Dickens had maintained Ellen in Peckham, and said she had born him a son

and Georgie wouldn't have stayed friends with an ex-mistress – which was arguable – and that it wouldn't have been accepted by a court of law – which was irrelevant. But in 1978 Miss Storey died, and her papers were found to include a precise note that Sir Henry Dickens had told her, on September 8, 1928, that he knew Ellen to have been his father's mistress, and had so informed Geoffrey Robinson. Another note supported the claim that a son had died in infancy. One may dislike the gleeful spoliation

who died in infancy. She denied knowing anything about Wright's revelations, and certainly could not have known that he had written privately to two Dickens Fellowship officials that there had been "children" from the liaison.

The controversy was heated. Smart young writers wanted to damn all Victorians as hypocrites. Dickens could now be put down as a leading humbug: the apostle of purity who seduced a young girl. For the next thirty years Dickensian apologists fought back, saying that the evidence didn't prove a sexual relationship beyond all doubt – which was true – and that respectable Mamie

of traditional pieties, and detest a subsequent undercurrent of pseudo-scholarly detective work hinting that Dickens "really" died with Ellen and the family "covered up" by smuggling the body back to Gad's Hill. But there is no longer any serious historical hope of denying that Ellen Ternan was Charles Dickens' mistress. Exactly when; for exactly how long; exactly how happily – these secrets remain properly private but what once seemed scandalous must be accepted as true. The value of "the immortal memory" is undimmed. Its real basis was always brilliant writing, not saintly morality.

DICKENS ASSISTING THE INJURED AT THE STAPLEHURST RAILWAY DISASTER.

Hostile Criticism

WHEN HUGH KINGSMILL used Wright's revelations to attack Dickens in *The Sentimental Journey* the new scandal was adduced in support of some old objections. Dickens had never won the ungrudging admiration of the English intelligentsia. Harvard professors loved him. Scientists like Owen and Lyell were friends. Carlyle admired him as "a unique of talent" while retaining a certain stiff distance from mere entertainment. But those who expounded literature in the universities withheld their approval. Among academics, only Charles Calverley was a notable Dickensian, giving his pupils a spoof examination on *Pickwick*, and Calverley was more a wit and lawyer than a scholar.

Dickens' day boasted no university departments of English Literature: those mixed blessings which can do so much for uncreative students and have done so much for literary history and so little for literature. The Victorian scholar was trained in the classics. If he transferred his learning to English then, like Harness and Dyce, who wept with Carlyle at Dickens' reading of *The Chimes*, he probably sought a church benefice for his income and concentrated on Shakespeare and the Early English Texts Society. True scholarship was editing texts. There was no place for contemporary literature.

Sir Leslie Stephen, the father of the *Dictionary of National Biography* – and of Virginia Woolf and Vanessa Bell – was really the father of a modern intellectual approach to English literature. His essays "Hours in a Library" were the work of a former Cambridge don who was up-to-date enough to have gone in for Crisparklean outdoor sports, excelling at running and mountaineering, and who wrote seriously and intelligently about literature in English. He left academe and resigned holy orders when his agnosticism unfitted him for either. His transition to intellectual journalism gave him the Johnsonian opportunity to make a mark in soil less arid than the lost Greek letter digamma or textual cruces in Thucydides. He was a founder of the Radical *Pall Mall Gazette*, and he succeeded Thackeray as editor of the *Cornhill*. The entries he composed for the *Dictionary of National Biography* gave formal recognition to recently deceased writers, and a very long entry on Dickens conceded his manifest importance as a great figure on the Victorian scene and – but, oh, so grudgingly! – a great novelist.

Quite simply, Stephen didn't care for Dickens. He didn't like the sentimentality that stood in for tragedy. He didn't enjoy grotesque caricatures. He didn't approve of slapstick humour and boisterousness and a gargantuan delight in feasts and fairgrounds. He didn't think that unphilosophically based emotional appeals were really helpful to the liberal progressive causes he favoured. Dickens was a great writer because – well, really because a lot of people liked him! Which didn't mean that intellectuals had to endorse their liking.

George Eliot's grounding in German scholarship and the higher criticism made her more worthy of the, intelligent reader's respect. If novels were to be humorous, then surely Jane Austen's showed better taste than Dickens'? Wasn't there something boorish about his continued preference for her slightly cruder predecessor Fanny Burney, even when he finally brought himself to read Jane?

The men who agitated for the academic study of English literature and successfully brought it onto university syllabuses were rather of Stephen's way of thinking. Churton Collins and Walter Raleigh wanted the study of Shakespeare; wanted a patriotic respect for glorious British poetry; but when it came to the novel, wanted a more perfect and mandarin prose than Dickens' exuberance. Even Quiller Couch, the rather surprising first Professor of English Literature at Cambridge, shared his generation's peculiar admiration for Robert Louis Stevenson as the great stylist. Though the author of *The Astonishing History of Troy Town* recognized Dickens as first of the Great Victorians.

Not that "Q's" entertainments and romances were part of any real School of Dickens. It was, indeed, another drawback that Charles seemed to have no serious successors. The "young men" he brought on in *All the Year Round* – Edwin Yates and Percy Fitzgerald and G.A. Sala – proved rather flashy second-rate journalists. The social "sensation novelists" who apparently imitated or learned from him – Wilkie Collins and Charles Reade – were not really glories of late Victorian literature. Wells and Bennett shared Dickens' unusual sympathetic understanding of the lower-middle-classes, but were, at best, only fitfully Dickensian. Evelyn Waugh was the one writer who really recaptured and developed Dickens' spirit of wonderfully comic grotesquerie, but his unpopular political and religious stance debarred him from proper critical appreciation for much of his lifetime. J.B. Priestley followed Dickens' sentimentally comic endorsement of progressive populism and the rights of the Little Man. Priestley however, unlike Dickens, didn't really enjoy broad vulgar entertainment. He might describe soubrettes and hoofers sympathetically in *The Good Companions*, but in the end he clung to the sentimental dream that a socialist society would make all the workers love poetry and classical music. Priestley would never be the object of academic admiration.

Q's greatest pupils in Cambridge did more than anyone else to hold back Dickens' intellectual reputation. F.R. and Q.D. Leavis, the most influential critics in mid-twentieth century English Literarture, almost wrote him off. Queenie Leavis's *Fiction and the Reading Public* looked rather disparagingly at "best-sellers", apparently defining them by the length of authors' entries in *Histories of Literature*. Dickens was accused of trying to pack in something for everyone, with disastrous results. F.R. Leavis's *The Great Tradition* (of the English novel) explicitly excluded Fielding, Smollett, Sterne, Thackeray and Trollope. Dickens was acknowledged as a "great classic", but a classic "of entertainment", with the implication that this was something inferior to literature. The Leavises were themselves controversial. But for many years there were no critics capable of confuting them. C.S. Lewis, who tried, was too often bluffly off the point, and, anyway, didn't push the case of Dickens, preferring convoluted Christian apologetics for Milton or corkscrewy intellectual gymnastics over Donne and Dryden.

Counter Revolution

IRONICALLY, the Ellen scandal tended to boost Dickens' reputation with intellectuals. There were always individual writers, from George Gissing to George Orwell, who appreciated him; the latter, indeed, coined a brilliant phrase to define the Chestertonian vision of Dickens: "Rotten architecture with wonderful gargoyles." But the great turn-around in the higher educated reaction came in 1941 when Edmund Wilson published his essay "Dickens: the Two Scrooges". Wilson believed that Ellen Lawless Ternan's name, and therefore personality, were reflected in the heroines of Dickens' last three books: Est[ell]a Prov[is] – a bit forced, that one! – B[ell]a Wilfer –and that!– and H[elen]a Landless –that seems nearer the mark. Estella was incapable of love for most of the book. Bella had to be trained out of a mercenary nature. Helena had the ungovernable spirit of a girl who had dressed in boy's clothes to run away from home. So through loving a very unsympathetic and un-Victorian woman at the end of his life, Dickens, it seemed, reached an unpredicted maturity.

This claim seems a bit forced, today. We don't really know what Ellen Ternan was like. We can see a rather different unifying theme in the late heroines. Bella Wilfer and Rosa Budd have both been "willed away" to predetermined marriages, so the one is pettishly mercenary as the other is wilfully childish. Estella's emotions, too, are the toy of an adult guardian, though she combines this with development from a line of handsome *Belles Dames Sans Merci* like Edith Dombey and Rosa Dartle and Miss Wade who seem to evoke some masochistic anxiety in Dickens. Helena Landless just seems cut out for an admirable second heroine. But the rightness or wrongness of Wilson's biographical interpretation didn't matter. He was a competent critic making positive points about Dickens, who fitted his Philoctetean model of the artist: the man who possessed the bow of creative ability in balance with a suppurating wound of psychological trauma which forced him to write.

As an American, Wilson drew attention to English writers whom their intellectual fellow-countrymen disparaged. "The Kipling Nobody Read" was another of his essays restoring a neglected reputation. Lionel Trilling, urbane and gentlemanly professor of English Literature at Columbia University, followed his lead with favourable essays on Dickens and Kipling in his collection *The Liberal Imagination*.

Both Wilson and Trilling moved away from the old exclusive passion for early and humorous Dickens. Both were interested in *Bleak House* and *Little Dorrit*. And the darker Dickens was appreciated when the generation brought up on Wilson and Trilling produced their own studies. The American scholar Edgar Johnson wrote a massive standard life in 1953, calling it *Charles Dickens: His Tragedy and Triumph*. Forster hadn't felt that the triumphant life was blotted by tragedy. But other titles and sub-titles from the rash of critical books produced in the late 1950s and early 1960s showed that the simple humorist, or Friend of the Poor, or evoker of familiar places and buildings was no longer to the critical forefront. *The Flint and the Flame, The Melancholy Man, The Dreamer's Stance, The Confessional Fictions, The Violent Effigy*: Dickens books had moved a long way from *Bozland*, or *London Rambles*, or even *The Social Reformer* or *Dickens as an Educator*.

Those last titles, however, marked a scholarly strand which was revitalized in the mid-twentieth century. Oxford, always tending to the belief that the only good language is a dead language, had too much Anglo-Saxon on its English syllabus to allow undergraduates to study nineteenth-century literature until 1958. But its one literary Victorianist, Humphry House, produced a groundbreaking study in 1942, *The Dickens World*. This examined Dickens' recommended social reforms in the light of the conditions that produced them. It didn't judge the writing. It didn't approve or disapprove Dickens' opinions but it explained them. At a time when the Leavises in England and the New Critics in America were insisting that the proper work of the commentator was to evaluate words on the page, and not substitute anecdotes about authors, it was not always appreciated. But it laid the groundwork for one of the best lines of study. Philip Collins' *Dickens and Crime* and *Dickens and Education* in the early 1960s, gave us a much greater understanding of the way the social commentator worked.

Understanding, too, was generated by John Butt and Kathleen Tillotson's *Dickens at Work*, which examined the *aide-mémoires* and pre-designed part-issue wrappers to see just what effect serial writing had on the planning and form of the novels. Dickens research was now far removed from the activity Orwell had caricatured as looking for beds where Mr Pickwick had slept! The Pilgrim Trust financed a massive attempt to collect and publish all his letters. The Clarendon Press started a proper scholarly edition of the novels.

By 1970, practically every critic of serious repute agreed that Dickens was the greatest exponent of the Victorian novel. Henry James's claim that these were "loose baggy monsters" couldn't disguise the fact that the, common reader, with whom Dr Johnson sensibly rejoiced to concur, persisted in reading Dickens and spitting out James with disgust. And the Leavises capitulated. They produced a book in praise of Dickens. Fashionably and predictably they praised the later, darker Dickens. Equally predictably they mixed perceptive observations, especially from F.R, with some pretentious silliness, especially from Q.D. But absolutely unforgivably, they pretended that they had never disparaged Dickens. And with ineffable impertinence, they could be heard claiming that their book had put Dickens on the critical map during the few years they had left to live!

Intellectual respectability carried its hazards, especially in an age of expanding universities whose teachers had to publish or perish. An American reviewer remarked that a book for students with chapter titles like "Social satire: caricature of class or institution", was a bit too po-faced to put across Dickens' humour. As the offending author, I had to concede the point! A paper I once heard on "Mrs Gamp as a Jungian Earth-Mother" was solemnly absurd. Book titles like *Sexual Analysis of Dickens' Props* and *Dickens and the Suspended Quotation* and *Dickens's Conflicting Self- and Object-Representation* make one long for a writer to place all of us with our distinguished predecessor, Professor Dingo (of European reputation).

"BLEAK HOUSE" —
DARKER DICKENS.

Dickens ON THE Stage

FOR A CENTURY AND A HALF, many people's strongest impression of Dickens has come from actors portraying his characters. His original plays were no great triumphs. His two "burlettas" – light sentimental comedies with songs by John Hullah – were performed at the St James's Theatre, but not revived for second runs. Nor was his farce *The Strange Gentleman*, based on the Boz Sketch "The Great Winglebury Duel". A second farce, *The Lamplighter*, was not even given a performance. But in the same programme as his burletta *Is She His Wife?* a comedian delivered a monologue in the character of Mr Pickwick. And before that gentleman's *Papers* were complete, three other theatres had mounted dramatized versions of his adventures.

The young Dickens was flattered. He didn't object when six managements piratically produced dramatizations of *Oliver Twist*, although one of them was so bad that he lay on the floor of his box rather than watch it. He was a little more concerned that adaptors devised endings for *Nicholas Nickleby* before he did. But he still enjoyed the theatrical presentation of his creations as much as actors and actresses enjoyed realizing them, and Mrs Keeley's affecting performance as Smike particularly touched him.

By the time he came to *The Old Curiosity Shop* he was determined to oversee productions to his own satisfaction. When his profits from the commercially valuable *Christmas Books* were threatened by piracy, he made careful arrangements to have approved dramatizations appear almost simultaneously, scripted by friends and acquaintances. They secured that control over his cre-

ations which became ever more important to Dickens.

By the end of his life dramatizations of his works were almost a theatrical sub-genre. Stories with pathetic child roles were especially popular. If they were undemanding, like Tiny Tim, they would be played by real children. If they demanded sentimental melodrama, like Smike or Oliver or Nell, then an actress would take them. Leading comic actors enjoyed bravura roles like Buzfuz. Melodramatists found life in Fagin and Quilp. Before Dickens' death, the actor J.L.Toole was committed to a career based on Dickens' characters. In the age of the great actor-managers, Henry Irving, in a light moment, played Mr Jingle. Beerbohm Tree made Fagin a role to tear a cat in, spying on Nancy from a niche of London Bridge on a stage flooded with real water which lapped against a facsimile of the real bridge.

If audiences didn't insist on Dickens in the theatre, actors would. Laurence Olivier once remarked that there are no cameos in Dickens: all the roles are gems. Sir John Martin Harvey's success ultimately refined itself to a one-role career as Sydney Carton. This was so essential to him that in 1935 he begged the young John Gielgud not to mount a new production of *A Tale of Two Cities* with Peggy Ashcroft as Lucie Manette. Martin Harvey feared that he would need to revive his own version shortly. And Gielgud good-naturedly agreed, starring Peggy Ashcroft as Juliet to his Romeo instead.

Since then, musicals have usually dominated the Dickensian stage. Harry Secombe's Mr Pickwick had a hit with "If I Ruled the World". Lionel Bart's *Oliver!* is deservedly one of the most popular and frequently revived of all musicals. But the greatest Dickensian triumph of the last twenty years was not a musical. Terry Hands' production of *Nicholas Nickleby* at the Royal Shakespeare Company climactically culminated the sequence of "marathon" productions which had started with attempts to pack Shakespeare history sequences into unified entertainments. *Nickleby* was turned into two three-hour plays, which really determined spectators could watch back to back with a break for a meal. The strain on actors who had to double secondary roles as well as working immensely long hours was alleviated by the knowledge that they were in one of the outstanding productions of the century. The problem of breaking between Part One and Part Two was brilliantly solved by ending Part One with the newly-invented last act of the Crummles' company's *Romeo and Juliet,* and reducing the audience to ever more helpless laughter as, one after another, the tragic dead turn up, alive after all, in Mr Crummles's happy ending. The problem of persuading the audience that it was really over, and nobody would see this great production ever again was harder to solve, and on the last night the cast were held on the stage with unbroken applause until they submitted to an adulatory discussion and question-and-answer session with the people they had delighted.

A climax (so far) is not a conclusion. At the time of writing *Oliver!* is again revived in the West End of London. The Northern Theatre Ballet danced a version of the *Carol* last Christmas. Staging Dickens will go on.

Dickens himself pioneered the other form of his theatre: the one-man show. He prepared his own scripts carefully, cutting and doctoring the text to make each

reading self-contained; marking expression, volume and pace changes, and like Sloppy, doing the roles "in different voices". As we have seen, Ellen Ternan followed him in giving readings from his work, and Canon Benham was not the only parson to recognize a healthy and elevating cultural entertainment he could provide.

When some amateur curates and professional actors developed the form further, using make-up and costumes to present monologues in characters adapted from Dickens, they soon discovered that the English passion for a drag show made Sairey Gamp and Betsey Trotwood highly favoured subjects. They also learned that Twinkletonian headmistresses might find ways of conveying their frosty disapproval of such ungracious cavortings, even while courteously expressing their thanks.

An imitation of Dickens himself, with wig, beard and evening dress, was brought to the stage by Emlyn Williams as *An Evening with Charles Dickens*. Professor Philip Collins went back to Dickens' original scripts and became well-known for his public readings from them even before he prepared them for publication. Indeed, his readings were sufficiently famous for his "Sikes and Nancy" to be televised. As were Simon Callow's brilliant later versions in the Emlyn Williams mode.

JONATHAN PRYCE
IN THE WEST-END
REVIVAL OF
"OLIVER!"

ROGER REES AS
NICHOLAS AND
DAVID THRELFALL
IN AN OUTSTANDING
PERFORMANCE AS
SMIKE: THE ROYAL
SHAKESPEARE
COMPANY'S "NICHOLAS
NICKLEBY", 1980.

DICKENS ON THE STAGE

Dickens
ON THE Screen

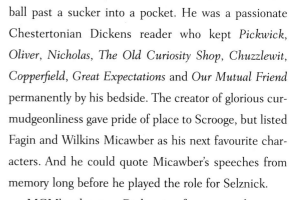

I N 1934, DAVID O. SELZNICK, MGM's *wunderkind*, employed Hugh Walpole to make a screenplay of *David Copperfield*. Walpole reduced the book's essence to 133 minutes playing time. George Cukor directed, his sensitivity with women giving great strength to David and Dora's marriage, as well as securing predictable triumphs with the childhood sweethearting of David and Em'ly and the golden-hearted ferocity of Betsey Trotwood. Freddy Bartholomew captured filmgoers' hearts as the boy David, and barring some chocolate-boxy cottage exteriors, the sets and costumes gave a satisfying vista from Blunderstone via Daniel Pegotty's (Lionel Barrymore's) boat home and the Yarmouth moles and jetties to London and Kent. It is an unsurpassed Dickens film.

Selznick's surprise triumph was casting W.C. Fields as Mr Micawber. How could this ultra-American incarnation of disreputable bottle-nosed bachelordom ever bring off David's totally British surrogate father? In the event, Fields restrained many familiar mannerisms and offered a respectful interpretation of Dickens' character. He enunciated with Victorian pomposity; used none of the boozy, leering irritability he had made his own, and gave one of his greatest performances. It would have surprised the world less had it known that Fields was no semi-literate barfly whose sole amusement was hitting a ball past a sucker into a pocket. He was a passionate Chestertonian Dickens reader who kept *Pickwick*, *Oliver*, *Nicholas*, *The Old Curiosity Shop*, *Chuzzlewit*, *Copperfield*, *Great Expectations* and *Our Mutual Friend* permanently by his bedside. The creator of glorious curmudgeonliness gave pride of place to Scrooge, but listed Fagin and Wilkins Micawber as his next favourite characters. And he could quote Micawber's speeches from memory long before he played the role for Selznick.

MGM's other two Dickensian forays were less successful. *A Tale of Two Cities* stormed the Bastille better than any previous or subsequent enactment. But Ronald Colman was not as whole-hearted a tear-jerker as Sir John Martin Harvey: indeed, the studio rather prided itself on having kept the melodrama restrained, which rather lost the point! And the hope that Lionel Barrymore would repeat on screen his annual radio triumph as Scrooge was dashed when he proved too lamed by old age to take the role and Reginald Owen had to substitute.

Subsequent filmed successes were British. David Lean's *Great Expectations*, like Walpole's *Copperfield*, gave a brilliant impression of retaining Dickens' essential creation while actually editing, simplifying and clarifying usefully. Jean Simmons, the rising juvenile of the 1940s, was impressive in the earlier scenes, before Valerie Hobson and John Mills took over from her and Anthony Wager as Estella and Pip. Forty-three years later Jean Simmons would appear in a televised version as Miss Havisham, the role in which Martita Hunt had schooled her own Estella in despising men.

Alec Guinness repeated for Lean a stage success he had enjoyed with Herbert Pocket. And two years later his

Fagin was the foremost figure in Lean's *OliverTwist*, which grimly flicked between blazing firesides and dark London streets. Some Dickens lovers felt that he, like Francis L. Sullivan as Bumble and (especially) Robert Newton as Sikes, lacked the full horror of the original characters. Even so, Guinness, in a nose that would have done credit to a macaw, was too much for American Jewry, and the film has rarely been screened in the USA and never shown on American television.

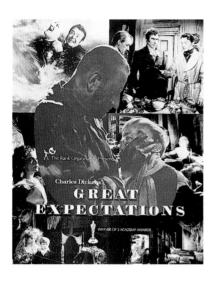

Three more Dickens films confirmed that near-square black-and-white films best captured his art. James Hayter's *Pickwick* was surrounded by Pickwickians who almost perfectly realized Seymour's and Phiz's visual inventions. Dirk Bogarde used quiet melancholy and apparent detachment from his surroundings to recreate the self-contempt from which Sydney Carton's heroic moment springs. And Alistair Sim created a Scrooge which took its place annually on American televisions screens as Lionel Barrymore's had once filled the radio. It still seems the best version of the *Carol*, despite excellent colour versions starring Albert Finney and George C. Scott.

Colour and the wide screen, in fact, have offered little advance. Their one big success has been Carol Reed's *Oliver!*, charmingly reproducing Bart's stage musical. Ron Moody and Jack Wild exploited to the full Bart's reduction of Fagin and the Dodger to lovable rogues, so there has been no problem with showing the film in America. More recently, a star-studded *Little Dorrit* tried rather awkwardly to make sense of the book by dividing it into Clennam's view of events and Amy's, as separate parts.

BBC Radio had long made a success of serial Dickens dramatizations and some very fine readings like Derek Hart's *David Copperfield* in "A Book at Bedtime". Increasingly its television productions have been mounted as classic prestige series. There have been fine and memorable performances: Patrick Troughton's Quilp in black and white, and slapstick comedian Charlie Drake's Grandfather Smallweed – as surprising a delight as Fields' Micawber. That colour *Bleak House* was notable for its pioneering atmospheric amber lighting; for its demonstration that the late "dark" Dickens was now sufficiently esteemed for Mr Turveydrop to be cut, alas!; and for the demonstration that an actress could make something of Esther Summerson where Dickens had failed. And Tom Wilkinson achieved what might have been thought impossible by creating an absolutely convincing Mr Pecksniff in a *Chuzzlewit* that was unreasonably criticized for cutting the American excursus.

But television budgets are smaller than film budgets, which means perfect sets and costumes may be harder to achieve. One remembers Nigel Stock, haplessly trying to convey Mr Pickwick in skintight trousers and tummy that just didn't fit him, while surrounded by Pickwickians in a ludicrous array of Technicolor blue and green velvet top hats and coats.

Perhaps the oddest television adaptation was a 1994 *Hard Times*, whose commendable attempt to replace nostalgic Victorianism with industrial drabness made for very spare flat settings. The writers, presumably influenced by today's politics, turned Gradgrind and Harthouse's loco-foco Utilitarian Liberals into a Conservative Party! And far from showing sheep-like trade unionists swayed by Slackbridge to victimize Stephen Blackpool, three noble sons of toil under a union banner regretted as much as Stephen himself that his inexplicable obstinacy – as he himself agreed – left no alternative but his dismissal to Coventry! Sadly, we still await the perfect translation of a Dickens novel to the small screen.

POSTER FOR DAVID LEAN'S "GREAT EXPECTATIONS" (1946).

BBC TELEVISION'S BRAVE ATTEMPT AT "HARD TIMES".

Dickens Today

AS BRITAIN becomes increasingly a tourist destination, Dickens makes a large contribution to the industry. The visitor will notice immediately that pubs, restaurants, wine-bars and hotel-rooms often take their names from Dickens characters. Or from Dickens himself. Famous old inns like Jack Straw's Castle on Hampstead Heath and the Star and Garter at Richmond proudly remember that they were the venue of his celebratory dinners with friends. Tourists all over Britain can enjoy the old pleasure of looking at places in the novels, from the Five Sisters windows and "Dotheboys Hall" in Yorkshire, to Ding Dong mine and the Longships lighthouse in Cornwall.

Guided walking-tours in Rochester give a well-informed introduction to the most Dickensian of provincial cities. And London? It was said that Dickens described it "like a special correspondent for posterity".

BETSY TROTWOOD'S PARLOUR, RE-CREATED IN DICKENS HOUSE MUSEUM, BROADSTAIRS.

We are that posterity, and can usually still see his streetlines if not always his buildings.So much of *Bleak House* takes place in such a tight area around Lincoln's Inn and Chancery Lane that forty minutes will take the pedestrian from Tulkinghorne's house, where Forster had his chambers, past "Miss Flite's garden" and the Old Hall where the court of Chancery sat, with a glance down toward Gridley's and Charley's lodgings; out of Lincoln's Inn back gate to the little alley, rebuilt and cleaned up recently, but still narrow and enclosed, where Krook lived and Dickens renamed the pub after the Sol's Arms in Hampstead Road; across Chancery Lane to Quality Court where Vholes lurked; down the road to Took's Court and the Snagsby home, and up the road again to Holborn and, first Snagsby's rural retreat of Staple's Inn, and then the Jellybys' neighbourhood of Thavies Inn. Really good guides in the City of London will know the church of St Ghastly Grim which the Uncommercial Traveller visited by lightning, and where Pepys worshipped before him, and the little churchyard where Charley Hexam reduced Lizzie to tears and Riah found her by the gate. Many tours go to the site of the Marshalsea and take in The George, the only surviving Borough High Street Inn to preserve part of the galleried courtyards of Dickens' day. Too few tours go on to St George's church to think of *Little Dorrit*, though the journey would take them past Horsemonger Lane where the Chiverys had their tobacconists' shop, and where Dickens saw the unforgettable spectacle of Mrs Manning, stiffly upright in her corsetted black bombazine, swinging from the gallows.

The Dickensian-minded visitor to England will be

struck by the museums and visitor-centres available: the birthplace in Portsmouth; the first marital home in Doughty Street, with wonderful exhibits including the desk-ornaments without which Dickens could not work, and the wooden midshipman made famous in *Dombey*; Miss Strong's house in Broadstairs, with its front room decorated and furnished to replicate Phiz's illustration of Betsey Trotwood's parlour; "Bleak House" in the same town, with Dickens' desk placed where he loved it, over-looking the sea; the Rochester Dickens Centre in the old building Dickens appropriated for Miss Twinkleton's Academy, now exhibiting a sound-and-waxwork exhibition and, most excitingly, the chalet Dickens was given by the actor Fechter and which he used as his summer workroom at the end of his life. For many years, Gad's Hill Place was a private school closed to the public. But since the school's last change of hands, it has been opened on the first Sunday of every month, and guides from the staff and the friends of the school and the city of Rochester conduct visitors through the famous ground-floor rooms: the reconstruction of the conserva-tory Dickens added, and his study with its desk and chair in the window as depicted by Luke Fildes and Buss, and the facetiously titled dummy-books disguising the door and wall: "Lady Godiva on The Horse" and "Hansard's Guide to Refreshing Sleep" and the like. The replica of Dickens' desk between his long, narrow mirrors flanking the window was made by his direct descendants, who have established a business making beautifully crafted Dickensian furniture. Four times a year, too, the school plays host to interested members of the public who enjoy Dickensian entertainments: lectures, or readings, or musical evenings, or even conjuring.

In the early summer, Broadstairs and Rochester both have annual Dickens Festivals. Many people turn out in Victorian costumes, as, indeed, elderly people do every Thursday all summer in St Peter's Village, Broadstairs. Lectures, demonstrations, exhibitions and all manner of Victorian entertainments and jollifications take place, and the public may have the good fortune to meet Mr Cedric Dickens and decide that wonderful bonhomie and a tremendous sense of fun have been genetically transmit-ted to him from his great-grandfather; or they may hear his nephew Mr Gerald Dickens reading, and conclude that Charles handed down a gift for the uninhibited histrionic realization of wickedly funny characterizations.

There is, in fact, a range of gifted readers following in Philip Collins' footsteps. It is, perhaps, especially pleasing that one of the best of them is another Professor of English, Malcolm Andrews, the current editor of *The Dickensian*. In his editorship he succeeds Professor Michael Slater, and they together with Professor Angus Easson, are a welcome token that the English professori-ate, which treated Dickens so scurvily for so long, is now making handsome reparation with scholar-ship that constantly contributes to our appreciative understanding of the works and redresses the imbal-ances of past prejudice. America has never failed in this respect, and scholars gather annually to enjoy specialist papers on Dickens in a panel at the Modern Language Association convention.

Nothing is definitive in today's fast-moving scholar-ship. Fred Kaplan produced an excellent biography of Dickens in the 1980s, correcting and tightening aspects of Edgar Johnson's work. It was followed very shortly by nov-elist Peter Ackroyd's biography which makes a massive and impressive effort to digest every book written on Dickens. Its quirks are tiny: a curious belief that Dickens at 5ft 9ins was obsessed with being short, and a writer's conviction that things were only real to Dickens when he wrote about them. Its virtues are outstanding, especially the constant awareness that Dickens interests us as a writer. For Dickens was a man who cared so much about the words on the page that he protested in his will against the legal language his lawyers dictated. That lover of language, the creator of ideas and people in words, is the Dickens who matters today, tomorrow, and every day our language lasts.

THE CHALET DICKENS USED AS A STUDY, NOW STANDING IN THE DICKENS CENTRE, EASTGATE HOUSE, ROCHESTER, ENGLAND.

Index

Acknowledgements

It is impossible to thank everybody who has contributed to my knowledge and awareness of Dickens: my grandmother for collecting the incomplete London Edition of the works, which stood out so bravely on the bookshelves and tempted me to read *David Copperfield*; *Oliver Twist* and *Nicholas Nickleby* before I was nine. My mother and her friends who advised that if I hadn't read all the novels by the time I was 21 I probably never would, and later encouraged as much laughter as possible in life; colleagues and librarians at all institutions where I have studied or taught; Roger Tyrrell, the best walking-tour guide in London; staff and curators at the British Library, the Guildhall Library, Canterbury Public Library and Reference Library, Dickens House (Doughty Street), Dickens House Museum (Broadstairs), Dickens' Birthplace, the Dickens Heritage Centre, Bleak House, and above all, Ms Betty Copleston and all at Gad's Hill Place.

As usual, there would be no book, but for Paul Savory. My agent Richard Jeffs and editor Sarah Larter have encouraged me when necessary and, equally helpfully, left me alone to get on with it when necessary. Paul and Keith spared me the later stages of unwelcome correspondence about Jack the Ripper. And Karen has born with patches of my ferociously bad temper when working under pressure.

MARTIN FIDO
CANTERBURY 1997

The publishers would like to thank the following sources for their kind permission to reproduce the pictures in this book:

Jane Austen Memorial Trust 133. ©BBC Picture Archives 43, 53, 54, 69, 77, 135, 139b. Barnardos Photographic Archive 90. The Bridgeman Art Library, London: Scrooge & the Ghost of Christmas Past from Dickens A Christmas Carol by Arthur Rackham 4/Bradford Art Galleries & Museums: Painting of Little Nell leaving the Church (From The Old Curiosity Shop by Dickens) by John Hodgson Lobley (b.1878) 47l/Dickens House Museum, London: The Pickwickians start from the Bull Hotel at Rochester by Cecil Aldin 2; Fagin, Illustration from Cope's cigarette card 119/Fine Art Society: Kate Nickleby by Thomas Faed 63/Forbes Magazine Collection, New York: Queen Victoria, 1867 by Jacob Thompson 104/Geffrye Museum, London: Wedding painting Changing Homes by George Elgar Hicks 48/Giraudon, Musee de la Ville De Paris, Musee Carnavalet: Execution of Marie-Antoinette 16 Oct. 1793 Danish School 108/Guildhall Library, Corporation of London: Workhouse, St.James's Parish from Ackermann's Microcosm of London by T.Rowlandson & A.C. Pugin 93; Metropolitan Railway, Praed St., Paddington, by Kell Bros. 1860, 112; New Stock Exchange from Ackermann's Microcosm of London by Rowlandson T. & A.C. Pugin 113/National Gallery, London: Dido building Carthage or The Rise of the Carthaginian Empire, 1815 by Joseph Mallord William 15/O'Shea Gallery, London: St Mary le Strand church from A book of the Prospects of the Remarkable Places in and about the city of London by Bob Morden17/Private Collection: The Ragged School, West St., Smithfield 94/Russell-Cotes Art Gallery & Museum, Bournemouth: The Beggar 1886 by Henry Gillard Glindoni 102/Scottish National Portrait Gallery, Edinburgh: Sir Walter Scott, 1822 by Sir Henry Raeburn 14/Stapleton Collection: Charles Darwin (1809-82) photograph by Julia Margaret Cameron 114/University College Museum, London 96/Victoria & Albert Museum, London: The Grave of Little Nell by George Cattermole 5, William Macready as Macbeth by M&B Skelt 25; Sailor with Union Jack, Mr. E.F. Saville as Union Jack, By Redington 120/The Trustees of the Weston Park Foundation, Disraeli, Earl of Beaconsfield, 1877 by Theodore Blake Wirgman 13bc. City of Rochester upon Medway 129b, 141. Reproduced by courtesy of the Dickens House Museum, London 1, 6, 7, 10, 16, 18, 19, 20, 21, 22, 23, 24, 26-31, 33, 38, 42, 45, 46, 47r, 49, 50, 52, 55, 56, 58, 59, 62, 64-68, 70, 71br, 72-76, 78, 81, 82, 84, 86-89, 95t, 98, 99, 106, 111, 115, 117, 121, 124, 128, 129t, 130, 131, 140. ET Archive/V&A 107. Mary Evans Picture Library 13tr, 35, 36, 37, 39, 41, 51, 61tc, 71tl, 79, 97, 101, 103, 109, 110, 116, 123, 125, 132, 136.
The Ronald Grant Archive/Columbia, Warwick, Romulus 1968Oliver 92/GFD, Cineguild 1948Oliver Twist 61br/MGM 1934David Copperfield 138/Rank 1958ATale ofTwo Cities 83/Rank, Cineguild 1946Great Expectations 85, 134, 139t/Renown 1951 Scrooge 40.
Hulton-Getty 3, 34, 44, 95b, 100, 118, 122.
Kinema Collection 126.
Performing Arts Library/Fritz Curzon 137t, Michael Le Poer Trench 60.
Photostage/Donald Cooper 137b.
Rex Features Ltd./Sands, Cannon 80.

Every effort has been made to acknowledge correctly and contact the source and/copyright holder of each picture, and Carlton Books Limited apologizes for any unintentional errors or omissions which will be corrected in future editions of this book.

ACKNOWLEDGEMENTS